THE MAG
YOUR MI

D0406265

by U.S. Andersen

This book reveals a mental magic that guarantees increased achievement and assures success. Many people have locked themselves in prisons of their own making because they have the impression that they have been unsuccessful. *The Magic in Your Mind* teaches the magic by which men become free and begin to grow into the image of the Secret Self.

Perfect action and perfect works stem from an inner conviction of the mental cause behind all things. A man changes the state of his outer world by first changing the state of his inner world. Everything that comes to him from outside is the result of his own consciousness. When he changes that consciousness he alters his perception and thus the world he sees. By understanding the process and effect of mental imagery, he goes directly along the correct path to his goal.

The Magic in Your Mind offers a program for training the image power of the mind, so that a scene cast up in consciousness will arrive in three dimensions, with color and sound, pulsing with life, as real to you as the outside world. The salvation of each of us is to train his image power to obey him. In this manner it is possible to become free from frustration and failure, and even from disease, destruction and death. He whose inner power of vision transcends the stimuli of the outer world is truly master of his fate.

By U. S. Andersen
Three Magic Words
The Secret of Secrets

THE MAGIC
IN
YOUR MIND

U. S. Andersen

Melvin Powers
Wilshire Book Company

12015 Sherman Road, No. Hollywood, CA 91605

TO
L. S. BARKSDALE

Published by special arrangement
with Thomas Nelson & Sons—N.Y.

Library of Congress Catalog Card No.: 61-7959

PRINTED IN THE UNITED STATES OF AMERICA

ISBN 0-87980-089-5

FOREWORD

This book reveals a mental magic that assures success, that absolutely guarantees increased achievement, whether your profession is in the arts or business, in science or sales, in sports, war, or politics. Here you will learn the secret way in which your mind is tied to the source of all power; you will learn how you are capable of becoming anything and doing anything you can visualize.

Every man's consciousness is constantly changing, is trapped at the knife-edge overlap of past and future, reacts rather than acts, is incomplete and partial, eternally seeks itself, for since the mere state of being throws no light on that state, consciousness learns of itself through reaction to outside stimuli. If a man comes to believe he is unsuccessful, it is because he carries the impression he has *been* unsuccessful, and this conclusion, once adopted, inescapably molds him into the shape of the thing he believes, locks him in a prison of his own making.

The magic by which a man becomes free is imagination. By training himself to cast up mental pictures of the thing he desires, by resisting sensual stimuli, even envisaging the exact opposite, he tends to assume a factual position in accordance with his vision, for his vision then becomes his experience, rather than the sensual stimuli that moved him before. Consciousness always assumes a form to suit its knowledge of itself, and where such knowledge breaks beyond the limits imposed by sensory experience, man begins to grow into the image of the Secret Self.

There is only one mind in all creation; that mind is in everyone, is in its true state of being not confined to anyone, not confined to the body. It is a central, knowing consciousness in which everything dwells, which dwells in everything. In a bodily-confined state it assumes the limitations imposed upon it by the knowledge of itself which it receives through the senses, but when bondage to those senses is broken by development of an inner power to perceive and know directly, then slavery to its embodiment is at an end.

Perfect action and perfect works stem from an inner conviction of the mental cause behind all things. A man changes the state of his outer world by first changing the state of his inner world. Everything that comes to him from outside is the result of his own consciousness. When he changes that consciousness he alters his perception and thus the world he sees. By coming to a clear understanding of the process and effect of mental imagery he is led irrevocably along the correct path to his goal. By working with this cause of all things —his own consciousness—he achieves infallibility in works, for inasmuch as his mental imagery propels him into action, that action is always true to the picture in his mind and will deliver him its material counterpart certainly.

In this book you will find a program for training the image power of the mind, so that a scene or situation cast up in consciousness will arrive in three dimensions, with color and sound, pulsing with life, as real for you as the outside world. Haven't you ever dreamed such dreams? Haven't you sometimes in sleep become immersed in a mental and spiritual world with such solidity and dimension that you were certain it was real and the material world a delusion? If ever you have known the overwhelming power of mental imagery to influence your attitude and perception, then you will quickly see that the salvation of each of us is to train his image power to obey him. In this manner it is possible to become free from the promptings and urgings of nature, from death and disease and destruction, from ineffectuality and frustration. For the man whose inner power of vision transcends the constantly distracting stimuli of the outer world has taken charge of his own life, is truly master of his fate.

CONTENTS

FOREWORD   7

1. THE HIDDEN CAUSE OF ALL THINGS   13

2. DISCOVERING THE SECRET SELF   39

3. THE GREATEST MAGIC OF ALL   64

4. SELF-MASTERY   85

5. MIND OVER MATTER   107

6. MENTAL IMAGERY   129

7. THE POWER OF CHOICE   150

8. OVERCOMING OPPOSITION   169

9. DEVELOPING SKILLS   190

10. CREATING YOUR OWN TALENT   208

11. HOW TO USE YOUR SIXTH SENSE   229

12. THE MENTAL ATTITUDE THAT
    NEVER FAILS   244

I give you the end of a golden string:
Only wind it into a ball,—
It will lead you in at Heaven's gate,
Built in Jerusalem's wall.

WILLIAM BLAKE

1 THE HIDDEN CAUSE OF ALL THINGS

Shakespeare's Hamlet in his famed soliloquy pondered, "To be or not to be," and thus faced squarely the primary challenge of life. Most people only exist, never truly *are* at all. They exist as predictable equations, reacting rather than acting, walking compendiums of aphorisms and taboos, reflexes and syndromes. Surely the gods must chuckle at the ironic spectacle of robots fancying themselves free, but still, when finally the embodied consciousness rises above the pain-pleasure principle of nature, then the true meaning of freedom is made apparent at last.

ACTION VERSUS REACTION

We exist in order that we may become something more than we are, not through favorable circumstance or auspicious occurrence, but through an inner search for increased awareness. To be, to become, these are the commandments of evolving life, which is going somewhere, aspires to some unscaled heights, and the awakened soul answers the call, seeks, grows, expands. To do less is to sink into the reactive prison of the ego, with all its pain, suffering, limitation, decay, and death. The man who lives through reaction to the world about him is the victim of every change in his environment, now happy, now sad, now victorious, now defeated, affected but never affecting. He may live many years in this manner, rapt with sensory perception and the ups and downs of his surface self, but one day pain so outweighs pleasure that he suddenly perceives his ego is illusory, a product of outside circumstances only. Then he either sinks into complete animal lethargy or, turning away from the senses, seeks inner awareness and self-mastery. Then he is on the road to really living, truly becoming; then he begins to uncover his real potential; then he discovers the miracle of his own consciousness, the magic in his mind.

Mastery over life is not attained by dominion over material things, but by mental perception of their true cause and nature. The wise man does not attempt to bend the world to fit his way or to coerce events into a replica of his desires, but instead strives for a higher consciousness that enables him to perceive the secret cause behind all things. Thus he finds a prominent place in events; by his utter harmony with them he actually appears to be molding them. He moves effortlessly through the most strenuous action, the most perilous times, because his attunement with the mental force that controls the universe guides him to perform the work that needs to be done.

ELECTRO-MAGNETIC MIND

This mental force that controls the universe may be called anything you like and visualized any way you choose. The important thing is to understand that it exists, to know some·· thing about how it works, what your relationship to it is. It might, for instance, be likened to an enormous electromagnetic field. All conscious forms of life then would be tiny electro-magnetic fields within the universal field and finding positions within it, each according to the kind and quality of its field. Where each individual field would wind up within the main field then would be a matter of inexorable law and absolutely unavoidable, as is illustrated by the millions of people who perform the same tasks over and over with absolutely the same results, almost as if following ritual. Perhaps they are always sick, always defeated, "just barely missers," perhaps always broke, always out of a job. If we give just the slightest reflection to our own lives we cannot help but be startled by how we seem dogged by the same situation in all things, year after year, time after time. This deadly recurrence is the source of most frustration and mental illness, is the bottom root of all failure.

Yet it is avoidable. And the way by which it is avoidable brings complete emancipation of the mind and spirit. *For the tiny electro-magnetic field has inherent within it the ability to change the kind and quality of its field, so that it will be moved about within the main field with all the power and sureness of the main field until it arrives at the position its new quality of consciousness demands.*

The important thing to remember about this illustration is that the tiny electro-magnetic field does not move itself. It is moved by the large field. And behind its movement lies all the power of the large field. Any attempt by it to move itself is obviously futile since it is held in place by a power infinitely greater than itself. And it is held *where* it is because of *what* it is. The moment a change occurs within itself, it is moved by a power outside itself to a new position in the field, one in keeping with its new potential.

THE MENTAL WORLD

The foregoing is admittedly an analogy, but nevertheless S.W. Tromp in his remarkable book, *Psychical Physics,* has proved beyond all doubt that the human being exudes certain electro-magnetic fields, that the earth itself gives off an electro-magnetic field, and his illustrations are so impeccably documented that there cannot possibly be any scientific quarrel with them. We indeed may be on the very threshold of scientific proof of those invisible areas of human aspiration that have hitherto been the province of philosophers, diviners, and priests. Departments of investigation into the paranormal abilities of the human psyche have been established at our leading universities, and it is now surely only a matter of time until we are faced with the final irrevocable proof of our intuitive perception—the power of mind over matter.

It is a mental world we live in, not a physical one at all. The physical is merely an extension of the mental, and an imperfect extension at that. Everything we see, hear, and feel is not a hard and inescapable fact at all, but only the imperfect revelation to the senses of an idea held in mind. Preoccupation with sensory experience has focused attention on effects instead of causes, has led scientific investigation down a blind alley where everything grows smaller into infinity or larger into infinity and walls man off from the secrets that lie behind life. It is not the planets and stars, the elements and winds, or even the existence of life itself that is the miracle that demands our attention. It is consciousness. It is the mere fact of being, the ability to say, "I." Consciousness is an indisputable fact, the greatest miracle of all, and all the sights and sounds of the world are merely side-effects.

THE HIDDEN "I"

To be conscious is to be conscious; there are not different kinds. The "I" that is in your neighbor is the exact same "I" within you. It may appear to be different through being attached to different sensory experience, but that is only because it has allowed itself to be conditioned by such experience. In point of actual fact consciousness is never the result of experience but the cause instead, and wherever we find it, it is primarily aware of existing, of being "I." There is only one basic consciousness in all creation; it takes up its residence in all things, appears to be different according to the things it enters into, but in essence is never changed at all. It is intelligence, awareness, energy, power, creativeness, the stuff from which all things are made. It is the alpha and omega of existence, first cause; it is you.

"Everything in Nature contains all the powers of Nature. Everything is made of one hidden stuff," wrote Ralph Waldo Emerson. He pierced the veil, perceived behind the sense-enamoring dance of nature's myriad forms the workings of the one mind and one intelligence from which all life and aspiration spring. There can be no inner peace or surety of action without this basic spiritual knowledge. The man who lives isolated from the roots of his being has cut himself off from the source of all power and dwells alone and without resource in a hostile and threatening world. Let him once perceive the true nature of life and his relationship to it and he soon sees that the world always reflects his thoughts.

THE MASK

The surface mind or sense-self or ego is the villain of the play that is being enacted on the human stage at present. Man as a form of life is sufficiently evolved so as to understand his separateness and uniqueness. He looks in the mirror and understands that the reflected animal is he. He is concerned with the appearance and welfare of this animal and ponders its relationships with the world and others. He does not truly understand what he is, only that he is conscious and confined within a particular body, and the experience and knowledge he acquires, together with his disposition as to their use, he labels "I," and thus he is deluded into calling a ghost by his own name.

Hidden behind this ghost, obscured by its struggles and fancies, is the Secret Self, which even though hidden, ignored, or misunderstood, nevertheless moves all things on the chessboard of life according to their natures and aspirations. We are never ego or sense-self. These are masks we don as we play at the parts we find in life. What we truly are is not a changing thing, but is whole and entire, powerful and serene, limitless and eternal. It springs from the inexhaustible source of life itself, and when we learn to identify ourselves with it, then we have hitched a ride on a power so far beyond our tiny temporal selves that our lives are changed in the most amazing manner.

THE IMPRISONED SELF

"To be what we are and to become what we are capable of being," wrote Robert Louis Stevenson, "is the only end of life." But when we stultify our divine birthright in manacles of mental and spiritual limitation, then we have no alternative but stagnation and pain. As long as we are responsive solely to the stimuli that impinge upon our senses from the outer world, we have no choice but to be victims of every circumstance. Locked to the senses, we reel under each stimulus, now aggressive, now afraid, now joyful, now sad, now seeking death, now life, but always our inner serenity and equilibrium are in the hands of something we neither understand nor control; and so we are puppets, pulled by invisible and unknown strings, swirling in the maelstrom of life like scraps of paper in the wind; and if perchance we garner knowledge enough to perceive our helplessness, then we often are overcome with such depths of sadness as to make effort against our bonds an almost unimaginable thing.

But the moment that we pause long enough in the headlong rush of life to see that we are not moving in accord with or in response to our own decisions but rather in reaction to the world around us, then we have taken the first step toward freedom. Only one who knows his slavery can aspire to be free, just as true freedom is possible only to one who has experienced chains. Our hates, loves, fears, envies, aspirations, deceits are for the most part products of circumstance, of false and limiting codes and mores—more often innate terrors of mountains that are molehills; and the solution to all of them is to stand foresquare before them, daring them to do their utmost, exposing them for what they are, thus foreswearing allegience to the cupidity of the deluding and blinding ego which forever keeps us thinking we are greater than others and less than we truly are.

THE LIBERATING POWER

It is not necessary to become a mystic, even a philosopher, certainly not a melancholy metaphysician in order to come to grips with the spiritual side of existence, to establish a mental causation in your life that will give you control of circumstance. What *is* necessary, however, is that you do not immediately throw out the door everything that has to do with spirit simply because it is the established province of religion. You may be a Christian or a Hindu, a Moslem or a Buddhist, a Taoist or Shintoist, but that only increases your individual human responsibility to think through all issues that bear on the world and life and death and your individual being. Only when you come to grips with your own mental essence, only when you arrive at a realization of the ephemeral, ever-changing nature of "I" will it become apparent that everything is in a constant state of growth and development and aspiration, and there are no limits and finalities and defeats, and anything is possible to one who first conceives the image in his mind.

There is within us a power of complete liberation, descended there from whatever mind or intelligence lies behind creation, and through it we are capable of becoming anything and doing anything we can visualize. The mental stuff of which we are made is of such kind and quality that it responds to the formation of images within it by the creation of a counterpart that is discernible to the senses. Thus any picture we hold in our minds is bound to resolve in the material world. We cannot help ourselves in this. As long as we live and think, we will hold images in our minds, and these images develop into the things of our lives, and so long as we think a certain way we must live a certain way, and no amount of willing or wishing will change it, only the vision we carry within.

THE LAW OF LIFE

It is astounding and sad to see the many thousands of people whose mental machinery keeps delivering to them the very effects they say they do not want. They bewail the fact that they are poor, but that doesn't make them richer. They complain about their aches and pains, but they keep right on being sick. They say that nobody likes them, which means they don't like anybody. They aren't bold, they aren't aggressive, they aren't imaginative; mentally they quiver and quake and are bound to negative delusions. It simply doesn't matter what the picture in your mind is, it is delivered nonetheless, with the same amount of faithfullness and promptness if it is a picture of poverty or disease or fear or failure as it would be if it were a picture of wealth or health or courage or success. The law of life is this: all things both good and evil are constructed from an image held in mind.

A tightrope walker edges swiftly out on his elastic and minuscule support. High in the air, wavering, suspended on a thin black line, he seems to transgress all normal laws of behavior. What is astonishing is not that he is able to do this thing so well but that he dares attempt it at all. Yet what he is doing is an inescapable result of mental law. Long before he set his first uncertain steps on the taut wire, he made a picture in his mind. Throughout his early bumbling attempts the picture persisted. He saw himself, agile, balanced, adroitly crossing the swaying wire, and this vision sustained him through all early failures, Now he flaunts his skill and courage in the very face of death, nonchalantly, as the spectators gasp. He is sure, poised, confident, delivered of all fear and mishap by the sustaining picture within.

IMAGE POWER

The image power of the mind is imagination, but just what imagination is and where it comes from nobody seems to know. A famous surgeon is reputed to have remarked that he had sliced open many a brain without ever having seen a picture or found a thought. The imagination certainly is no more exclusive property of the brain than of an arm, a leg, or the stomach. Thinking is performed not by a part of the body or even the whole body but by the inhabitant within. It is that function which enables consciousness to know its surroundings and to know itself. Only one who thinks is able to say, "I." Only one who can say, "I," is able to cast up pictures within his own being, known to no others.

The eternal striving for knowledge and capacity, the most apparent thing about life, is resolved always by two principal elements of the strife—the knower and the thing to be known. By definition these appear to be separate, and we observe that a man ordinarily copes with the outer world by tabulating the manner in which it impinges upon his senses. A thing is so long and so wide and weighs so much and is so hard and a certain color. A name is given it, and as long as each subsequent time it is encountered it maintains the majority of its original characteristics, a man recognizes it for what it is and knows it when he sees it. If you ask him if it is near, he is able to answer instantly, simply by glancing around. If its presence produces some particular effect upon him, like fear or anger or love or tension, then the mere presence or absence of this object may be said to materially affect his life. In that case, his state of mind is not a matter of his own determination, but instead is the direct result of the object as he encounters it or avoids it in the outer-world.

INNER VISION

Life in animal and vegetable forms is purely a matter of reaction. There is first the organism, then there are the elements that intrude their presence upon it. The conflict thus engendered resolves itself in the process of evolution as each organism attempts to overcome the obstacles it meets, but this influence, through the lower stages of evolution, apparently comes only from outside and is the result of processes and forces beyond the control of the organism. Nature holds the world and life in an iron grip, and lower animal as well as vegetable life is led inexorably along a path it neither understands nor can avoid. A thing is the kind of thing it is through a creative process that appears to be outside it; existence itself, in any shape or form, appears to be beyond the power and scope of the individual being. We are born and we die, and nothing within our known powers or knowledge can aid or stop these events. And insofar as we live in response to the senses, we are automatons only, and the shape of our lives is predestined by the circumstances we encounter.

Imagination is the tool by which we may be delivered from

our bondage. We can decide what we will think. We can decide to originate thought from some secret wellspring within rather than in response to the stimuli of the outer world. We can resolve that the images in our minds will no longer be products of the conditions we meet, but instead that our visualization will be the result of our inner resources and strength, in conformance with our goals and desires. Thus the quality of our consciousness will be tempered by our true motivations and we are freed at once of the trap of defeating our purposes through giving credence to every obstacle. The unalterable law is this: only that which takes root in mind can become a fact in the world. Thus the man whose consciousness is influenced only by the goals and purposes he has set within is delivered of all defeat and failure, for obstacles then are only temporary and have no effect upon his inner being. Only that which conforms to his inner vision is accepted home at last and allowed to take root in the plastic, creative medium of the Secret Self.

THE SECRET SELF

It is knowledge about and faith in this Secret Self that is the key to correct use of the imagination. No man lives in the dark when he learns where the light is. To understand the Secret Self is to free oneself from bondage to circumstance, to loose within a power compounded upon itself, to provide life with perfect working and perfect serenity. This entity within each of us, not the ego, not experience, not time or circumstance or place or position, but consciousness only, the "I" divested of all accoutrements except pure sense of existence, this is the self that contains all power, whose essence is greater than the individual, greater than ten thousand individuals, for it is the supporting structure upon which all things are built, the evolving self of the universe. It is not confined to the body, to a time or place or condition, but is in all times and places and conditions. It is infinite and eternal and only one, but being so as easily manifests as the finite and temporal and many. All are contained within it, yet each contains it all, for by its very nature all of it is everyplace at the same moment. The Secret Self is timeless and eternal. It is the self of the universe and it is the self of each of us, the self of you. It was never born and it will never die. It enters into each of its creations and becomes that creation. What is going on in life and the world and the universe is completely its working and the result of its secret purpose and undivulged goal. The nature of its being is mental; its essence is dynamic and creative. It is the eternal stuff that occupies all space and time and within which there is no dimension. It is all ends and middles and opposites and extremes, and it is infinitely creative. The myriad forms of life are but a tiny indication of its vast potential for plastic multiplicity out of its essential oneness.

MENTAL ASCENDENCY

The Secret Self is within you. It is not visited upon a fortunate few and withheld from others, but is totally existent in the heart of each of us. Insofar as we are able to divorce ourselves from the world and the ego and sensual stimuli we will become increasingly aware of its existence within and consciously strive to identify ourselves with it. It is through this identification that the seeds of power are sown. One who is able to cast off the limitations of ego and improve the quality of his consciousness through disciplinary use of the imagination is able by means of direct identification to become one with the Secret Self and thus attain to a measure of its power for perfection. The potential for achieving this astounding goal lies within each of us. By means of inner mental ascendency and pictorial definition a man may become one with the purposes of the Secret Self and thus become infallible in his works and his goals.

This is a pretty big capsule to swallow. Our materialistic society with its reverence for the products of science has excised three-quarters of our mentality. We have concerned ourselves too much with the world, what it is, what is in it, how we can use it, and today we know little more of the origins and purposes of life than we did before men were able to read and write. It is difficult when we know something of the principles of the gasoline engine, the generation and transmission of electricity, the refining and tempering of steel, of electronic and radio transmission, to admit the possibility that something radically opposed to the viewpoint of science could have a foundation in fact. Science says, "The laws of nature are supreme, and man must learn to live with them in order to prosper." Now comes this diametrically opposed theory, "Nature is subservient to mind, not the mind of man as we know it, but the Supreme Mind or Secret Self that lies behind life, and this Secret Self is within each of us. We can come to know it and to use it, and thus transcend the laws of nature and free ourselves from bondage to the senses and the material world."

THOUGHTS BECOME THINGS

What is going on in life is the evolution of the individual to complete oneness with the Secret Self. The universal being that lies behind creation has differentiated into finite form, taken disguise, so to speak, in order to work out the manifold sides of its infinite and eternal nature. Therefore the man who expands his consciousness is fulfilling the fondest wish of life. It is not necessary that we become saints to understand as much of the Secret Self as is necessary to use its power in our affairs. To know this law is enough: whatever we accept as a permanent mental image in our consciousness must manifest in our world, for we become in life what we are in consciousness, and nothing can alter that fact.

It takes a great deal of courage to admit to yourself that if you are sick, frightened, frustrated, or defeated you have brought these conditions on yourself and no one but yourself can get rid of them. Occasionally someone so afflicted will experiment with the power of his mind to cure him, but will give it only the most cursory trial. If, for example, he is ill and in pain, he might say, "I visualized myself well and happy, but I hurt just as much as ever." What he didn't do above all things was visualize himself well and happy. He visualized himself sick and in pain. The moment he began to visualize himself well and happy, he would become well and happy. This is not a law that works once in a while or part of the time or on auspicious occasions. It works all of the time and it works in the exact same way, and it is returning to you right now in the material world the images you maintain in your mind. You cannot escape them. They surround you, sustain you, or torment you. They are good or evil or uplifting or degrading or exalting or painful according to the vision that prompts them, and as long as you are alive, as long as you think and imagine, you are literally surrounded day and night by the images that predominate in your consciousness.

THOUGHT CONTROL

The startling power of the Secret Self is that it always makes manifest the image it beholds. Nothing illustrates this fact better than the current experiments with hypnosis. A man may be in such excruciating pain that even narcotics will not relieve him, but he can be put under deep hypnosis and told that there is no pain at all, and presto, there is no pain. He may have a deep and abiding fear of crowds, but under hypnosis it can be suggested to him that he likes crowds, and lo and behold, he enjoys them most of all. He can become stronger, healed of disease, smarter, more aggressive, possessed of endurance and indomitableness, all because these things are impressed upon his psyche as facts and the image in his mind grows from them.

"Aha!" the cry goes up, "find me a good hypnotist. I want to be smart and strong and successful and all those good things and to be rid of weakness and pain and failure." And hypnosis can do it too, if you are willing to abdicate as the person in charge of your life. If you are willing that someone else run it every hour of every day throughout the whole of it, then you can turn your life over to a hypnotist and he can remake it in the image you outline. However, it will make small difference to you. You may still be in the vehicle, but you no longer will be driving. If effort and strife and the overcoming of obstacles are the spurs to growth that the Secret Self intends them to be, then surely you will have abdicated from life itself.

You need no hypnotist to put the power of the Secret Self to constructive work in your life. No hypnotist can overcome the negative image making of your mind unless he is with you twenty-four hours a day. You are the only one in constant rapport with yourself, and thus you are the only one able to police the thoughts and images you entertain. If you let the image be prompted by something outside you, then you exercise no control over your life. If you accept images only in accord with your desires, then life will deliver your inner goals. In any case, the magnificent promise of the Secret Self is this: *you can change your life by altering the images in your mind, for what comes to you in the end is only that which you have been accepting in consciousness.*

Now there are many people who agree with this premise but are quick to point out that the images in the consciousness of most persons are projected there from the subconscious and are not of their own choosing. Most schools of psychotherapy apparently feel this way, for they propose a tedious and time-consuming treatment bent on expurgating from the subconscious memories of painful and bitter occasions which might prompt unpleasant images in the mind. Seven or eight years of this process have not noticeably emptied painful memories from the subconscious of most patients, and in any case, if a treatment is truly efficacious, it cannot possibly consume so long a time. The saddest thing about the modern "put the blame elsewhere" school of psychoanalysis is that the person undergoing it accepts it as justification for his failure to police his consciousness and thereafter expects such policing to be accomplished by having the neighborhood rid of criminals. If he achieves some semblance of a changed consciousness in the hands of the psychiatrist, he soon goes back to a world full of negative thoughts and ideas, and just because he does not police his own mind, they readily find acceptance there. You may not be able to alter the positions of the stars, to stop the earth from revolving, to cause the winds to blow or the sea to calm, but you *can* choose what you will think. You can think what you want to think. You can think only in response to an inner vision and a secret goal, and if you take your stand with a firm heart and a high resolve you will be successful and you will not be intimidated and you will project your image clear and true and its counterpart will return to you in the world.

DRY HOLE CASEY

In a little village on the western slopes of the Great Divide lived a man whose entire life had followed one ignominious pattern. For thirty-five years he had been an oil well driller and had followed the frontiers of oil exploration throughout the United States. During that time he had drilled forty-four wildcat wells and not one of them had made a strike. He had drilled in Texas, Oklahoma, Kansas, Louisiana, California, New Mexico, Arizona, Colorado, Wyoming, and still he had not hit. Oil operators wouldn't hire him anymore. He became known as "Dry Hole" Casey, a nice guy, but strictly out of luck. Finally he took a job in a Colorado mine and eked out his days without hope. He kept his drilling rig, though. It was his first love. Weekends would find him in the backyard, lubricating and cleaning its parts, handling them with ritualistic care.

One day in late spring, when the snow stood in broad glittering fields on the slopes of the mountains and the rivers and streams were high and roily, he wandered up into the woods and sat gazing over the valley. The valley was a basin hemmed in on three sides by precipitious intrusions of granite, and these mountains had been productive of many minerals, lead, zinc, silver, tungsten, manganese. Our friend gazed to the west, to where the basin sloped down to a plateau. Suddenly his mind formed the perfect picture of a faulted anticline, a predominant type of subsurface oil trap.

The image seemed superimposed over the scene before his eyes, so that he could almost see the oil below the surface of the ground. He trembled before his vision, could not resist it. It seemed like a sudden visitation from heaven, and he left the mountainside absolutely certain that within the small valley lay a major oil field.

Next day he quit his job in the mine and with his savings managed to procure oil lease options on the land he visualized as being the most favorable. Now he had to raise capital to complete his leasing arrangements and provide funds to drill an initial well, a gargantuan task, since everyone who knew him knew also his history of failure. But the vision in his mind persisted. It led him to take a bus to an eastern city in quest of funds. It led him after a week of discouragement to a park bench and a seat alongside an elderly man who quietly and patiently fed the squirrels.

It was a bright warm day, and the squirrels were active, playing and clowning over the proffered food, and the two men laughed at their antics, and each told stories of other squirrels and other times and agreed that the foibles of humanity were not shared by animals. Warmed at each other's company, they agreed to lunch together at a nearby restaurant. In the course of the luncheon, the oil driller told his new-found friend of his vision and his problem. His friend was interested, questioned him closely about the vision he had had on the mountainside, seemed impressed that it persisted.

"How much money do you need?" he asked.

"Fifty thousand dollars," replied the oil well driller.

"I will provide it," the man said suddenly. "We will be equal partners."

It seemed incredible, but there it was—a chance acquaintanceship on a park bench, and the money was provided. It is almost anticlimactic to relate that the subsequent well discovered a rich oil field. There simply was no alternative. And the man who put up the money knew that it would. He had had sufficient experience with the power of inner vision to manifest in the world to be absolutely sure of his position. He did not dwell for a moment on his partner's previous failures, only on the vision that possessed him now.

DISSOLVING THE MASK OF VANITY

What strange alchemy prompted our oil driller to have this clear vision in his mind, a vision that subsequently made him a rich man, when his whole previous life had been one unbroken line of failure? Surely the wells he had drilled before had been drilled in response to a vision too. Why should they have failed?

They failed because the vision he possessed then was one of failure. Sure, he would have denied it, but it was true. Perhaps a sense of the great hazard connected with searching for oil lay at the crux of his subconscious. Perhaps he felt that the odds were against him. Perhaps he was conscious of the fact that there are millions of acres of land without oil under them. In any case, his vision was one of failure, from whatever cause, and he was led into those arrangements that would inevitably cause him to put his drillbit down in barren soil. And in two cases, where he actually had drilled on productive land, he once had ceased making hole only twenty-seven feet above the productive formation and another time failed to make a test of a sand that later produced several million barrels. But he could not help himself. He was only following the dictates of the vision in his mind.

See how different his behavior was in the discovery of the basin field. He *saw* the oil. He *knew* it was there. There was not the slightest doubt in his mind, and that is the way he acted. There was no resisting him this time. His vision was for production, and that is what resulted.

Why? Why did he finally have a positive vision after harboring a negative one for so many years? Such a question could not be answered with certainty without making an intensive study of the man, but in all probability the debilitating and crippling factor was fear. Fear more than any other single thing warps and distorts our vision. Our oil driller most likely was afraid of failure, and his apprehension twisted his inner vision from success to defeat. He couldn't win as long as the fear stayed with him. Finally, when he had reached the absolute bottom, when the business he loved had rejected him and the men in it no longer would hire him, fear simply left him. Everything bad had happened already, what more was there to fear? And in this psychologically relieved attitude, the Secret Self was able to get through the mask of vanity, and the ensuing vision inevitably brought success.

MIND OVER MATTER

"It is computed," wrote Jonathan Swift, "that eleven thousand persons have, at several times, suffered death rather than submit to break their eggs at the smaller end." The resistance of the human mind to change is amazing, especially when it appears so obvious that life itself is nothing more than change. Multitudes of people, many of them very intelligent, argue that all cause is in the physical world and that mentality only observes. They seem determined to go down to their deaths with this frightfully erroneous viewpoint, even though their own inner attitudes belie their stand, even though their slogans extoll the power of mind over matter.

On locker room doors and conference room walls the framed and placarded slogans emblazon their messages: "A quitter never wins. A winner never quits." "A team that won't be beat, can't be beat." "Put your heart in it. All else will follow." "Make up your mind, and you make up the future." But these verbal expositions to thoughtful vision are regarded as having precedence only in such matters as team effort, to bind together the group for a purpose, and their tremendous importance to individual creativeness is largely overlooked. From the inner vision all things are done —the bridge is built, the tower constructed, the oil well drilled, the motion picture made, the book written, the picture painted, music composed, outer space probed, secrets of the atom exposed.

There is absolutely no such thing as accomplishment unless it is preceded by a vision of that accomplishment. You simply can't reach across the table and pick up a dish unless you first have the mental image. All things come to all people according to the pictures that form in their minds, and the effort that is expended in this world to escape fates that are inevitable is sufficient to construct a tower to the sun. No amount of movement, of physical energy expended, can prevail against a wrong mental image. Similarly, the possessor of the correct mental image is guided to perform the work to be done, effortlessly, almost nonchalantly. Most of the struggling and striving in the world is done by people who are trapped into unwanted circumstances through incorrect mental visualization, and the fact that they visualize the very thing that they profess to abhor is the contradictory situation that is filling our psychiatrists' couches.

MASTERY OVER FATE

Bernard Spinoza wrote, "So long as a man imagines that he cannot do this or that, so long is he determined not to do it; and consequently, so long is it impossible to him that he should do it." The picture that forms in the mind, whether for good or ill, will deliver its inevitable consequence. The problem is not with the mental or spiritual fact of physical fulfillment of mental visualization, but rather of finding a key that will enable each person to cast up mental images at will, hold them until realization, and not have other images intruded by the recalcitrant subconscious, which so often runs contrary to the wishes of the conscious mind. In the deeper reaches of the human psyche the seeds are formed that motivate a whole life, and a man either accedes to or takes command of these invisible prompters. If he accedes, his life will be run from a source beyond his conscious control. If he takes command, he becomes master of his fate.

Taking command is never as simple as it sounds. It requires a firmness and boldness that only few people innately possess. Most of us live as complete slaves to reaction, absolute victims of the commands of the subconscious, and we seldom if ever even think it possible that we can overcome our feelings and react in an entirely different way than circumstances would have us do. For example, if you participate in a test and defeat seems inevitable, you only make it certain by acceding. But if you keep alive your spirit by a vision of victory, by an absolute resistance to the importunities of defeat and disaster, who knows what miracles may occur? The mental vision that resists all sensual stimuli becomes at length a thing unto itself and its resolution as objective fact in the material world cries out for utterance and will not be stifled. Nature's vast creativity springs from the infinite potentiality of the Secret Self. Anything possible of conception is sure to eventually be created as a solid material fact for all the world to witness. There is no such thing as an idea without a visible resolution, for the great plasticity of the Secret Self shapes every idea contained within it, and whoever is possessed of a thought is possessed of a thing as well, as long as he holds his image clear.

CREATIVITY

Creativeness is not part of the surface self, of the ego, the conscious mind, the physical or sensual being. It emanates upward through the levels of consciousness from the Secret Self, takes shape and form through a power greatly beyond and infinitely more powerful than the small individual "I." That part of a man which is most powerful of all is invisible, seems apart from him completely, is hidden in the deepest recesses of his being, is not callable by name, is not recognizable through the physical senses, cannot be coerced, but responds innately and completely to image. This is the great plastic Secret Self from which all things are made, the creative self of the universe, maintaining a sameness in all differentiations, being eternally one in the midst of multiplicity; this is the Secret Self within you, which is not different from you, which in final analysis is altogether you. You are not conscious mind or ego or memory or sensual being, but were born directly from the mind that formulated and constructed the universe, and you are not different from that mind but attached to it by a mental and spiritual construction that makes you and it the same.

Abandonment of the surface self and seeking self-balance in the deeper regions of consciousness is the pathway to power and perfection in works. For when a man attunes himself to the life force and mental entity that gives him consciousness and lives within him, then he takes on by a process of identification the effectiveness and potency of the infinite and eternal entity from which his individual life has sprung. His horizons expand, his consciousness widens; there wells up from secret and subterranean springs a constantly increasing and never-ceasing power for perfection and perfect understanding. His faith is placed with simplicity and unfailing trust in the inherent power of the Secret Self to return in material fact those mental images that live within him, and he need not have the key that unlocks the universe in order to use effectively this basic law. It bothers him not that there exist doors in the mental and spiritual realm that thus far have not yielded. He need not know all and understand all to use those truths he thus far has discovered, and he lives in the consciousness that life is a mental adventure and not a physical journey.

KNOWLEDGE—THE GREAT LEVER

We all have seen people achieve great ends effortlessly. We have seen others strive frantically toward some goal only to consistently fall short. We are assured on all sides that hard work makes the successful man, yet we discern almost immediately that hard work sometimes fails of accomplishment while fortune often smiles on the man who seems to make little effort at all. Shakespeare wrote, "There is a tide in the affairs of men which taken at the flood leads on to fortune." The story is told of the man whose furnace refused to work and who subsequently called a repair man. The repair man struck the furnace a blow with his hammer, and it promptly resumed working. He presented a bill for one hundred dollars. "Outrageous," sputtered the irate householder. "I want that bill itemized." "All right," answered the repair man. He scribbled on the bill, "Striking one blow with hammer—one dollar. Knowing where to strike—ninety-nine dollars."

It is not how hard we work that matters, but what we get done. It is not the wailing and gnashing of teeth that is the show, but the things that are built and accomplished. The knowledge of the simple lever six thousand years ago might have saved a million hours of backbreaking labor, and had television existed in the time of Christ a different shape indeed might have been given the Christian Church. Knowing where and when to strike, just as the repair man so aptly illustrated, is the goal to be sought, and not the energy to run a million circles around a field which does not need to be circled even once. Knowledge is the thing, not physical effort; all things exist because of mental causes, have risen in the physical world in response to ideas held in mind. Mind is first cause, and he who is guided by this knowledge discovers the fountain of power.

Your Secret Self is a giant self, dwarfing into nothingness your surface mind and ego. It is a self without limits in space and time, and anything is possible to it. Its manifestations on the human scene sometimes seem supernatural. It outcrops in our geniuses, in those with "second sight," in our artists, our explorers, our pioneers, our adventurers. Its presence may be intimately felt in the fields of parapsychology, extrasensory perception, precognition, clairvoyance, thought transference. It stands behind all human endeavor and aspiration as the guiding intelligence of evolution. Life is going somewhere high and lofty and worthwhile, and the path by which the heights are to be scaled is safe and secure and well-known. Only in partial knowledge is there confusion, and only through the separate and incomplete view of the surface self are we rendered impotent and afraid in a world that should be ours. The little mind that sits immediately behind our eyes has not the horizons nor the expanded consciousness to see the larger picture, the worthier and greater goal of the

Secret Self. All individual suffering, frustration, and failure stem from the failure of the surface mind to find and properly identify itself with the Divine. In isolating ourselves from the true roots of our being, we are thrown out of kilter with the power and surety of the Supreme. By fancying ourselves to be sense-minded only, we are like the severed tail of a snake, possessed of movement still, but senseless now, without purpose or entity, helter-skelter, scratching out a crazy pattern in the dust.

THE GIANT WITHIN

We are one body only, one mind only, one deep and abiding intelligence. We are not tiny infinitesimal parts of an infinite and incomprehensible whole, but we are that very whole, that entire mind, that great and vast intelligence from which the universe has evolved, and everything contained within the universe is contained within us, and if we truly understand ourselves we understand the world and everything in it.

You can be anything you want to be, do anything you want to do, tread any path you will to tread, become master of your fate, ordain your future, but you will not do these things by railing against circumstance, by throwing yourself frantically against events and persons simply because they do not seem to be in accord with your plans. Only by perceiving the hidden purpose behind events, the true motivations that actuate people, will you be able to attune yourself to life, to act in accord with the gigantic tides that bring the future. This faculty is yours once you have gleaned the existence of the Secret Self and have set about striving to live in accord with it rather than with the surface self that has moved you heretofore.

We all aspire to goals, desire to improve our understanding and our abilities. We would not be alive if growth were not inherent in us. But oftentimes our growth becomes calcified through being ringed around with impermeable layers of selfishness and conceit. This selfishness is not necessarily just acquisitiveness; it may even be exemplified by an overwhelming generosity; it is simply primary concern for the ego, a living by and in accordance with the little "I" that constitutes the average person's knowledge of himself. Such conceit makes knowledge of self a constant judgment, a comparison with others, favorably or unfavorably. It feeds on flattery and victory, is decimated by criticism and defeat. It has no true existence, but depends entirely upon circumstance and the reactions those circumstances set up within it. As a consequence, it is always exultant or sad, for its impression of itself is that it is either better than or worse than everything that confronts it. It has absolutely no knowledge of equality.

THE ULTIMATE RESOURCE

Breaking through the limiting boundaries of the ego into the unimpaired vision and knowledge and joy of the Secret Self is the undoubted goal of evolution, the purpose of life. This transformation, truly a transfiguration of the mind and spirit, is not an absolute thing but a matter of degree, is partially achieved at this moment by thousands of living persons, is possible of limited attainment by anyone who lives. To exist immersed in the ego is to live a restricted life, to realize only a small fraction of your potentiality. Such deliberate subordination to the dictates of nature is a subjection to pain and suffering and death and decay. Such subjection is normal to lower forms of life, seems part of the plan by which the Secret Self is emerging from matter, but when consciousness has reached the point where it recognizes its imprisonment, when it sees its subjection to circumstance and pleasure and pain, then it must strive to be free, to establish a truer order for its development. It then must break through the barriers of its awareness, cease living in the ego and attain the widened horizons and powers of the Secret Self, or it will fall back into the inertia of the sensual nature, lose its capacity for growth and development and so cease to represent the Secret Self at all. To the person trapped and resigned to be trapped in the ego, there is no final end but suffering and pain. Only in the Divine lie the ultimate resources that overcome all obstacles, and only in seeking to discover the Secret Self has a man firmly set foot on the one and only path that leads to success, serenity, and joy.

STRUGGLE AND SACRIFICE

Nothing, of course, can be accomplished without a fight. Life itself is a struggle, and each of us enters it daily. It is simply a question of where to expend the effort: pursuing the material wraiths of the physical world that constantly seem to elude us or concentrate on an inner resource that controls the outer world. It is a wise man who expends his energies developing his consciousness. He shortly will find that all the aspects of the world have assumed an order and a benignity he would not have thought possible. All things appear to do his bidding, not because he truly bids them, but because he understands them. It is this knowledge, attained by inner perception, of the potentiality of each thing and circumstance, that leads to beneficent power, that allows a man to move through the most intense conflicts with serenity and surety. He sees the thing to be done because he knows the outcome that must be achieved, and because of this inherent perception of the laws of life and nature, he appears to be modelling each event, shaping each thing, yet it is not he who does this but the Secret Self within him, to which he has entrusted himself completely and which guides his steps and actions with omnipotent assurance.

Will you have the power and assurance and serenity of the Secret Self? Then there is something you must give up. You must give up the ego, that thing within you that you always have thought to be your very self. You must seek to shed that sense of separateness that is a product of your surface mind and to search deep within your consciousness for the pure core of being that is the self of all things. It will not be easy. The sensual nature with its constantly distracting stimuli brings daily clarion calls from the outer world. But if your life has provided you full measure of pain and frustration from chasing these tempters and deceivers, then you will face them with resistance and resolve to pursue them no more. The path to power lies within you. All things will be found there. The fight is not between the world and you, but between your ego and your true self. Simply choose to find your true self, and in the end you cannot lose.

When the fight begins within himself,
A man's worth something.

—Robert Browning

2 DISCOVERING THE SECRET SELF

Human personality is immensely complex. A person is far more than a name and certain physical, mental, and emotional characteristics. It is strange that we ever feel we know others at all, when the slightest examination of our own psyche reveals at once that we know scarcely anything about ourselves. We do not even dwell alone in our own bodies, are for the most part a battleground for opposing sides of our nature; and as one assumes command, then another, we present the constantly changing colors of a chameleon.

OUR MANY SELVES

A man engaged in concentrated effort often talks to himself. One part of him sits in judgment on the other, so that he gives vent to little exclamations of exasperation such as, "You can do better than that, Henry, old boy," or "Don't be such a bonehead, you can get it!" In this apparent division of the self, one half assumes a nature that appears above reproach while the other apparently has the personality of a mischievous, recalcitrant child. If you ask Henry which of the two he is, he answers that he is Henry. If you ask him who is talking to Henry, he achieves a look of utter blankness, manages to answer at last that he's only talking to himself.

Well, it isn't just a way that Henry has, it's a way that all of us have. We house within us not one nature, but many, not one self, but a whole myriad of selves superimposed upon each other like endless reflections in opposing mirrors; and not one of these selves is our true self, not even all taken together, but another truer being hidden within, timeless and eternal and unchanging.

The conflicts and oppositions of the many sides of our surface nature are directly responsible for the prevalence of that psychological disorder called schizophrenia. The schizophrenic is disoriented with the world and himself through intense inner conflicts waged by several of his different natures. In extreme cases, one, then the other, takes over, so that he is possessed of several distinct personalities, each as different from the other as night from day. A number of clinical cases of this nature have been studied extensively, one has even been made into a best-selling book, so that by and large people are finally becoming aware of the wavering, mystical being each of us really is.

The psychologically sound person is one who takes charge of his own personality, refuses to allow himself to be influenced by the wind, imposes a discipline upon himself predicated upon the goals he wishes to achieve. Yet despite this "taking charge," despite the discipline imposed upon the surface nature and inner parts of the psyche, the psychologically sound person must remain subservient to an inner hidden part of his being, that indestructible and bright core within that sustains him and gives him life. If he does not, then a sickness of all his parts aggrandizes his ego, disassociates him from reality, causes him to assume the psychologically functional disorder known as paranoia. His blown-up ego then has shut him off from the supporting and sustaining Secret Self, and he is heading directly for destruction. Most of the dictators of our modern political systems have been of this type, carrying their countries and themselves to destruction in a blind and headlong rush.

INFINITY IN THE FINITE

It becomes obvious, once we give it close consideration, that man not only is at war with nature, but actually is at war with himself. We are such battlegrounds within that often we cannot contain our turmoil and our entire psyche becomes permeated with a sickness that makes it of little use to the world or ourselves. Whatever the human being is, he is more than a physical body, and the misty shape of his invisible aura is something that cannot be contained within boundaries or assigned categories or weighed or measured or counted. All that we are and can hope to be is mental, is the essence of some gigantic intelligence in the lap of which we nestle and from which we are fed and nurtured as if from subterranean springs. This gigantic intelligence is the Secret Self of the universe; it is also, paradoxically enough, the Secret Self of each of us.

No amount of rhetoric prevails against disbelief; no argument dissuades the man of faith. Still, the enigma is there. How is it possible that something infinite in size and scope, like a universal mind, can be housed within the tiny, finite body of an individual man? To be infinite is to be one. More than one of anything infinite automatically is not infinite, for anything infinite occupies all the space there is and therefore does not leave room for anything else. Thus anything infinite is exactly the same as anything within it, for all of anything infinite has to be at each particular place at each particular time. Now this may be a pretty hard dose to swallow, but it is perhaps as scientifically sound as the Quantum Theory of physics, and what it essentially means is this: if there is intelligence behind life, and there is every reason to believe there must be, then all of that intelligence is innate in each creation of that intelligence. Thus universal mind or the Secret Self is complete and entire within each of us. We have only to discover it for its power and perfection to be ours.

But neither the search nor the finding are easy. We are so steeped in our egotism, so encysted within our myriad surface selves, that vision to penetrate the illusion is hard to acquire, is developed only by arduous mental effort and spiritual discipline. Underlying all the turmoil, supporting the contest between the surface selves, giving each life direction and purpose, is the garden from which springs personality, the Secret Self, a place of calm and certitude within each of us. There is no struggle in the Secret Self. It *knows.* Its mere act of perception is an act of creation, for seeing precedes being in this most mental of all places where thought and idea are always prior to physical fact.

BEHIND THE WALL

Carl Jung has stated that most people confuse "self-knowledge" with knowledge of their conscious ego personalities, so that anyone with any ego at all takes it for granted that he knows himself. Actually, he knows only the ego and its contents and seldom has little if any knowledge of the vast and shadowy areas of the subconscious from whence all the impulsions and compulsions that form his active life spring. No man is free who feels that his motivations originate in his conscious ego personality. He is moved about in life like a puppet by the subconscious, and all his elaborate reasonings and painful arrivals at conscious perceptions are made after the fact of his commitment to certain ideas and actions, never before. Between the surface self and the Secret Self lies an opaque wall, impenetrable to the gaze of the ego and yielding its secrets only to one who has expanded his consciousness beyond the limits of his conscious mind. The materialist who prides himself on never accepting anything but a proven physical fact has merely accepted blindness as a condition of his being, and what he thinks is freedom is simply servitude of the highest degree. Turning one's back on the subconscious does not obliterate it. The individual is sprung into being not by an effort of self, but comes preformed by something other than the ego that fronts his consciousness during life. The question is, who is the true resident within, the ego that grows from experience, or the life force that animates from the beginning? Reflection leads us inescapably to the conclusion that the true person within is the hidden dweller in *all* things, that the ego is only a mask donned by this dweller for a moment in some inscrutable play being acted out for its secret delight.

The constant search of the psyche of man, as long as it confines itself to the ego and the surface nature, must continue to be fruitless, for it concerns itself with a wraith. To truly know man, his actual nature, origin, purpose, destiny, the deeper regions of consciousness must be probed. These are all subconscient, make up the vast, jumbled, tremendously powerful, even frightening mental area below consciousness. Who knows what things are possible to this area of man's being? Sigmund Freud, having exposed its awesome powers, is reported once to have confessed that he created the dogma of his sexual theory of human behavior because some powerful bulwark of reason was needed against the black flood of occultism that might spring from the subconscious. Yet it is just that occultism, just that black flood that most needs to be studied, for the Secret Self lies there.

THE UNUTTERED PART OF LIFE

The ouija board and divining rod are not just parlor games or the tools of crackpots but are the best of illustrations that within us there is a being enormously different from our surface selves and which has powers of perception and knowledge vastly greater than our conscious minds. A man with a forked hazel stick can find water beneath the surface of the ground, and this remarkable feat is true not because there is any affinity between the water and the hazel stick, but because there exists in the subconscious of the man a means of perceiving that water underlies a particular piece of ground. The stick turns downward and points out the water because of unconscious muscular reactions on the part of the man, but he will swear it does so of its own volition; and to the degree that the turning down is originated by the Secret Self and not by his surface self, his claim is true. In any case, the stick turns down, the well is dug, and water is there. The man couldn't have seen the water, the stick couldn't have known it was there. Some other thing, some invisible force was at work. That thing, that force, is the Secret Self.

Thomas Carlyle wrote, "The uttered part of man's life, let

us always repeat, bears to the unuttered, unconscious part a small unknown proportion. He himself never knows it, much less do others." We wend our unheeding oblivious ways through life, captives of forces we neither understand nor are aware exist, and we labor under the delusion that we are free. This blindness has not been forced upon us because of our relationship to life, nor is it necessary in order to preserve our sanity or individuality as some casuists would have us believe. It is simply an inevitable step in the evolution of mind out of matter, and even now is being transcended by those individuals sufficiently evolved to correctly perceive the Secret Self and its existence within. Mind seeks to know; its goal is a constantly increasing awareness. Expanding consciousness is apparent wherever we look, almost as if a mental explosion had taken place in the heart of the universe and now speeds outward in all directions, encompassing everything.

LIBERATION FROM BONDAGE

The surface mind is not the true mind, is but the barest fractional part of the true mind, and we never know our power and effectuality until we turn away from this troublesome false self and originate thought and action on the deeper planes of our being. Then we become as a power doubled upon itself, have "hitched a ride" on illimitable energy. Below the surface self and the conscious mind, sustaining and supporting both but remaining infinitely greater than either, is universal subconscious mind, the vast mind that springs into being all living things, that underlies life like a great and infinite ocean of intelligence and energy. This subconscious mind is not just a hodgepodge reservoir of instincts, urges, and long forgotten memories individual to each man, neither a kind of cell memory of pain and pleasure as some psychologists would have us believe, but encompasses infinitely more, the whole scope of creation, of space and time and knowledge and purpose, and all of this mind is in every person and no one has a larger share of it than others, and all of it is available to each of us this very moment, is actually the sustaining self of every one of us.

Frustration and suffering are the human lot in this stage of evolution because we have separated ourselves from the root source of our power. This has been done as consciousness has evolved into self-consciousness, for the particular stage of self-consciousness at which we have arrived is embryonic, is only self-consciousness in the narrowest sense of the word, delimits itself by the boundaries of the physical senses and therefore makes of itself a tiny speck in an infinitely large and living universe. It is small wonder that we are blinded to the beginnings and ends of life, so tiny is our newly-acquired sense of being. Yet even now it reaches groping and hopeful hands toward an alliance with its greater self, and it is this alliance that will finally liberate it from bondage to the flesh, from the limitations of space and time and matter.

THE OTHER PERSON IN YOU

All this may sound pretty obscure, even occult, and since the average person today is so grounded and steeped in materialism, there may be those of you who balk at this point and say, "Prove it. Show me evidence of Universal Subconscious Mind." There is evidence aplenty.

Various hypnotic techniques are continually exposing layers of the subconscious that indicate that they are not the personal property of the person under hypnosis. For example, Miss Jones may be hypnotized and recall intimate details of a life not her own, so that the unwary researcher will be led to believe that she is recalling a life lived previously. Such evidence is continually offered in support of the reincarnation thesis, but no such actual proof ever has been forthcoming. People under hypnosis have spoken languages they neither consciously understood nor ever had heard, described in detail places and times where they had never been and could not have conscious knowledge of, literally performed all manner of clairvoyant feats that indicate the amazing power and scope of the subconscious; and the indisputable evidence is of a single entity only, existing in all persons but the individual property of none.

Someone else lives in your body other than the surface mind which you have long regarded as yourself, a bigger, finer, more dynamic, more gifted, and powerful person than you ever have imagined yourself to be, but your true self nevertheless, the real you. Its action and power are behind every thought and move you make, and if your conscious mind is opposed to this real self, then you are torn on the rack of indecision and opposition and meet nothing but frustration and disappointment wherever you turn. But once your conscious mind and surface self are lent as tools to this subconscious self, then of a sudden you are a whole and glorious thing and you find yourself proceeding along life's pathways with surety and power.

YOUR SENIOR PARTNER

To fully uncover the Secret Self is no doubt the final goal of evolution. When the inhabiting spirit has fully emerged from matter, then the Godhead will be revealed at last with all its conscious power and infinite realization. The man who joins this irresistible tide is swept onward by unsuspected energies to accomplish feats far beyond his poor mortal self. He has hitched a ride on cosmic power, and his energies and inspirations spill over the boundaries of his surface self and touch all those with whom he associates. He becomes a leader, a doer, a creator, and achieves a kind of omnipotence because he is led in performance by an infallible and irresistible force.

You can talk to the Secret Self. You can go into conference with it much as you might consult an all-wise and benevolent father or the president of the business that employs you. Once you have the hang of it and come to fully realize beyond any shadow of doubt its potentiality and possibility, then daily conference will be as natural and fitting to your mode of living as the act of breathing. This is "the Father that dwells within you," spoken of by Jesus. This is the senior side of your dual personality, the detached one that judges the action and is untouched by it. This is the subconscious mind referred to by psychologists, the mind that never sleeps, thinks when all is still, works with surety and calmness in the midst of the greatest turmoil. This is the talisman that delivers you the "hunch," that brings your fortune, the idea for your book, painting, or composition, an inner vision, a new path to tread. This is the deep center of your being to which you retreat in meditation and prayer, where joy, serenity, and bliss reign because all is known and truly understood.

Haven't you ever contacted it? Set that right at once. As soon as you know the Secret Self is there, your close relationship to it is assured, for who would turn his back on the source of his redemption from pain and suffering and frustration?

AN EXPERIMENT

Take a simple finger ring. Tie it to a thin thread about twelve inches long. Hold the loose end of the thread between your thumb and forefinger. Let the ring dangle. Now tell the Secret Self that you are going to ask it some questions, that if the ring moves in a small circle you will understand the answer to be "yes," that if it sways back and forth in a linear path you will understand the answer to be "no." Ask the question aloud; hold the ring and wait. Don't try to stop it from moving, and make no attempt to start it moving. It will move. At first, the movement will be erratic, but soon it will settle into a back and forth or circular motion. Eventually, your questions will be answered instantaneously. Then you will have made a direct contact with the Secret Self, and you will realize with comprehending awe that someone infinitely aware dwells within you.

There is no limit to the power of the Secret Self. Your whole effort from the moment of your realization of its existence should be to become acquainted with it, to explore its infinite facets and discover the keys that unlock its powers. Once you begin to guide your life in accordance with its perceptions and motivations you will begin to take on an infallibility in works that bodes success in every undertaking, every relationship. You will find that you are accompanied always by a feeling of inner joy and energy and well-being where before you were always gnawed at by vague anxieties and fears and feelings of lethargy and fatigue. The color of the sky will change; the world will take on a new and meaningful and exciting aspect. You will have placed yourself in tune with the guiding and motivating force of the universe, and it will buoy your spirits heavenward. No task will appear too great, no obstacle insurmountable.

SUPPORTER OF THE WORLDS

Arthur Schopenhauer wrote, "Every man takes the limits of his own field of vision for the limits of the world." And it is this blinding quality of the surface psyche, that it cannot see beyond the limits it imposes upon itself, that gives inherent characteristics of weakness and incapability to every mortal man. Even so, the degree is markedly different in the limitations men impose upon themselves. Some men build towers to the sky, challenge nature in her most inaccessible places, make their whole lives a constant attack on mental and physical barriers. Other men accept all the limitations they encounter, live in fear of self-manufactured ogres, cannot challenge, expand, or grow because they are slaves of the tiny surface self and have not glimpsed or understood the giant within them. There is hope for the man who aspires; his place among the gods is assured. But he who hangs back and never dares and never takes action is withering on the tree of life, and all his wishes will not change anything as long as they are not strong enough to prompt him to attack his fear-created walls.

Once you have discovered the Secret Self within, then it becomes a gradual process of turning over your work, your goals and aspirations to it. You cannot build a perfect life on the imperfect foundation of the surface self. It will not support even the flimsiest edifice, will crumble under the slightest pressure. All must be built on the Secret Self, which already supports the worlds and the universes and will support your life, be you savant or saint, and without the slightest tremor.

Of all the causes that conspire to blind
Man's erring judgment, and misguide the mind,
What the weak head with strongest bias rules,
Is pride, the never-failing vice of fools.

—Alexander Pope

FACING FEAR

It is vanity, or pride if you will, which is the true enemy of the Secret Self. For with consciousness centered in the surface self, with the vanity that self-centeredness brings, an opaque veil is drawn over all spiritual perception, and a man lives isolated from the well-springs of his being. He may struggle through life many years in this manner, attacking his problems and pursuing his goals with the persistent energy of an enterprising fly, but eventually he must be brought up short by the realization that he simply is ineffectual and he had best find a new blueprint of thought and action or give up the ghost altogether. One ant alone does not topple a rubber tree plant. Only the concerted effort and teamwork of thousands of ants make this feat possible; and the energy and effort of one human being is nothing by itself, but is everything when it proceeds from the source of all energy, for then it is attuned to the tides and forces of the cosmos, becomes in a manner an irresistible force, a kind of infallible action.

Success stories often are fictions concocted by the human desire to achieve supremacy over circumstance. Most people fit into a kind of equation. They react a certain way when confronted with certain circumstances, and therefore *must* act a certain way *always* when confronted with those same circumstances. For example, suppose a man is afraid of groups of people when he is unacquainted with them and expected to circulate amongst them and communicate. If early in life he gives in to his fear and avoids new groups, such behavior becomes a habit and one that he eventually finds impossible to break. Therefore, all through his life, when confronted with a strange social situation, he will avoid it through one pretense or another, simply because he has built up a habit of acceding to fear. He is absolutely predictive in each circumstance of this type, and he is predictive because he is not free, because he is a slave to his fears. He has become an automaton led around by the nose, a victim of circumstances because he is not master of his feelings. He tends to regard circumstance itself as the evil, says, "People in groups are uninteresting. They bore me." They don't bore him at all; they scare hell out of him; so much so that he avoids them at all costs, leaves a large blank in a portion of his psyche and is completely frustrated in this area of his growth. And it is his own fault. He simply cannot bring himself to muster the courage necessary to face his fear.

OVERCOMING WEAKNESS

"You cannot run away from a weakness; you must sometime fight it out or perish; and if that be so, why not now, and where you stand?" Fittingly enough, these lines were penned by a writer bedfast through illness, but he turned that illness into a great victory, eventually recovering his health and giving the world masterpieces of literature. His name—Robert Louis Stevenson.

We must not be soft with ourselves no matter what our goals or positions. All things fare best when they are constantly tested by opposition. The sturdiest grass is that which must grow through concrete. The coddled lawn burns clean away at first exposure to sun or wind. If we have an aching muscle we must learn to exercise it, not to rest it, and we will find the muscle soon healed. If our psyche is closing us in, cutting us off from life and growth and expansion, then we must learn to test and use and expand that psyche. If we do not, the psyche will atrophy, cut off completely all normal ties with life. Still, to be human is to be weak, is to be subject to sin and suffering and error, and as long as we live we never truly overcome any of these; but as long as we live we must try, for we truly live only when we try. What we finally have to learn is that we cannot expect an ultimate or even a satisfying victory over our infirmities when we meet them one by one, but only when we have found a way of assembling all on the same field of battle for one final showdown. What results then must be a complete step forward in our evolution as human beings, for no one is ever defeated who gathers courage to face his assembled weaknesses.

"How is this possible?" someone may ask. "How does one gather all his weaknesses in one spot and overcome them?" It is not simple or even apparent. In isolated areas, yes. If you have a tendency to be afraid of new situations, then you can build up confidence about them by forcing yourself to enter into them. Sooner or later you are bound to meet each new situation calmly, if not eagerly, for the general condition of newness has become familiar. This exercise of will power, however, while it will tend to give you courage in every aspect of your life simply because you have met fear in one area and defeated it, nevertheless will not overcome a tendency to be lazy, for example, or untruthful, or disloyal, or even to eat too much. As a matter of fact, it can readily be seen that his helter-skelter treatment of the unwhole psyche is much like a man trying to plug a series of leaks in a dike with his fingers. Eventually all ten fingers will be occupied, and still the new leaks come.

THE UNIVERSAL AUTHOR

What is needed is a new approach to the psyche, one that treats it as a single thing and not as a group of aberrations or incomplete perceptions, and the approach which gives one hundred per cent cures in one hundred per cent of cases is one in which the individual comes to know and be aware of his Secret Self.

Each of us faces life with an undeveloped psyche. It is undeveloped because it is less than whole, because it is only a partial manifestation of something greater than itself. Only insofar as it approaches awareness of this greater self does it approximate wholeness or self-sufficiency. That sense of self which we use in our daily rounds of effort is useful only insofar as it is larger than the task we undertake. It is perfectly up to peeling potatoes, for instance, but when something large is asked of it, then it may cower in the corner. Bridges are built by the Secret Self and not by the surface ego of man. Towers and highways and planes and automobiles and television are wrought by the Secret Self. All books are written by the same author, all pictures painted by the same artist, all music written by the same composer. The ego of the individual is simply not up to such tasks, and as long as a man lives entrapped in bondage to his surface self, then his efforts can only be crowned by such puny results as fit his ego. Only when he tears himself away, divorces himself from vanity and conceit and ego and surface self can he at last perceive the true dimensions of the being that dwells within him. Then he knows his true self, then he turns his life over to it. Then his efforts take on a grandeur and purpose that are bound to achieve noble and vigorous ends, for the power that engrosses him proceeds from outside him and carries him along on its surging tides and is greater than he in every way

Any man or woman whose life is aimed at creative effort is bound to discover the Secret Self sooner or later. No one can closet himself in the nebulous realm of the mental and spiritual without early coming to know that there dwells within him a mental being of enormous dimension and power, contact with which has the power to ennoble and illumine each moment. The author seeks his muse with all his heart. The painter pauses with raised brush, awaiting inspiration. We are moved from within toward each aspiration, provided it is loftier than the limitations of the surface self; and so the world belongs to those who aspire, who dare, who try, for all aspiration is only effort against the prison of the surface self, and all such effort is the alchemy by which the common clay of our little egos is transmuted into something transcendental and precious.

AN ARTIST FINDS HIS TALENT

A number of years ago there lived in a poor section of a large city a man who had given up the years of his youth to perfect his art. He lived meagerly on what few pennies he could earn making charcoal sketches in waterfront bars, and he spent every moment he could spare in front of his easel. He painted ships, every conceivable type and kind, at sea, becalmed and in storm, in port, loading and unloading, ships under sail, ships under steam, sleek yachts, wallowing freight ers, men o'war. He loved the sea and he loved to paint, and by the amount of time he had spent at each he should have mastered his art very well, but he hadn't. Somehow it escaped him. His paintings were not amateurish: they exhibited the hand of a craftsman; yet they always seemed clichés, as if they were saying something that had been said a thousand times before. People would look at them and even comment that they had seen them before. They hadn't, of course. The paintings just contrived to look like others that had been done.

The painter realized this fact only too well. His work was intensely dissatisfying to him. He often would relate that when he first was struck with an idea for a new subject he would be deeply elated and would set to work with a vengeance. Then, as the work progressed under his hand, he gradually would come to see that it was not a thing of inspiration at all, but wooden, pat, said before, a reproduction, and even before the work was finished he would be gripped by a depression so intense that he scarcely could finish. Still, he drove himself unremittingly. He felt a talent was within him, and he was determined to get it out. Once, in a rage at himself, he burned all the paintings in his studio, nearly setting fire to the building. Another time he was so furious at his hand for its clumsiness that he badly lacerated his fingers, intent on cutting them off. All this, of course, would indicate that our friend was not psychologically stable, but perhaps it was simply that his provocation was great, so enormous was the creative urge that constantly goaded him.

Like most of the great lessons that life teaches, his enlightenment came dear. When war broke out he had just finished a period of deep dissatisfaction with his painting. Disgustedly, he decided to turn his back on it forever. He shipped out as a merchant seaman aboard a freighter bound for Murmansk. The convoy was attacked by German planes and submarines as it skirted the Norwegian coast. Our painter's ship was sunk, and he wound up in a lifeboat on the frigid and stormy Arctic Ocean. For days and nights they drifted, fighting the freezing cold, trying to stay alive. At one juncture the skies cleared long enough for them to be sighted by German planes, and they were bombed and strafed. Five men were killed, three others seriously wounded, dying that night. A day later, two more died from exposure. Finally there were left in the boat only the painter and the ship's purser, an elderly and apparently frail man who surprisingly still survived.

"It's no use," said the painter at length. "There is no hope for us, and we might as well slip over the side right now and be done with it."

"That's not for us to decide," said the purser.

"Who then?" asked the painter.

The purser sat calmly, and his eyes were kind. "Do we decide to be born?" he asked. "Do we decide our nationality, our race, our heritage? Someone or something else does, I think. Get yourself quiet and listen. Perhaps you will hear a voice speak within you. Then you will learn whether you are to live or die."

The end seemed near. Surely it was useless to struggle further. For the first time in his life the painter was able to give over direction of his destiny to something other than his own ego. The bitter cold of approaching night descended on them. Just before dusk a British seaplane swooped out of the fog with a roar, saw them, landed on the sea, took them aboard. They were in a London hospital that night.

After some weeks of convalescence, our painter once again tried his hand at his easel. What emerged from the canvas startled him. It was as if a hand other than his own guided the brush, chose the colors, as though a mind other than his own envisaged the scene. Viewing the complete painting he felt a surge of joy. This was the talent he had fought to bring forth, and now it was flowing! In rapid succession he completed six paintings, packed them off to a London art dealer where they were received with open arms. They were an instantaneous success, launched him on a long and remarkable career.

Years later he was asked about his early period of struggle and how his talent happened to mature. "It didn't mature," he answered. "It was there all the time. I just never could bring it out because I thought it belonged to me. As soon as I was able to see that it belonged to a being greater than I, it emerged of its own accord and used me, where before I had been trying vainly to use it."

Mystical, yes, a kind of cosmic perception by the artist of his muse, but a far greater secret is hidden here. Our painter stumbled upon the psychological relationship of ego to Secret Self that brooks no failure, that inevitably leads to success, for it is a relationship in which all thought and action proceed out of a universal intelligence and omnipotent power that makes each work absolutely effective.

FALL FROM GRACE

Our consciousness is anchored falsely in our surface selves, and it is this delusion that is our fall from grace, for by it we do not know who we truly are and fancy ourselves as tiny isolated selves in a vast and overwhelming universe. The gradual opening and unfolding of consciousness to that point where the vistas within our psyche are revealed is the goal of evolution itself, as life and intelligence and being manifest out of matter, eventually control and dominate matter. As long as we remain chained to the illusion of the surface self we are but puppets of sensation, reacting this way or that to every situation that confronts us, little more than absolutely predictive ciphers in an equation aimed at producing the free, thinking, omnipotent man. Yet this condition of freedom and omnipotence needs only perception, for without doubt the mere act of perceiving the Secret Self is akin to becoming one with the Secret Self. How then shall we see? How shall our eyes be opened?

Perhaps the most important step in discerning the Secret Self is disillusionment with the effectiveness of the surface self, for how is it possible to see when we still rejoice in our blindness? So it is that spiritual awareness, psychic enlightenment, seldom come to one in youth, for youth is preoccupied with the senses, pursues all manner of sensual inamorata, and is for the most part completely oblivious of the prison which the senses have erected. Passing years bring the disappointments, the frustrations and inadequacies that cause the seeking soul to cast about within psychic realms for a new foundation on which to erect a more reliable and effective sense of self. When this comes, eventual enlightenment is assured, for no one seeks but he finds, knocks but the door is opened. The mere act of turning away from the senses and the surface self seems sufficient. The veil is removed, the blinder disintegrated, and an event in psychic life that was brought about by suffering and frustration and disillusionment turns out to be the greatest of blessings in disguise. A new world is revealed. The death of the surface self actually turns out to be a new birth. Resignation of the senses from control of the person turns out to be a seizing of the reins of the life by a new and dominant and effective force. When the inner eye of the soul is opened there descends upon the whole being a unity of parts and force, a vitality and serenity that remake that life completely, that lend magic and grandeur to everything that is touched or taken into consciousness.

> Who sees with equal eye, as God of all
> A hero perish or a sparrow fall
> Atoms or systems into ruin hurl'd
> And now a bubble burst, and now a world.
>   —Alexander Pope

PATH TO ILLUMINATION

While it is true that perception of the indwelling Secret Self ordinarily comes to harrassed mortals only after much suffering and disillusionment, nevertheless there is a path by which such suffering may be avoided in the main, provided that first the soul is dedicated and sincere in its desire to make the discovery. The Secret Self is never discovered alone within, but at the same time is discovered in all places, in all beings, and is found to be the same in all. Different forms of life are merely disguises donned for the moment by the single self that underlies all, that truly is all, a play in which for the moment the Divine is hidden, in which for that moment it actually has become in entirety each of the things it has become. All the power and effectiveness of the Supreme is within you, is yours to use, and is also in everyone and everything else, existing there behind the curtain of ego-consciousness, waiting to be discovered. Therefore there is a tremendous underlying equality to all things under the sun. Each is sprung from the same substance and has inherent within it the same omnipotent being, and we are not each of us different and individual and separate except insofar as we are incomplete. To be complete is to be the Secret Self, whole and entire, without reservation or error.

The most painless path to illumination, to perception of the Secret Self, is thus to arrive at a desire to know the truth that lies behind the surface façade of the senses and to seek this truth not only within but without, in every person you meet as well as in yourself. Once this sense of absolute equality of things and people begins to make itself known to you, then you will detect a presence in each stone and clod, in each tree and plant, in each animal and person you meet, locked in a prison dictated by its form to be sure, but a presence pure and simple of the Secret Self, which has chosen the masquerade for its own purposes and is not truly locked away from consciousness of its real self but even now is developing it as we brush at the veil that separates us from our heritage.

Once a man senses the presence of the Divine in all things he is able to arrive at a sense of equality that makes him in some secret and inviolable corner of his being untouched by victory or defeat, pleasure or pain, position or prestige. He becomes so intent on doing the work of the Secret Self that he abandons almost altogether the uses of the ego and so achieves a kind of selflessness in his appearance to the world. Equality is a perfect psychic position, but is impossible to the ego which seeks forever to be better than all the egos around it, and if it is not better it is convinced it is worse and so either becomes blown-up and blind or wounded and fearful and thus provides the worst of all psychic bases for dealing with life, love, and accomplishment. To be equal is to be unafraid. To know that there inhabits all others the same being that inhabits you is to achieve a psychic confidence that enables you to place your life and hopes and energies in the hands of this being without a qualm, with absolute certainty that you will be guided to perform that work that you must do, in the best of all possible ways, at the best of all possible times.

THE PHANTOM MATERIAL WORLD

It is an established fact that our five senses perceive but the tiniest portion of the almost infinite spectrum of vibrations that prevails in the universe, that a million times more remains untold about each thing than can possibly be perceived by sensual means. Whistles can be made which are imperceptible to the human ear but are easily heard by certain animals. The frequency of vibration we know as light is strictly bounded as to the range that has an effect on the human eye, but nevertheless we know there are variations in what people can see—some are color-blind, others nearsighted, others farsighted, some have an artist's vision, to others materializations appear, as to Bernadette at Lourdes. In short, the materialist who prides himself on accepting nothing but the evidence of his senses is accepting the sketchiest of evidence; he actually prides himself on his blindness, accepting things as facts on the basis of knowing a mere one billionth of their total qualities. He would not dream of entering a business deal with such meagre knowledge, but accepts the world and others and himself on such evidence and rears like a reluctant stallion when it is suggested to him that he lives among phantoms.

Focusing attention on the ego and the evidence of the senses is the veil that hides the Secret Self. The senses themselves are not the veil, only the impression they give that they are conveying to the observer the total aspect of things. Nor is ego inherently a veil, only the impression that it gives through completely dominating the consciousness that it is the actual self of the person. Hung up in his sensual world and totally immersed in the ego, a man has no chance to perceive the Secret Self. The clarion call sounds but his ears are not attuned. With his tiny and incomplete knowledge he keeps entering into things without perceiving their true nature and ultimate destiny and therefore his path through life is marked mainly by suffering and defeat, though occasionally the purposes of this ego will coincide with the ends of the Divine, in which case he willingly falls victim to his own duplicity, convinced that his little machinations have moved the world. The end of his ego is certain still, for it is but flotsam adrift on a surging tide and sooner or later destroys itself by pursuing its separate ends.

RESIGNATION AND ASPIRATION

To let go of ego is the thing to be done. To get outside of and free from the grip of the senses is the only path to discovery of the Secret Self. Many people are brought to their knees by life before they let go of self and achieve equality through resignation. Many of the most brilliantly recorded illuminations have happened in this manner. Out of the utmost defeat and degradation of the human soul have arisen its most inspirational moments, but it is doubtful if any human being would willingly choose such a path for an end that is vague to him in the first place. Mystics who have discovered the Secret Self through mental and spiritual concentration report that even they have experienced "a dark night of the soul" as the ego was surrendered. Evelyn Underhill chronicles many such transfigurations and all were preceded by a period of deep spiritual and emotional depression, such as Christ had in the Garden of Gethsemane. It is no easy thing to surrender ego. It is a kind of death. But it must be done before life can be enlarged by the expanded consciousness that results from complete possession of the individual by the Secret Self. The quality above all things that is required is courage. You must push off, the jump must be taken. Lyrically, it is almost exactly as recorded by Dustin Smith, a free fall parachutist.

"The first time you go into a free fall is the weirdest. You have no idea what is going to happen. You are terrified on the first step. Then you look down, like God. And the ultimate is going away from the plane. In this you're free and you're purely responsible for yourself. There is a real moment of truth when you reach for the cord. You come down absolutely elated. You've done something that in one way seems ridiculous, but in another way makes great sense."

Now it is not recommended that any seeker after truth adopt parachuting as a means to illumination, but there can be no doubt from Mr. Smith's observations that pushing off from the safety of an airplane into the unknown dangers of the sky is almost exactly like the spiritual step of pushing away from the ego and surrendering one's life to the unknown guidance of the Secret Self. They both require courage; they both exemplify a search. They both typify man's aspiration to pierce the veils that blind him.

THE COUNTRY BEYOND

The end result of transfiguration, of illumination, is for the ego to be properly subordinated to the Divine, but before the Secret Self can even appear to the aspiring soul there must be a prior period of time in which the edge of the importance of the ego is gradually whittled down until it no longer occupies the whole consciousness, until there is room within the awareness for light to enter, for the Divine to be revealed. Some people are so immersed in the workings of the ego that they haven't the faintest idea what is meant by subordinating it to another principle. To them the ego is the beginning and end, the sum of all existence, and according to how they gratify this surface self by power and position and victory they feel they have achieved success in life. The truth is that the surest way to insure *against* success in life— the success of arriving at a grasp of the meaning of existence— is to continually gratify the ego. What results then is a blindness by limitation, for the ego, being small, cannot see beyond itself.

Jesus, a great mystic and a master of spiritual knowledge, pronounced it to be more difficult for a rich man to enter the kingdom of heaven than for a camel to go through the eye of a needle. This observation of his, of course, is largely parable. It is not strictly rich men Jesus referred to, for some rich men are most spiritual, but rather men who live to gratify the senses and their own ingrown vanity; these are the ones to whom expanded consciousness is unavailable. It is denied for no moral reason, but a purely scientific one. If one chooses to look through a crack in the wall there is revealed a partial world. If one goes *through* the wall, the true aspect of the country beyond is revealed at last. Forsaking ego and uniting with the Secret Self makes this view possible to the aspiring soul.

EXPANDING CONSCIOUSNESS

Consciousness is the key to discovering the Secret Self. To become aware that consciousness is the same in all people is a big step on the road to illumination. Once you have become struck by the enormity of this situation you will never again be the same, for you will innately perceive that at work in the universe is not a multitude of aspiring and searching souls, but one individual only, and you are it and it is all others, and so in a very real sense you and your neighbor are one. Once the magnificent implications of this fact have come home to you, you will see that the secret of effective living is not the exerting of your individual will as you have always supposed it to be, but rather in growing to know and understand events and objects so that you can correctly perceive their true purpose and destiny. And you will not do that by observing the surface facts as recorded by the ego self, but only by expanding your consciousness to the point where objects and events become a part of you, as they surely are in actuality, for both you and they are the Secret Self.

To expand consciousness infinitely would be to grow into oneness with the one force, the one power, the one mind that truly exists. Perhaps this goal in this age and at this stage of evolution is impossible, but nevertheless we can expand our present consciousness a thousandfold, if not to include the universe, certainly to include our friends and neighbors and the events and circumstances that surround us. By a process of identification we can come to know other things and other people and outside events even as we know ourselves, and possessed by this knowledge we can act in the midst of all things in complete accord with their true nature and destiny, and so our actions take on a kind of omnipotence, our works a kind of absolute effectiveness, so that we appear to be molding and changing the world about us when in truth we are only acting in conformity with its real but unrevealed nature.

MAGIC ALCHEMY

"It is not I, but a power greater than I" is the first acknowledgment we must make to the Secret Self. Once this is done, we have by a kind of surrender placed our fate where it should be, in the hands of something infinitely more informed and more capable. To forsake the urgings and promptings of the surface nature and ego is the first step, for as long as we are bound to this ineffective and tiny microcosm we cannot be effective in our works or serene in our spiritual development. We must turn away from that which we have always considered self and embrace that which we have always considered other than self, and in that turning away and in that embracing lies our salvation. "It is not I who doeth the works," stated Jesus, "but the Father that dwelleth within me." And when his transfiguration was complete: "I and the Father are one."

The surface self will not surrender lightly. Its struggles and misguided urgings will be constant. Wise is the man and extremely enlightened who manages to control his ego at all times. To be human is to be subject to error, but to discover within the image of perfection and joy is to find a way out of the morass of physical sensation in which we find ourselves entrapped in life. Salvation for all of us is as near as ourselves, for there dwells within each of us a hallowed light, a hidden self that can relieve our sufferings and frustrations, no matter how painful or enduring. We have only to discover and embrace it, for it to become our true selves and to work its magic in our lives.

3 THE GREATEST MAGIC OF ALL

Mechanistic notions of life are all too prevalent in society today. Most people believe a thing is what it is because of being made out of, by, and from other things, and most of us are intent on moving this thing by hand, as if fancying ourselves chess players and life the board and the pieces the things we are concerned with. All too soon we find we are opposed by an inscrutable and ruthless opponent, and our end is inevitable. We have concerned ourselves with only the surface aspect of the game, and such a viewpoint never can fathom life's nuances and real significance.

IMMORTAL HAND AND EYE

Material concepts of existence wind up depressingly sterile, for after the complex machinery of the human body is reduced to its tiniest cell, still the animating presence is not found; nothing is there but the yawning abyss of a dead and unheeding universe to greet the material researcher. The form of a thing suits its function, and its function suits its purpose, and inherent in each is a complex and highly intelligent design, far surpassing anything yet possible to the surface mind of man. It is not so much the form that we must be concerned with, but the idea that lies behind form, the intelligent purpose that gives that form perfect function.

> Tiger, tiger, burning bright
> In the forests of the night

What immortal hand or eye
Could frame thy fearful symmetry?
—William Blake

Witness the pacing of the sleek and powerful tiger in the cages of a zoo and you know at once that you are seeing a creature consummately designed for a specific function, without a wasted motion, without a spare or useless part. Examine the myriad geometrical designs of snowflakes and you become immediately aware that behind creation lies a supreme mathematical mind, a millionfold more comprehending than that of the most erudite of scientists. The ordered spinning of the planets in space, the arrangement of solar systems in the universe, the design of the atom, the deep and inscrutable mystery of animation; surely we are blind if we fail to recognize the working of a supreme intelligence, guiding, molding, directing with purpose. Out of the infinite plastic creativeness of this intelligence have all things sprung. It makes all, fashions everything from itself. Man does not hold the fate of the universe in his hands; that fate is safe and sure in the hands of its creator, and that creator has incarnated in man all of its potentiality and power.

The ends of evolution were assured long before man arrived upon the earthly scene; they were assured from the very beginning. That intelligence of sufficient scope to have within it the power to originate the concepts of space and time and matter, to create the countless forms of life and animate them with its own presence, surely would not, in any crisis, abdicate, give over control to one of its partially developed and fractionally aware creations. This, however, is the conclusion that some of our thinkers have come to, those, at least, who believe that man controls the universe and his own destiny, the material man, the surface man, the ego-centered, partially aware man.

STEPS AMONG THE STARS

There is a hidden cause of all things, hidden because it is not visible, invisible because it takes no special form, fits no special description. It lies eternally and omnisciently behind the consciousness of every living thing, and it determines all fates, all consequences, all conflicts and resolutions. It is not thwarted in a single aspect of its being or purpose; there are within it no loose ends, no unresolved conflicts. It is universal mind, divine intelligence, the Secret Self that animates every living thing. It is as large as infinity, there are no limits upon its capabilities or powers, and it resides completely and entirely within you. Hidden though it be from your surface mind, it is your own immortal self.

This is the self whose steps are visible in the stars, in the infinitesimal and complex design of the germinating seed, in the color and grandeur and bustling energy of evolving life. It brings all forms into existence, crumbles and dissipates them when the idea behind them has been expressed. It is the sole being, the one mind, the solitary life, the only true presence, the one real self in existence. Immortal, never born, never dying, the infinite sides of its manifold nature are expressed on the stage of life, and each of its creations contains within it all of the essence and power and intelligence of the creator, each has within it the Secret Self.

LIFE TAPS US ON THE SHOULDER

"What good is it," a man sometimes asks. "to have a self that is so far beyond your comprehension, that isn't even the you that you've always thought yourself to be?" There is a very great deal of good. If you focus yourself in the surface mind, then the dimensions of life are forever hidden from you; you do not know where you came from and you do not know where you are going; you even wonder if one day you might suddenly cease to be. You cannot fathom the billions of miles of distance to the nearest star or the billions of years since the earth first swung into orbit around the sun. You cannot see the mind of another person, understand what animates a living being, comprehend the purpose of life. All is mystery, all dwarfs the little ego, which literally cannot see beyond its own nose and grasps even that but vaguely.

Unless we are as uncomprehending as cows in the field, we cannot help but be sick when we live focused in the ego; the world is just too big. Fear and futility and guilt and frustration are our daily lot when we are small and inadequate and know that we are small and inadequate. We may be mice and roar like lions, but we will soon know that we are mice if we live absorbed in the ego. Life taps each man on the shoulder. He either listens or he gets knocked down. No individual reigns supreme; we are all part and parcel of one mind, one self, one supreme intelligence; and inasmuch as we understand this transforming fact that intelligence enters completely into us and possesses us and uses us for its work in the world, so that we perform to the zenith of our human capabilities.

TUNNEL VISION

Implicit in the universe is first cause, original impetus, and this first cause is a primal intelligence from which all things have sprung. It is involved in expressing itself, and the result is the infinite variety and design of life, the endless series of evolving forms that inhabit the world. Each form is not a separate creation of the original intelligence, but rather is an expression of it, so that there dwells in each the original intelligence itself, masquerading as the form and limited to that extent, but in essence remaining infinite and eternal and omniscient. You are not the limited surface self and ego that you have always fancied yourself to be, but you are that very primal intelligence that has manifested all the forms of the universe.

Reflection on the nature of intelligence and consciousness reveals why this is so. When our attention is focused upon a certain thing, inasmuch as our absorption is complete, we become the thing that has our attention. This "tunnel vision" quality of consciousness is responsible for the remarkable phenomena of hypnosis. Where hypnosis is deep and consciousness may be directed toward a single object, subject becomes object and does not know himself in any other way.

If told that he is a duck, he quacks and waddles. If told that he is a bear, he growls. If told that he is a statesman, he delivers orations. He knows himself only as a duck when a duck, only as a bear when a bear, only as a statesman when a statesman. Surely universal intelligence itself must be so absorbed in each of its manifestations, becoming the thing it has become with complete amnesia for its true state and all other manifestations of its nature. This is why we do not know what we truly are and become the thing that our consciousness is focused upon.

CONCEPTUAL UNIVERSE

It would seem that universal mind or primal intelligence has the ability to become anything it would become, or rather, that its inherent nature is to become anything that takes root within it as idea, as thought. The existence of this universal mind must be purely mental. Chief and perhaps solely its activity is thought. It is thinking, and each of its thoughts is manifested as a form in the material world. Each thought contains within it all of the intelligence of the thinker, so that a thought is a thing capable of developing other thoughts. Thus, if a man is a thought in the mind of ʾn eternal thinker, then all of the intelligence of that eternal thinker is latent in the man, and thus the seed of liberation from a directed and focused consciousness is implicit in each of us. We can, in effect, become anything, do anything, since behind our focused awareness lies a universal and omniscient mind. The seed of all possibilities lies within us.

> Short arm needs man to reach to Heaven
> So ready is Heaven to stoop to him.
> —Francis Thompson

The metaphysical aspects of the relationship of universal mind with your own surface mind must be grasped in some manner before it is possible to free yourself from bondage to sensual reaction and slavery to circumstance. It is perfectly all right to admonish a sufferer from circumstance to think positively, but all too often he has not the resources within him to accomplish this, any more than he is able to take arms against the physical events that attack him. It takes a wealth of spiritual resource to produce the courage necessary to free the soul from bondage to the surface self. And it takes a heap of courage to sustain one on that leap into the void of absolute freedom that comes with complete reliance on the Secret Self.

Generally speaking, motives of monetary gain or personal ascendency are simply not sufficient to produce the drive necessary to promote unity between the Secret Self and the surface nature. When we desire things through selfish motives we narrow our perceptual horizons to where it is impossible for us to glimpse the vast and powerful being that dwells within us. We can be beaten into complete submission, into abject humility, but such cessation of the urgings of the ego is all too often temporary, and when the equilibrium of our lives has been restored, then the ego gathers new strength, reconsiders its abdication, once again takes over the life to the sorrow of the person within. The only true and lasting conversion to unity with the Secret Self comes from possessing the facts of the mental and spiritual world we inhabit, so that all mind is seen one mind, all spirit one spirit, all persons one person, and such perception is not accepted on faith or belief but from a clear perception of the facts as they exist, on indisputable and irrevocable proof. Only mental understanding through increased awareness can accomplish this.

THE ETERNAL THINKER

Life for each of us is exactly as we construe it to be, and this is the mental law under which we live. Similarly, all notions of theology and metaphysics are, for each of us, exactly as we construe them to be, for the ideas that take root in our consciousness determine the scope and limitation of our consciousness. In short, God is as we fancy Him to be, and we have only to change our notion of Him in order to change

Him. He is idea only because He is mind, and that idea which is the largest, the most perfect, most workable, clearest, is therefore the nearest approximation of the Godhead. Our illness is caused by the little way we are able to see, and only as we enlarge our vision, push back our horizons, are we cured.

The metaphysic upon which this book is based is this. There is an eternal thinker eternally thinking, and each thought he thinks appears to be separate from him, but it is not; it represents the thinker only, but not entirely, and insofar as the thought exists at all it is the thinker, though not completely. The thinker is God, the thought is man, and God has absorbed himself in the thought but is not bound by this absorption, and may liberate himself at any time by expanding his awareness. As long as man is absorbed in the ego, he is absorbed in the thought and remains the thought, is bound by the idea that actuated him in the first place, but when he lays aside his absorption in the ego, then his entrancement has begun to shatter, and he is beginning to recognize himself as God. As soon as he makes any approximation of this psychic position whatever, he has arrived at a place where he can change the idea that actuated his ego in the first place, where he can make himself into an entirely different person simply by being able to accept an entirely new and different idea about himself.

We must penetrate the apparent duality of life before we are able to clearly understand our oneness with the Secret Self. There are not many different natures and beings at work in the world; only one. All are different aspects of this one being. In each is enclosed that amount of consciousness that determines the form of the thing, but the consciousness enclosed is still the consciousness of the Secret Self, limited and apparently separated because it is absorbed in the thing it has become. And this absorption, this limitation, is what we know as surface self, as ego, and it is the veil that separates us from knowledge of our vaster nature and true being. To get rid of ego then is the thing to be done. To subordinate it to the Secret Self, to place it in proper psychic position to its master and director, and above all to recognize it as primarily illusion, a changing thing, a temporary cloud that stands between us and pure and complete unity with the Divine, these are the steps a novitiate must take before his works in the world are marked by power and effectiveness.

CONDITIONING CONSCIOUSNESS

All lack, limitation, and malfunction that touches our lives is carried in our minds, is literally created there because it is a product of our limited and ego-centered consciousness. We stumble because we do not see, and this condition of not-seeing places the obstacle in our path. Edward Carpenter stated, "It should be as easy to expel an obnoxious thought out of your mind as to shake a stone out of your shoe," but, alas, it is not so. The obnoxious thought is not a thing of itself, but rather the lack of a thing. Negative conditions are imperfect perceptions. It is when we are not able to perceive that we falter. You simply cannot turn your mind upside down and shake out something that is not there in the first place. The reason the obnoxious thought exists is because the consciousness is too small, and simply does not see. The remedy, rather than trying to cast out something that is not truly there, is to expand consciousness until it can be seen that lack and limitation and malfunction only exist by virtue of imperfect mental perception. This is why there is such a great deal of failure on the part of persons who try to create positive conditions in their lives by thinking positively. Usually such positive thoughts center around money, health, love, security, inner peace. A person who lives in a constant state of apprehension is told that all he has to do to develop courage is to tell himself that he is brave. Still, no lion-hearted warrior, he. All positive statements to himself avail nothing, and he is left just as cringing and tension-filled after his self-treatment as before, perhaps more so, for now even the little confidence he once had has been stripped away.

It is simply no good telling yourself that something is white when your eyes tell you that it is black. In order for that something to become white it must *appear* white, and the only way it will appear white is for you to be able, by psychic development, to penetrate the illusion of its blackness. Fear is not inherent in circumstance, it is inherent in our *reaction* to circumstance. If we wish to conquer fear, we must develop such knowledge and perception as enable us to see control and safety in those situations we formerly found threatening. There is nothing wrong with being afraid of a lion. But if we wish to conquer that fear we are going about it the wrong way when we try to hide the fear from ourselves and step out to meet the lion in ignorance, thereby providing the beast a tasty meal. The only way to conquer fear of lions is to learn to handle lions. Once we have learned control, we step out to meet the lion in perfect safety.

> It is not strength, but art obtains the prize
> And to be swift is less than to be wise.
> —Alexander Pope

THE PROPER PSYCHIC POSITION

The single cause of all things is the Secret Self. Out of it all is made. The infinite procession of animate forms in the world is a manifestation of its many-sided and eternal nature. The Secret Self is purely mental. Its essence is light, electricity. It is signified by the enormous at-balance energy in the atom, by the curious invisible prison that locks molecules into certain form and gives them the shape of a tree, a rock. The wonderful, emancipating, hopeful fact is this: the interaction of the Secret Self with its creations is the cause of evolution in the species and the cause of evolution in the individual. A man can change himself, make himself better, by achieving proper relationship with it.

What is this proper relationship? It is not a groveling debasement, not a tearful submission, not an abject resignation. It is a conscious and controlled turning over of the life to a power more fitted to use and develop it than the ego of the individual. The ego remains, to be sure, the surface mind remains, but subordinated now, vehicles of a greater power, a vaster consciousness than directed the life before. To find the proper relationship between the ego and the Secret Self is to discover that psychic position from which all things are possible, that vortex of energy and creativeness that makes a giant out of the most humble of men.

Learn to listen. There are voices that speak within the soul. When you consciously give over direction of your life to something other than the ego, the voice of the Divine becomes unmistakable. Inner sight comes with this inner voice, so that you will intuitively perceive the truth in situations where formerly it was hidden. Mysteriously, the boundaries of consciousness widen, encompassing persons, things, situations, so that you move in accord with their natures, so that your actions begin to take on a kind of infallibility through being perfectly attuned with your surroundings and the persons with whom you come in contact.

UNLOCKING THE PRISON OF SELF

Imagination is the key that unlocks the prison of self. Each of us is contained within the poor four walls of his ego, and it is this containment, this restriction that visits our ills upon us, that locks us away from the source of our power. The mental essence of the Secret Self is imagination. In one quick instant imagination can span all boundaries, all space, all time. Man, the physical animal, is only an infinitesimal creature struggling in the gigantic abyss of space and time, but man, the mental being, has the same stature as the universe itself, for his mind can perceive all and understand all, the very structure of matter and life. Imagination propels him into such understanding. Imagination is his link with the Secret Self.

John Masefield wrote, "Man consists of body, mind, and imagination. His body is faulty, his mind untrustworthy, but his imagination has made him remarkable. In some centuries, his imagination has made life on this planet an intense practice of all the lovelier energies."

It has been established that whatever is maintained as an

image in the mind will make its way into the outer world and manifest as a physical fact. This is not because we have changed the outer world but because we are able to see there only those things that our consciousness is conditioned to perceive. By changing our consciousness we alter our perception. Consciousness is generally altered by stimuli from the outer world. One born into money tends to develop a prosperity consciousness and thus to live all his life in a condition of plenty. Similarly, one born into a condition of poverty tends to develop a scarcity consciousness and thus to live all his life in a condition of scarcity. Insofar as this is true of each of us, we are slaves to our environment. Yet the liberating tool lies within—imagination. According to how we use this consciousness-conditioning power of our minds we are able to remake our lives.

Imagination can condition your consciousness any way you choose. Properly used, it can make you master of all events, all circumstances. No longer need you exist as an equation of reaction to the things and events that surround you, but instead you may cast up within your mental being those images that most suit your inner goals and intents. Seeing these instead of opposition and discouragement, nothing under the sun can stop you from achieving them.

VISUALIZATION

What a lovely thing is the power of the mind to visualize! Pageants, scenes, whole arenas of action may be cast up within the imagination, in full color and sound, at a moment's notice. What we choose to see within our minds we see, and this is the principal fact of our existence. We are always no more or less than the things that take root in our consciousness, and when we determine to keep out all that detracts and restricts and limits, then we have taken our first step in making our lives a self-determined affair rather than a reaction. The God-like part of man is mental, spiritual. What is so astounding about his existence is not his hands or eyes or heart or liver or even brain, but the fact that he thinks, visualizes, conceives, originates. By an amazing gift of some genie he is able to choose what he will think and thereby determine his fate.

All creativity stems from the relationship of the surface self with the Secret Self, and from the dynamic effect of imagination upon the Secret Self. An author puts himself in tune with his muse by first subordinating his surface self to some power within which he knows to be great and vastly effective. He then focuses his imagination on his story and his characters, and by a process that seems entirely independent of him they begin to move and reveal themselves, and the story unfolds. He is not "making it up." It is as real to him, more real in fact, than the chairs and desks in his room. What is happening in his mind is happening *within* him, and he acknowledges it immediately as being part of him, as changing him, as making him different than he was before the story came and the characters performed. Upon the moving screen of his mind an intensely significant and highly symbolic drama is played, for what he visualizes there is taken unto him and becomes a part of him, and his consciousness is altered by it. It is not the author who creates the book, but the book that creates the author, just as we all are creations of the mental images and ideas and thoughts that have found a home in our minds.

THE SEED OF PERFECTION

Each of us is an infant in the metamorphosis of the soul through myriad forms and an eternity of changings. We fancy ourselves as concrete things, something with boundaries, unchanging, and when we have occasion to refer to ourselves or examine ourselves introspectively, we believe we know what we refer to and are adamant in our avowal of self. The truth is we neither know ourselves nor are we the same from one moment in our lives to the next. If we think of ourselves as bodies, our changing self becomes apparent. It is nearly impossible even for families to recognize a loved one after thirty years of absence, so greatly has the self altered. And a little reflection upon the changing quality of consciousness is sure to give us some insight into the numberless selves our surface minds and egos have become since first appearing in the world. "First the infant, muling and puking, then the schoolboy with his shining morning-face, then the lover, sighing like a furnace, then the soldier, full of strange oaths, then the justice, in fair round belly, then the lean and slippered pantaloon, then second childishness, sans teeth, sans eyes, sans taste, sans everything." Shakespeare indeed perceived the many masks donned by the Secret Self in its journey through life, and the man who points to himself, and charging his surface mind and ego to be recognized, says, "I am this" or "I am that," only bespeaks his tendency to become like the image in his mind. The rest is illusion.

The emerging knowledge of self naturally brings with it a fear of the vast and impenetrable universe. There is no such fear in a cow, who, chewing cud and contented with pasture, does not know itself as a cow or as anything. It simply exists as a complex bundle of nerves and blood and tissue, reacting to situations that surround it according to a set of established reflexes called instincts. Since it does not see the stars, it does not wonder about the size of the world, about whether it is separate from it or a part of it or even existing. Only imagination and increased awareness know self, know ego and the surface mind, and this knowledge, this contained and refined consciousness makes man different from all other forms of life. To be aware of one's self is to be human, to have arrived at that currently highest stage of evolutionary development of the Secret Self. A number of individuals have evolved much further, however, and more are breaking through each day. Soon a new race of intellectual and spiritual giants will appear upon the earth, as higher in consciousness as present-day man is above the ape, to whom the secrets of space and time and dimension will be revealed, making the entire universe home, journeying from planet to planet, star to star.

> In this broad earth of ours,
> Amid the measureless grossness and the slag,
> Enclosed and safe within its central heart,
> Nestles the seed of perfection.
> —Walt Whitman

STAR GAZER

It is often true that men who make astronomy their vocation have a philosophical turn of mind. Perhaps this is because the focus of their consciousness is among spaces that dwarf their physical selves, and they cannot help but be concerned with the beginnings and ends of life, with the destiny of man. It does seem impossible to gaze into the incredible glowing vault of the heavens without becoming reverent with awe at the obvious handiwork of a supreme intelligence. In any case, Sterling became a student of philosophy at very nearly the same time that he became a student of astronomy, and he maintained throughout his career that one activity was simply an extension of the other. Yet despite his efforts in both directions, throughout the major part of his life he had achieved no notable success in either.

He would say, "I suppose I'm just a reasonably good mechanic. Some people are born to put the pieces together after others think up the ideas. I put pieces together." Yet it was easy to discern that he was far from pleased with this judgment of himself, even though it seemed true. In whatever observatory he worked, he was given chartwork to do. Theoretical probabilities and exploratory work were left to others.

Even in his philosophical endeavors, Sterling took a like path. He became a walking compendium of all the philosophy ever written. He could quote page and number from the works of Plato, Descartes, Hume, Locke, Lao Tze, the *Bhagavad-Gita*, but even though he embraced all, none took root within him, and he professed no particular philosophy. Despite all his learning and all his studies, he seemed in an intellectual bog, as if ideas simply would not take root in a soil so barren of germinating power.

As it must to all men, time finally brought Sterling to a point in his life where he could look as far backward as it was possible to look forward, and what he saw distressed him. He suddenly was aware that the routine moves of his existence would not be bearable for another thirty years. He de-

cided that he either must find some other profession or discover new meaning in the one he had. He sought help.

"What is it," he asked, "that I am missing? It is almost as
if some ingredient had been left out of me at birth, so that I
am incapable of grasping the meaning of life. I see the design in all, in the heavens, in the logic and concentration of
man's intellectual effort, but I cannot see what it has to do
with me, why the simple fact of my existence has anything to
do with the world and what is going on in it."

"Can you imagine a world without yourself in it?" he was
asked.

"Certainly. And I often think it would be much better."

"If you think it is possible that you once never existed at
all, how can you feel you will continue to exist after this life
is finished."

"I don't. I figure this is all. When the curtain comes down
here, that's finis."

"But what about the design you mention, the obvious concerted effort of life toward some common goal?"

"That belongs to somebody else, not to me. I can't even
understand it, let alone be a part of it."

"How can you isolate yourself from the things you see
about you? If all of life seems to be part of some central, guiding intelligence, surely you can see that you must be too. If
whatever is being done here is being done through the incar-
nations of some supreme being, then each incarnation represents that supreme being and is not different or isolated
from it."

"Perhaps not. Logic seems to support you. I can only tell
you how I feel, and I feel left out, not a part of what is going
on."

"Then your trouble must be selfishness."

Sterling nearly leaped out of his chair. "Selfishness!" he
exclaimed. "I have a wife and four children, and I provide
for them all. I serve on the board of my church, on the
chamber of commerce, and I belong to four service clubs.
Seems to me that half my life is spent serving others. How
can you say I am selfish?"

"I didn't mean that you lack concern for others. I mean you are over-concerned with yourself. Anyone who completely delimits and isolates his own being is selfish, is egoistic. Because he cannot expand his consciousness beyond the limits he has imposed upon it, he has no chance whatever of perceiving his unity with all life, with all beings."

"How does one go about this?"

"By trying. By making an attempt. As long as you continue to rail against the meaninglessness of life, so long will you add substance to the veil, for you are encysting the ego, giving it a reality that it does not truly have, and therefore you are blinding yourself with it."

"Do you mean that simply by trying to know a higher consciousness one automatically achieves a higher consciousness?"

"Perhaps it is that simple. Certainly when the human psyche opens itself to reception of a knowledge that lies beyond it, then and only then is it in a position to receive such knowledge. Is not this a change in consciousness? What was closed and impenetrable now is open and receptive. That is the secret of increased awareness."

"Is this a solitary thing? Must one retire from the active life in order to achieve it?"

"By no means. The best spot of all is the area of your daily work and activity. If you will get outside yourself in each thing you do and make a deliberate effort to feel and think from the standpoint of others who are involved in events with you, then you will find that door in your consciousness will be opened. Light will shine through."

Sterling decided to give it a try. He stated that his exploration of the heavens had always been a thing apart from him. He had peered into space as if he were an interloper, and the only thing that had been revealed to him was that he was an indiscernible speck upon an indiscernible speck. He decided to work on the theory that the entire heavens were within his own consciousness. The idea intrigued him.

Several months later he discovered a new novae. Within a year he presented a paper elucidating upon the constant creation of hydrogen. It was widely acclaimed. He made this statement to his friends:

"It is impossible to penetrate the heart of a matter if one is detached from it. In some kind of mysterious way we all share the same consciousness, and when we manage to break down the walls that separate us from the things we are doing, we are able to grasp their meaning by a kind of direct apprehension. I suppose you could call this intuition, but actually it is a great deal more. It is absolute knowing through being the thing you are attempting to know. If this sounds mysterious I can only say it happened to me. I found a novae not because I saw it but because I knew it was there. I was able to help on the Constant Creation Theory not because I am a mathematical genius but because I knew deep inside me that it was so."

EXPRESSING THE UNEXPRESSED

Carl Jung wrote, "Since we cannot develop backwards into animal consciousness, there remains only the more strenuous way forwards into higher consciousness." Nearly all human ills, fears, guilts, hostilities, and frustrations stem from the fact that we no longer have the insentience of animals but have not as yet expanded our awareness beyond the limits of our surface selves. As long as we remained chained to our surface selves, life will be a burden which we are not fit to cope with."

Strange, how different it is to convey this simple message. The delusion of separate ego-self is so strong in many people that no amount of persuasion, example, or proof can dissuade them from their illusory consciousness. "As long as it works, it's okay with me," seems to be their conclusion, and they do not see that it isn't working at all, that they are only automatons moved about by their reaction to outside stimuli. As long as they acquire sufficient material comforts they are satisfied with the present level of their consciousness, are bound to insentience, do not aspire, so cannot possibly expand. To live in the somnolent awareness of the animal fulfills no areas of the soul. If man carries within him any portion of that which is infinite and eternal, then it becomes his obligation to express it. If he does not, he loses his soul. That which is unexpressed, in the end becomes non-existent.

Something has moved constantly upward and onward through the eons of time since the beginning of the universe. It gathered itself through the slime and mist of first creation, animated the darkest corners of the earth, the depths of the sea, the most arid of deserts. Wherever space and substance is, there also life must be, for nothing truly is inanimate in all creation. One mind, one intelligence, one life seeks an ever more complete and manifold expression of its hidden and unrevealed self. All things are made from one thing, develop in one direction, and all paths converge in some infinite place where each shall find his home in the heart of the Secret Self. We are that very thing that has fashioned the earth and the planets, whose infinite intelligence and myriad design is found in the complex geometry of four-dimensional space, the complicated cohesion of the atom. We have only to resign the mask we present to others and ourselves, to let go of ego and seek residence in a wider range of consciousness, and there will be revealed to us at once a living universe of which we are not only the center but which we completely contain.

HIGHER PLANES OF CONSCIOUSNESS

There are planes of consciousness that no one yet has penetrated. Waiting for the intellectual adventurer is a whole host of unexplored realms of the mind. Man may have crossed the oceans and visited the poles, may even now be venturing into space, but thus far he does not even know his origin or his destiny; these lie hidden in the dormant layers of his consciousness. The unavoidable cause of all things is mind. Before anything material, anything substantive was ever made, there had to be prior knowledge of such creation, and that prior knowledge could only be held by an intellectual being, a mind. It therefore follows that in the crucible of creation the thought always precedes the thing, that thoughts themselves are things in the process of being formed. The nature of existence is to be conscious. To be conscious is to think. To think is to give form to thought, for all consciousness is motor, and the moment a thought impresses itself upon consciousness, consciousness sets about giving it form. Everything that exists, then, exists by virtue of consciousness. It is made from nothing but primal intelligence, exists because it is idea or thought in the mind of primal intelligence. Insofar as the creation of things embodies a degree of the primal intelligence, the thing so created and the intelligence so embodied approximates the intelligence of the creator. The thing created becomes ever more like its creator, is only different because of the limitations imposed upon it by the idea which gave it form.

POWER TO CHANGE

Insofar as increased awareness creeps into each created thing, so there comes to it a liberation from bondage to the idea that originally gave it form, so it becomes possible for the created thing, because of its reaching out to unite with the dynamic of primal intelligence, to achieve the power of that intelligence in direct ratio to its apprehension. In other words, a man is not bound to his limitations because he has been created a certain way. He can turn to the wider consciousness that lies within him, call upon it to manifest in his life, to expand his awareness, perception, knowledge, effectively becoming a different and better person than he thus far has grown to be.

Surely this must be the purpose of life itself, that the created expressions of some great and primal intelligence grow into full knowledge and awareness of that intelligence, and by so doing, unite. The world and all within it is the expression of the Divine, which is never more than partially revealed in each of its numberless and varied expressions, but which is fully inherent in each of those expressions. All the power of the Secret Self lies within you. Some tiny portion of this great creator was not cut off and installed; all of it is hidden within you, lies dormant there, ready and able to enlarge your life to the same degree that you are able to free yourself from ego-imposed bonds. The hidden cause of all things is the primal mind that lies behind creation, and it delivers to each creature according to the consciousness of each creature, according to the image in the mind. What we are witness to in the world is an incessant parade of thoughts becoming things, not because thoughts create things, but because we only perceive the things that occupy our consciousness as thought. In essence, all things possible of mental visualizing are already in existence, for in order that they be visualized at all, they must already have been conceived in the mind of the ultimate intelligence. Therefore, there is no such thing as a new thought or new idea from the standpoint of the Secret Self, but each idea or thought is only new from the standpoint of the individual consciousness which apprehends it. As soon as this idea takes root in individual consciousness, the individual soon perceives its material counterpart in the world. It then seems that the idea created the thing, but in actuality the thing was there all the while; it existed in the mind of the Secret Self and awaited only perception by the individual consciousness.

WE SEE ONLY WHAT WE ARE

It is established fact that a half dozen people can stand on a street corner and each see things that are imperceptible to the others because of the different qualities of their consciousness. One man might be a realtor and be primarily concerned with the value of a vacant lot. Another might be a doctor and be preoccupied with the erratic gate of a pedestrian. Another might be an advertising man with his attention focused on a vacant billboard atop the drugstore. Still another might be an old lady concerned with the speed of the traffic. There might be an automobile salesman whose attention is riveted upon the new model of a competitor.

There might be a contractor who observes that the drugstore needs painting. Such a list is endless. Because of the infinite variety of the human species, it would surely be impossible for any two people out of any number of combinations to see exactly the same things on the same street corner. What we see is always a result of our consciousness. We see only that which already has been cast up as mental image in our minds, and we see only that which we are.

There is no liberation from this fact. It is the basic law of existence. It can be used to restrict consciousness or it can be used to expand consciousness, but work it must, and always. By using it, and we cannot help using it, we either shrivel our souls or expand them, there is no in-between. We are cursed or blessed from within, and upon the judgment seat sits our ego, a false judge to be sure, an illusion to begin with. When we subordinate ego to Secret Self, then we are able to expand consciousness and increase awareness, to fully use the law of growth and power. But as long as the ego remains king, that long will we be slaves to a tyrant which imprisons our consciousness within narrow boundaries.

TRAIL BLAZERS

The path that mankind treads toward discovery of unity with the Secret Self is sure. Such discovery is the goal of evolution. The earth one day will be occupied by a race of intellectual and spiritual giants, in whom the Secret Self is fully revealed. Meanwhile the path is not blazoned, and trail breakers proceed singly. Set off along it, if you will. There will be as much satisfaction in the journey as in the destination, for adventure is here, soul-stirring excitement, profound intellectual stimulation. Behind you, aroused slightly, coming slowly, but always following, is all humanity.

Wrote Thomas Carlyle: "The lightning-spark of Thought, generated or say rather heaven-kindled, in the solitary mind, awakens its express likeness in another mind, in a thousand other minds, and all blaze up together in a combined fire."

4 SELF-MASTERY

Bernard Berenson is quoted as stating, "A complete life may be one ending in so full an identification with the not-self that there is no self left to die." Unquestionably such spiritual aspiration is aimed at achieving an asymmetrical and proper relationship between the ego-self and the supreme self, thereby arriving at the finely honed discipline of self-mastery.

It is foolhardy to attempt control of the ego-self through the ego-self. Control connotes an element to be controlled and an element to exercise control; *ergo,* a duality; and if the element to be controlled attempts domain over itself, there is no hope of achieving balance and direction in the personality. It is the ego-self that must be controlled; it is the Secret Self which must exercise control; and true self-mastery is only arrived at when the individual achieves identification with the Supreme in the deeper recesses of his being. Then he is able, by a kind of unity with primal life force, to mold his own ego-self, to exercise control over it, to knead and shape it to fit the ends of his life.

SUBCONSCIOUS PROMPTINGS

Innate in each ego personality are thousands of subconscious urgings and instincts that tend to lead each of us around by the spiritual nose. We seldom if ever make decisions in an area of our consciousness that is free from the guilt, fears, and envies of our ego-self. In consequence, we are never truly free to decide anything. Each decision wells up in us from the subconscious, reminding us below the level of awareness of some long-forgotten incident in which the ego suffered or had pleasure, and now, in this present instance, we must follow a path dictated by ego-reaction, and so we remain slaves to the past. It just is not possible to fight this reaction. Someone who has an inordinate fear of heights, for example, is never cured of his fear simply by being exposed to height. In fact, such treatment is likely to end in complete personality displacement, in an all-consuming fear hysteria. In the final analysis, such a sufferer is only able to overcome his fear by modifying the importance of his ego-self, by displacing it from the frontal awareness of his consciousness, taking unto himself a deeper, more heightened sense of being through identification with the Secret Self; and so his life begins to be guided by a mental and spiritual essence rather than a protoplasmic pain-pleasure reaction.

The ego-self is not master of itself, cannot be master, only deludes itself when it attempts such mastery. Most people are so entirely frustrated in the will-power area of their psyches that they seek desperately for deliverance from the all too apparent fact that they can never make themselves do what they want to do. If they are fat, for example, they know that they can grow slim by eating less, and they desire to be slim, but the psyche knots upon itself, the contemplated pleasure of being slim pulls against the present pleasure of eating, and the person eats and stays fat. As sorry as this may be in the matter of his personal appearance, it is nothing compared to the damage wreaked upon his already injured psyche. Now he knows that he cannot make himself do something that he ought to do, and he realizes all too well that he is not in control of his life; something else is, and he senses this something to be undesirable, to be constructed of whim and mood and urge and sensualness; and he would be free of it, but cannot help himself, for he is attempting to make both subject and object out of the exact same thing—his ego-self. In every action, as proved by physics, there is a mover and a thing to be moved, and by the very nature of space and energy and substance, an object cannot move itself without having something to act upon or against. The ego-self is a thing to be moved, and it needs a prime mover—the Secret Self.

WILL EQUALS INTELLECT

Benedict Spinoza wrote, "The will and intellect are one and the same thing." In other words, we always do the thing that our understanding prompts us to do. Wishing does not make it so, and desire itself is only a key that unlocks the door of understanding. Knowledge moves the world. We cannot make ourselves or anybody else do anything that we are not capable of controlling through having a complete knowledge of all the factors involved. There is a law that follows all accomplishment, all attainment, all creation, all action, and that is the law of sacrifice. Nothing in this world is gained except by giving up something else, for nothing occupies and absorbs consciousness except that it displaces something else from that position; and whatever occupies consciousness receives the total energy and thought and imagination of the individual, absorbs him as it were, and tends to come into his life as a complete and whole thing. You do not achieve your goal simply by wanting it; you achieve it primarily through thinking about it. Through thinking about it, you grow into understanding of it, and it is this understanding that delivers the goal in the end.

The first kind of understanding that must be achieved is an understanding of the psyche, how it is divided, how it consists of the little "I," the ego, and the big "I," the Secret Self, how the relationship between these two determines the mental health and effectiveness of the individual. Self-mastery starts with the knowledge of mistaken identity, how you always have regarded yourself wrongly; and when you perceive, no matter how dimly, the giant person you really are, then you are able to regard with compassion the struggling little pygmy of your ego, to educate it, direct it, enlarge it, and so enlarge your life.

"No discipline can be without pain," wrote Havelock Ellis, and when the ego seeks beyond itself for a method of discipline and growth, there must be a breaking of bounds, a throwing off of chains, an expansion into new territories of aspiration, and all that is old and restricting must be left behind, and all that was routine and secure must be left there too, and the soul must take flight to a new and higher area of consciousness, on brave wings, daring and aspiring, and just as ecstasy is close to pain, so pain will come, then ecstasy, then pain again, and the encysting shell will be broken, and understanding will come.

SELF DISCIPLINE

The surface self has neither the scope nor the power to effect control of itself. When it attempts to impose such discipline it achieves a kind of sideshow effect, remaining surface ego entirely but dressing itself in inhibitions and restraints that make it a grotesque parody of itself. Discipline is only possible through subjection. The individual must acknowledge a being or a principle greater than he in order to follow its guidance. Once such acknowledgment is made, then the whole life is caught up in the work that is involved, a power descends into the person from beyond him, and works are performed that before were completely beyond his scope.

Most efforts at self-discipline are either pathetic or humorous, for the ego-self simply is not capable of controlling the subconscious. The feelings that proceed out of the subconscious are the motivating forces of our lives, and all logic and reasoning are merely rationalizations after the fact that we must do certain things or must not do them because we are so impelled or restrained by the subconscious. If we desire one thing consciously and its opposite keeps appearing in our lives, it is because our conscious desires do not conform to our subconscious desires. What we subconsciously desire is always delivered to us finally. No amount of willing or wishing or hoping can change this immutable law, for the subconscious has an umbilical tie with the supreme mind, and what is impressed upon it as a thought, an idea, a desire, is inevitably delivered into the world of the individual.

MAN AGAINST HIMSELF

In point of actual fact, it is impossible for the conscious mind to truly entertain an image that is in direct opposition to subconscious feelings. For instance, if we are afraid to dive off a diving board and resolve to overcome this fear, we must first condition the subconscious not to be afraid. If we do not, we have absolutely no chance of diving off the board. We may climb up on it. We may look down at the water. We may command our limbs to throw us forward through the air, but they simply will not respond. The fear-created image in the subconscious holds us back, protects us from the danger it fears. That conditioned image was placed in the subconscious by the impact of conscious mind, but imagination and a new conditioned image, free of fear, may be placed there also by conscious mind, and when it is, we are free to dive off the board and will.

Will power itself is a much overrated and misunderstood thing. Like a rattlesnake the will often turns on its tormentor and delivers a painful laceration instead of the obeisance sought. The story is told of the man who had become obsessed with the power of his mind and his will. He believed he was able to command all animate things to do his bidding, and now sought to prove the effectiveness of his thought upon inanimate objects. He secluded himself in his study, placed a small block of wood upon his desk, sat down in a chair opposite it, sought to move it by the power of his mind. Three days later relatives, failing to elicit response to their knocks and calls, broke down the door and found the poor man seated before his desk in a catatonic stupor from which he never recovered. Far from his having imbued the block of wood with his own volition, the block of wood seemed to have removed all volition from him. He never again, in the few remaining years of his life, evidenced any symptoms of will whatever. He had to be fed, dressed, completely cared for. He had expended his will completely.

In deepest truth, will is not something we develop, but something that is developed in us. It gathers itself out of a vaster, more highly developed and universal consciousness and makes itself manifest in us as a tendency to action or opinion that we have no desire to oppose. The vast majority of people in the world are not so much drivers as driven; and the unequivocal statement can be made that all those who fancy themselves as drivers are driven in reality. Will is not ego-dominance as modern fiction and drama would have us suppose. Inflated individuality is not the stuff that comprises the underlying motivation of the captains of industry, science, art, warfare. Rare is the man and wise indeed who rises to a pinnacle of world prominence and realizes that he has been brought to that point as an instrument, not as a prime mover, that he, himself, has been a servant each foot of the way, that something greater than he has moved in and through him to accomplish the ends that have been credited to him. Yet such a man is secure against the onslaughts of both time and change, and just because he is secure, just because he is equal to both victory and defeat, pleasure and pain, so his position in the world remains secure, for he has nothing further to learn by riding the eternal whirligig of opposites by which the one infinite and eternal intelligence plumbs the depths of its own knowledge and feeling.

THE TRUTH ABOUT WILL POWER

Usually, however, the world credits the man of accomplishment with a great determination, a great power of will to surmount obstacles. Modern civilization has a sense of drama, a sense of existence primarily derived from the stories of Cinderella, Frank Merriwell, and other exponents of the fairy tale that paints everything black or white with white winning an ultimate and inevitable victory. Our sense of values is always deeply shocked at learning that our heroes are tarnished in other areas than the one that made them heroes. We applaud the ruthless heavyweight champion who bludgeons his opponents into insensibility, but when we find that he sometimes does the same thing to his wife, we cannot understand what motivates him. Yet exactly the same thing motivates him in one activity as in the other. In both, the man is the same. The only thing that changes is society's view of him.

This duality of applause and condemnation exists in many other facets of our civilization. In wartime, we make a hero of the killer; in peacetime we put him in jail. Houses and cities are hacked from unsettled frontiers by men who are able to take by ruthlessness and hold by strength, but these same men, when society becomes more static, are put in jail for preying on weaker citizens of the society they helped create. Of all passing standards the most virulent is that which condemns people for being what they were born to be, as if it were their fault and they could change into something different or better if only they would. We are so sure that we are masters of our fate that we have blinded ourselves to the fact that practically the whole world is in chains, and rarer than Diogenes' honest man is his counterpart, a free one.

Will, in the end, does not belong to a man, but a man belongs to his will. There is in him, deep in the recesses of mind, spirit, consciousness, a motivation to be and to become, and for better or worse it is his to live with all his life. This is his fate, and he cannot fly it, must face it or die. And in the facing of it, he meets himself and comes to know himself or turn away from himself, is carried along to heights by the knowledge attained, or is crushed through the ignorance nurtured by his blindness. The path he follows is the path he *must* follow. Victory and defeat, success and failure, knowledge and ignorance are all there. He will experience them all as he threads his way forward toward an ever greater self-knowledge.

Will power, then, is merely the shining through personality of an inner power to become something other than the role the individual is cast in at the moment. A man is born poor and impoverished and grows up to become rich and powerful, and we say he became successful through the exercise of a superior will power. Yet, in most cases, such a man did not take stock and then consciously make the decision to strive for wealth and power; his environment conditioned his subconscious to it. The hurts and rebuffs of his childhood accumulated to place in his subconsciousness an inordinate desire for conditions of plenty and power, and so his entire adult life was spent in pursuit of such gratifications. He is no more free than the man who attains no success at all; he was led to it through an uncontrolled subconscious; he is a prisoner still, a dweller in chains.

THE UNREVEALED QUEST

In our society it certainly is considered eminently more desirable to wind up wealthy and in a position of power than it is to wind up stone poor and in a position of dependency, but if life is a spiritual quest and not a material one, then it matters little where on the scale of material acquisition a man arrives as long as he attains a wisdom about living and discovers his immortal soul. There is evident behind all living things an animate being resident in each, and it cannot matter much to this being which of its manifestations manages to accumulate more than the others. Life is going somewhere, is involved in a paramount but unrevealed quest, and those who conform most nearly to the ends sought are those who unravel the secrets, contribute to progressive understanding and enlightenment. The will to know, to understand, to grow, to become, is an integral part of each being; we cannot help ourselves in this. Each of us, however, must develop and expand along his own individual lines; no blueprint can be drawn for any man. We obey our own destiny best when we listen to our heart. No amount of conscious reasoning can prevail against this intuition, and only by following its dictates can we discover our true selves.

Each person is involved in becoming that thing that his subconscious mind wills him to be. To understand why we often behave contrary to our wishes, it is necessary to perceive that the long lines of our lives are controlled by our subconscious desires, and the only way to change our destiny is to change the aims of our subconscious. When a bomb goes off you do not behave in accord with your conscious mind, but in accord with your subconscious mind, and if in that instance you would like to behave like a hero, then you had better start right now conditioning your subconscious to make you behave bravely in the midst of noise, chaos, and confusion. In all emergencies, in all strenuous and heated action, we behave in accord with the subconscious, and no amount of willing or firm resolve will alter it, except if that resolve be put to work educating the subconscious prior to the emergency.

> Our remedies oft within ourselves do lie
> Which we ascribe to heaven.
> —William Shakespeare

ELEVATING CONSCIOUSNESS

Withal, we can develop a kind of will power, a will power which resolves itself in freedom from reaction to circumstance by recognizing that there is a greater power which will bring us to our fullest culmination as human souls when we allow it to use us completely, when we become instruments for its manifestation on earth. Then we are able by a kind of elevation of consciousness to transcend the constant goadings and urgings of the subconscious and to install in their stead the reasonable dictates of an illuminated intelligence. Then we rise above circumstance, above reaction. Then we take our fate into our own hands in the exact same measure that the ego abdicates as ruling power in our lives.

The first step in the development of will power is to seek outside the limited surface nature for the answers to all problems. One simply cannot instill the courage of a lion into the consciousness of a mouse, and a change in consciousness is the thing to be sought whenever discord lies in the life.

Attempting to coerce the ego through force of the will is like attempting to burst all the bubbles on the sea with a pin. A few will be broken, but the cause of their creation remains unchanged, and on and on they come. So the ego-will, which at most is only a kind of suppressor, dams for a moment the urges and instincts of the subconscious, but they will break through eventually and wreak double havoc through their pent-up force. To the extent that we delude ourselves that the exercise of ego-will can work a beneficence in our lives, we are led around by an illusion that must rob us eventually of all power and direction through being absolutely unable to provide any kind of control.

INSTINCTIVE AVATARS

Much of the suffering in this world is caused by the concealed guilts buried deep in the subconscious of unhappy persons who have set about remaking themselves by exercising ego-will against their defects. They bury these failures in the psyche where untold damage is done by repressing energy, robbing them of their natural vitality. The will of the ego when used to chain the natural energy of the self, restrains the whole personality, replaces boldness with timidity, optimism with pessimism, energy with lassitude. There is little help for the man who enslaves himself through bondage to the ego, through acceptance of restriction and limitation and lack as delineated by the necessity of conforming to some pre-existent standard that he was never made to conform to and could never truly conform to, no matter what.

We sometimes see men in whom life flourishes hugely, men who are cast in heroic mold whether their statures be large or small, for they fit into no pattern, are restrained by no fears or apprehensions, but seem by some stroke of great good fortune to possess themselves completely, confidently, compellingly. These men have not suffered to learn the "do not's" of life. They are unrestrained outlets for the energy and constructiveness of that constantly growing and evolving force that lies behind creation. Their appetites and enthusiasms are large. They take all into their scope, use all to grow by. They measure obstacles as opportunities to prove their strength, to improve their mastery. These lucky ones live in the lap of a nurturing and guiding fortune, for they have not cluttered their subconscious storehouses with a million chains and restraints. Life finds in them the joyous outlet it seeks, and these instinctive avatars are carried in a rush to the tops of their professions, are recognized and gathered around wherever they may be. Such dynamic unfoldment is possible to each of us, not in some humorless bending of the will toward a certain end, but by freeing ourselves of over-concern with the ego, by trusting in the great good ends of life, by placing our fates and our energies in everlasting hands.

> Thou are not idle; in thy higher sphere
> Thy spirit bends itself to loving tasks.
> —James Russell Lowell

EXPRESSING YOURSELF

The most important thing that any of us can learn about will power itself is that it avails nothing when accompanied by grim concern. The man who moves in accord with his inner self moves in accord with a force that no will power in the world can possibly alter in the minutest fraction, and he moves joyously. The grim concern of the ego-will is simply conscious desire out of joint with subconscious desire, and where these two meet head on, subconscious desire always wins. Far from exerting will against subconscious urgings, a man must first discover his true self by letting down all guards and prejudices and inhibitions, so that the power that makes him what he is can at last flow through. If the image then revealed is too repugnant to either his conscious mind or the laws and rules of society, then he must set about inculcating a new set of reflexes in the subconscious through a method of auto-conditioning; in short, he must remake his psyche. It will be a rare thing, however, if he remakes it in the exact image of his conscious desire; chances are such desire was false to begin with, having been accumulated in the subconscious through ego-conflict and social propaganda. Each of us is the product of a basic force at work in the universe, and each of us, because of the simple fact of his existence, is an integral part of the progress of that force through and out of primordial matter into consciousness, into superconsciousness, beyond. Only when we are our natural selves is it possible for us to project the power and mastery which is innate in us. Strangely, the majority of humanity lives in a straitjacket, restricted and repressed on every front of existence often knowledgeably so, but always justifying such restriction as being necessary to conformity, and this is the delusion that binds us. The one supreme power and vital mind that inhabits all creatures has not assumed its manifold masks for purposes of uniformity, but for purposes of variety and myriad expression. Conformity of any kind in the development of the psyche and character of the individual should never be anything more than happenstance, occurring only because the true nature of one individual happens to be like the true nature of another. The object all the while should be individual expression, and when this is the motivating force in the life of the person, he immediately increases his worth to society by acting as an absolutely unduplicated sounding rod in the cosmos, contributing his interpretation to all whom he contacts and therefore becoming a much more valuable member of society than the conformist with his preconceived ideas and predetermined reactions and basically unhappy psyche.

THE REVOLUTIONARY CONCEPT

So we are faced with the most revolutionary of concepts. One does not attain to self-mastery through an exercise of will, but rather through a search for his Secret Self, a hidden sense of being that overlays both the conscious and subconscious minds. He may exert will in this direction, insofar as dedication and determination are concerned, but even here he must exert it joyfully, with humor, else he is sure to be defeated. The door to all secrets is opened with a key; it is simply too strong for a battering ram.

A little effort expended in the right direction and at the right time has the power to move the worlds. If one plays golf he often sees small men of slight physique drive a golf ball many yards beyond their larger and more heavily muscled opponents. Understanding is the thing; timing and leverage produce the result; and no amount of human energy is sufficient to cause even the tiniest of events that daily occur on life's scene. But a little nudge here, a little pressure there, properly applied on the crescendoing force that is life itself, diverts that fantastic energy into an irresistible stream, and miracles are wrought, bridges and buildings built, societies constructed, all at the behest and after the understanding of an individual consciousness that has transcended its restrictions and limitations and created something surpassing itself.

THE OLYMPIAN TORCH

Ralph Waldo Emerson wrote, "He who has mastered any law in his private thoughts, is master to that extent of all men whose language he speaks, and of all those into whose language his own can be translated." An internal discipline sets each individual house in order, allows the self to be mastered and ruled by a power greater than the individual ego, and breeds the stuff of which heroes are made. Tenacity and determination are results of an ingrown faith and unshakable confidence in the great and good ends of life and the worthiness of human destiny. The man who throws up the sponge in the face of overwhelming odds does so only because the end he seeks does not seem worth the struggle, and any man who pursues his wraiths for ego-aggrandizement alone cannot possibly have the stuff which prevails when the crucible of conflict is heated white. When motivation springs from the depths of consciousness it is of such strength and irrepressiblity that nothing short of destruction of the individual will finally circumvent the goal.

An inner vision sustains each entrepreneur. Anyone who seeks to create something is first launched upon his enterprise through having envisaged it in his mind. To see is to believe, and seeing through the magic of imagination creates the prior vision necessary to action, to bringing an idea into material counterpart in the physical world. Just as nothing daunts the inner vision of seer and saint, so nothing can possibly mitigate against the inner vision of each of us, for there is a transforming power in consciousness that causes material results. In the scene surrounding a given observer there exists all possibilities, but he is touched only by those his inner awareness is conditioned to perceive. Determination and tenacity are products of inner vision, and are never more than symptoms of a consciousness that inspires positive action, steady optimism, and unflagging hope and humor.

The really important thing about the evolvement of the human being from out of the mass of half-aware, instinctive, probing protoplasm is the fact that he carries as an Olympian torch the seeds of an evolving consciousness that is struggling upward out of a nascent world of matter. A constantly expanding awareness, an ever greater understanding, and a growing mastery are the obvious ends of evolution, and this evolution now is not nearly so much a material one as a mental or spiritual one, involving consciousness and spirituality to the near exclusion of any physicalness whatever.

EVERYONE'S PRINCIPAL BUSINESS

A friend named Arthur sought his fortune in the world of industry. He had trained himself well for his task, had taken an engineering degree at one of the country's best technical colleges, had served a well-rounded apprenticeship in a major manufacturing company before venturing out on his own. Yet from the first his enterprise disappointed. It was a small company, subsisted mainly on contracts from larger firms, and there was no reason why it should immediately make him rich, but considering his personal skill and application and the fact that the process he rendered was sorely needed, it was strange that he barely managed to meet obligations. His company accumulated no capital, could not expand, and while dozens of ideas for manufacturing innovations seethed constantly in Arthur's mind, there was no means of fulfillment. Other men in positions like his own prospered, and he was sure he was being dogged by misfortune. The harder he fought against obstacles, the more real and immovable they became. At last he became a defeatist, confided to friends, "I've had lots of bad breaks, and I'm just plain tired. Let the god of misfortune load it on." The god of misfortune did. Arthur lost his business.

It was a deep shock. For a while he went about in a daze. The business bankrupted him, and he seemed incapable of going to work. His wife took a clerical job in an office, and they lived on her small salary. All motivation was gone from Arthur. He tried psychotherapy.

Seclusion in a monastery was prescribed. Though Arthur professed no religion, he finally agreed to take a four-month retreat, during which time he promised not to concern himself with business in any way, but to meditate on life, its origins and meanings, the question of who and what he was, what his destiny might be. He was given free access to the monastery library, and though he was required to perform the chores assigned him, nevertheless he spent long hours poring over the volumes recommended to him by his tutor. When he emerged from the retreat, he was a changed man.

There was about him a broader note, a more encompassing perception, a forbearance and understanding for all things that formerly had been narrowly confined to the business he worked in. He started a new business. Almost immediately it prospered. Within a few years it became one of the most successful in the country.

Arthur spoke of his transformation. "I always made the mistake," he said, "of thinking that a man could succeed by simply accumulating knowledge about the thing he wanted to do, but I was wrong. I learned during the retreat that something is going on in life that is far greater than making parts for airplanes. No man is here only to seek his livelihood. He carries within him the seed of a budding perfection, and it is only when he turns his eyes within and discovers this precious cargo that he is able to live his life with sufficient reverence for others to bring understanding to his tasks. My success in business has not been because I learned more about my business, but because I learned more about what was *outside* my business. In fact, it might be said that what I always thought was my business I discovered to be secondary, that my main business is spiritual instead."

GOLDEN TOWERS

There is fierce resolution in the heart of the man who sees golden towers beyond the hill. He is led across desert and wasteland; no matter the obstacles, his image propells him. The secret of never giving up is to implant upon the moving screen of consciousness a clear image of the goal to be attained. Let that image be your golden tower. Guard it from tarnishing, blurring, dissolving, and you need have no fear that you will falter on the way, or resign yourself to defeat, or give up altogether. Let no doubt assail you because the path you tread appears to diverge from the proper direction. There are as many ways to the promised land as there are pilgrims to undertake the journey, and each arrives in due course if only he keeps faith with his golden tower. We all move together toward the same ultimate destiny, but each of us is a separate and unique note in the universe, and each of us must travel his own path for the lessons to be learned there, for the experience to be gained.

Thomas Henry Huxley wrote, "Perhaps the most valuable result of all education is the ability to make yourself do the thing you have to do, when it ought to be done, whether you like it or not." And it is true that the picture in the mind does not always inspire in us the same enthusiasm for action. Sometimes we are beset by laziness and procrastination, and our resolve has to be nourished at the fount of renewed concentration. But it is no use expostulating, "Get to work, get to work," when the task at hand is repugnant. The first thing to do, if the job is to be accomplished at all, is to create an entirely new and attractive picture of the task.

If, for example, you are a salesman, and your job is to make ten calls each day on prospective purchasers, then you are making it extremely difficult for yourself if your mental image is making ten calls. With such a mental picture the wonder is that you are able to stir out of the house at all. Think about ten calls and they become repetitious, you become anxious to get them over with, to be free of their responsibility on you. Then you think of the driving to be done, the inevitable delays and irritations, then maybe so-and-so won't be in, maybe such-and-such isn't taking any more orders, so the entire day will be wasted and you might as well have stayed at home. Sure enough, that is what you wind up doing.

Now the other side of the coin. Instead of thinking of the ten calls, suppose the image within your consciousness is tied up with success and accomplishment. Your job then is not ten calls at all, but the systematic and congenial cultivation of every prospective purchaser of your product. The game always has to be worth the candle, and before you can throw yourself wholeheartedly into each challenge with determination and absorbtion, you must first be positive that right action will bring results. We are so constituted that we absolutely cannot act in any direction without the double-pronged spur of confidence and hope. Visualize your heart's desire. Keep the image fresh and clear. It will act as all the motivation you need to lead you into right and energetic actions.

APPROPRIATE DISCIPLINE

Suppose you are a writer, a painter, anyone whose work is creative and primarily conducted in solitude. When you sit before your easel or desk with idle hands and berate yourself for not working and struggle in the throes of lethargy, when your days become unfruitful and you are frustrated with the burden of your unproductivity, then give a thought to your imagination and the images that are playing upon the plastic creative screen of your mind. We are bound to do the thing that our consciouness is focused upon, and if the image we carry is far afield from the affairs of the world in which we are enmeshed, then we day-dream, cannot work, are enraptured by irrelevant pictures that pursue each other across our consciousness. Then we can call our will into play, not a will that attempts to force us to work, but a will that chooses the objects of its contemplation, so that instead of thinking of fishing in the Sierras we now concentrate our attention upon the task at hand. The mind takes the problem into focus. Possibilities and solutions are considered, and before long our fingers are busily at work, as if with volition of their own.

Impulses and whims occasionally spring out of a special attunement of the ego-self with the Secret Self, but far more often bubble up out of a capricious subconscious and are more to be controlled than given in to. Usually, impulses are creature comfort urges, and were we to live our lives in obedience to them it is doubtful we would ever accomplish anything. We would like to lie abed in the morning rather than get up and go to work, because lying in bed feels good, but if we stay there often enough we will soon be jobless and without means of support. We would like to load up on ice cream and cake and to eat the things we like as often as our stomach will allow us, but if we do we soon will have to be transported by truck, we will be so fat. We would like to play and have fun and never to have to worry about others, but if we take such a tack we one day find ourselves penniless, friendless, without family. The wise man soon learns that impulses and whims are simply the ego seeking surcease from the discipline being imposed upon it. Rather than relax that discipline, he applies it the more strongly. Every human desire must be tempered with appropriate discipline, else it becomes license, and the knowledge comes to all of us sooner or later that leisure is only valuable after work, eating after hunger, sleeping after tiredness, and it is absolutely impossible to experience a single pleasure in life without a concomitant measure of pain.

SUPER-KNOWLEDGE

Not to be confused with impulse and whim is the welling up out of the universal consciousness of a guidance or a direction that seizes the soul of the individual and directs him unfalteringly along a path that leads to his destiny. The unwary may easily be led to believe an impulse is such guidance or attunement, but once having experienced true rapport with the Secret Self any further delusion about which is impulse and which intuition is put finally to rest. In the wall that separates the human soul from its source a crack occasionally appears, revealing for a moment the mathematical perfection and utter rightness of the world beyond and the soul within it. It is this psychological state that is referred to in mysticism and in many religions as "attunement" or "grace," and once involved in it, the individual's choices and directions are as warrants from on high; everything does his bidding at the very moment his bidding is resolved.

This aspect of "super-knowledge" gives us our best indication of the nature and usefulness of the will. Once we understand that desire opposed to the aims of the Secret Self can avail the individual nothing but frustration, then we finally have been awakened to the principle of attunement, which is the secret of effective living. To actually decide is not within the scope of human knowledge, simply because human knowledge is limited to the scantiest fraction of total knowledge. It is just no good trying to make a decision about things when nearly the entire sum of their characteristics is hidden. Individual will exercised against events and people is the sheerest of vanities and avails nothing in the end but suffering and defeat.

Acts performed in the ego for advantages are acts performed without understanding of their true significance, and any success or satisfaction achieved through them is like froth on the crest of a wave, disappearing with the wave. Our consciousness is placed so frontally on our total psyche that we are forever being mesmerized by the blandishments, urgings, and pleadings of the ego. We aspire to conquer peaks that once climbed reveal themselves as the lowliest of plateaus, and force us to consider how false our gods have been. True goals are spiritual, and laziness, procrastination, and fear are overcome not by railing at the self, but by seeking the sustaining seeds of consciousness that lie deep within the nature.

THE LIBERATING LAW

As our understanding grows, so does our will power, but bear in mind the differentiation: true will power is effective, achieves results through the mere aiming; false will power never achieves results at all. As consciousness expands and takes in new levels of awareness, so the power of the individual increases. Achieving increased awareness and communing with higher heavenly powers are not things restricted to the isolated mystic or contemplative saint, but are available to all, and the reward is always complete effectiveness, whether in creative fields or executive, whether spiritual, mental, or material; for in understanding is power, in knowledge surety, and he who has arrived at enlarged consciousness must therefore be able to work his will and way on the world simply by becoming one with it.

To be what we truly are and to become what we are capable of becoming are the only courses of action open to the man who would live a fulfilled life. No matter the barbs of fate that frustrate you, no matter how stacked against you the cards of fortune, how you were born, where, into what kind of body, gifted with whatever native intelligence, there is a liberating law in the universe, and you can become the highest of the high, wisest of the wise, for you have within your very grasp a tool with which to achieve absolute freedom. Once you have acknowledged to yourself that within your body is that supreme consciousness that has authored the worlds and the universes, then at last you are bound to let the ego step down from the helm and allow a wiser force to chart your course through life. Once you have placed your fortunes and energies in the hands of the Secret Self you will know a peace and inner quietude that surpasses any joy you have known. Your life will grow into a whole thing. Each day will serve as a building block toward some definite goal or purpose. You will finally be amazed at the miracles wrought when the Secret Self takes over.

OVERCOMING GUILT AND HOSTILITY

Guilt and hostility are accoutrements of the ego, which arms itself with delusions in order to survive. If a nagging sense of guilt accompanies you, it is because the ego is made of accumulated things, teachings, blandishments, sensual impressions, none of which have much relation to eternal truth but nonetheless is a moral censor of every act performed by the individual. If you feel guilty, never make the intellectual mistake of thinking that your feelings arise from the censorship of the Secret Self, which makes no such lean and human judgments. Guilt is generally the accumulated teachings of society acting within the individual as a prompter or deterrent of certain actions. Such censorship seldom is based on lasting truth, since society's pressures for conformity are often at variance with the Divine's pressures for individuality. Hostility is simply the other face of guilt, manifesting as hostility in the aggressive person, just as guilt manifests in the more passive.There is certainly nothing good about either of these emotional blocks. They are products of the ego and vanish when the individual centers himself in the deeper regions of consciousness. Then it becomes nearly impossible to be emotionally involved in the vanities of the little self that is action servant of the Secret Self.

The way to peace of mind lies in abandoning the will as a tool of the ego, finally abandoning the ego also and centering the consciousness in the Divine. Through the widening of consciousness that this psychological transference brings, there comes to the individual an understanding that before was impossible to him. In a way that transcends material explanation he takes on a little of the identity of everything that crosses his awareness. In this manner he understands others through actually participating in the consciousness of others, and this super-knowledge, this deep intuition, brings to his action and work a high effectiveness and almost supernatural preordination. He moves in the center of events as if he were ordering events, because he moves in accord with their true nature, is guided in all by a principle that sees the end to be accomplished and the means of attaining it; and because he has abandoned ego and moves in response to this universal will, he acts with absolute surety, complete effectiveness, without hazard, anxiety or fear, is dominated henceforth by inner peace and absolute joy.

5 MIND OVER MATTER

The almost universal path that people follow is to accede to circumstance, to throw up their hands and say, "That's the way it goes." It is a curious and wry fact that when circum stances go against our personal desires we credit our frustration to bad luck, but when we are carried to some pinnacle of success it is no longer fortune but our superior skill that we credit. In actual fact, all luck and skill emanate from deepseated convictions in the subconscious mind of the individual.

DESIRE AND DESTINY

The average person never really decides whether mind rules matter or matter rules mind. He accepts the fact that mind rules matter in certain circumstances, but tends to regard these circumstances as the exception rather than the rule. He sees mental attitude determine the outcome of athletic contests, overcome physical disability, but when it comes to adopting completely a mind first approach to daily living, he never quite makes it.

If mind ever rules matter at all, it must do so as a result of an absolute principle properly applied. This absolute principle could not be a thing that worked some of the time or once in a while or capriciously responded to chance, but would have to be a law that always worked in exactly the same way. If, for example, someone adopted the mind over matter approach in a particular circumstance and failed to achieve the results he desired, it would not be the law that had failed but his understanding of the law and his application of its principles.

When we examine accomplishment, the first thing we notice is that the man who doesn't want to climb a mountain never climbs one. After that, we note that even among the men who definitely want to climb mountains a large number never climb any. From this, we deduce that the first ingredient essential to accomplishment is desire. After that, other more discretionary and therefore more obscure factors become involved.

It is difficult to say why people want anything. We observe that nearly everybody would rather experience pleasure than pain, but we are aware that certain persons not only stick pins into their bodies but maintain agonizing physical attitudes over protracted periods of time. Such people appear to have chosen pain instead of pleasure, at least in a physical sense, and to have done such a thing through an inner impulsion either above the pain-pleasure principle or related to it obscurely. Desire for a goal is the only thing that makes a pain-filled experience possible to bear. Desire is also an opiate. Many people involved in crucial physical exertions report no sense of pain whatever, though when the period of exertion is over wounds are found on their flesh, and joints and muscles are strained. Football players are a notable case in point.

If we carry our observations even further, we soon note that there is a great deal of difference in the degrees of desire. One man may want and hold out his hand, and that is the greatest effort possible to him. Another man may want and rend chains, so great is his need. Desire is a thing that impels. The greater the desire, the more it impels, and this impulsion is rooted in the inner vision that possesses the individual. To the degree that we are alive and imprisoned within reactive flesh, to that same degree we relentlessly pursue the visions that possess us. Whether our mental images are of buildings to be built or of banks to be robbed makes not the slightest difference to the motor impulse that develops within the creature. You can be absolutely certain that the things that occupy a man's mind will soon be part of life, if they are not already.

BLESSING AND CURSE

A curious thing has evolved in the human being. The quality of mental reflection which has slowly developed in his psyche over the eons of his evolution has enabled him to form pictures within his mind in complete variance to the world around him. He can, if he will, on a flight of fancy, transfer himself from rags to riches, Kansas to Istanbul, in the twinkling of an eye, and thus, in the conscious center of his being, no longer is a slave to the world in which he finds himself. Two principal phenomena have resulted, one stigmata, the other a blessing.

The stigmata are these. Life is largely a matter of disciplining one's self to endure pain in order to achieve a desired end, but the immature person often seizes on the image power of the mind to seek refuge from reality, and as a result develops a kind of wish-thinking that makes him absolutely ineffectual in all circumstances. He turns the power of the imagination upon itself, destroys its ability to influence the outer world by setting it to work on problems that have no relationship to the outer world. The victims of such delusions are legion. They populate our mental hospitals, derelict centers, flop houses. They constitute the majority of those admitted to sanitariums for the treatment of alcoholism. And they are to be found all over the world in zombie-like trance, making the movements of the living, but with one foot in another world.

On the other hand is the blessing that imagination brings. It is the mystic seeing that enables man to gaze upon his surroundings with x-ray eye and perceive in them their hidden potentiality. This harnessing of the image-making power of the mind to the outer world of things and events has transformed life on earth, has enabled man, in a few short centuries not only to achieve dominion over his immediate environment but to arrive at the verge of extending that dominion through the time-space continuum of the universe.

Most modern thinking conveniently divides the world into two different classes of things, one substance, the other intelligence. Science takes great pains to classify substance. It catalogues the elements and their various combinations, delineates the make-up of the molecules whose cohesion forms the elements, breaks down the molecule into various atomic weights, and even differentiates the atom into a nucleus and a certain number of encircling electrons. At this point, the difference between hydrogen and lead, for example, has become startlingly slight. Each has an invisible nucleus encircled by a certain number of electrons, more in the case of lead, but hardly appreciably more, and the difference between them appears to be one of degree rather than one of kind. Our confusion grows when, through the sudden process of nuclear fission, the atom itself is reduced to nothing measurable, disappearing in a burst of flame, and we are forced to inquire at last if substance is really substance after all but perhaps might not represent a vastly subtler conception, of idea only, intelligence itself.

BEHIND THE ATOM

If we examine any consciousness we inevitably find a body of some sort, a weight, scale, and dimension that houses the intelligence being examined and refuses any kind of scrutiny separate from it. It seems most probable that matter and intelligence are one and the same thing, that intelligence is only a higher manifestation of matter, becoming apparent only in that substance that takes on complexity. Once we have agreed that intelligence is a manifestation of form, it is but a step further to gain a glimmer of the truth, that intelligence is evolutionary in the growth of matter, which leads us inescapably to the conclusion that intelligence, while a manifestation of matter, is superior to and has basic control of that matter. In short, intelligence, or consciousness, or awareness, has inherent in itself control over all physical circumstances, all events.

Walter Russel is interesting here. "That which man calls matter or substance," he writes, "has no existence whatever. So-called matter is but waves of the motion of light, electrically divided into opposed pairs, then electrically conditioned and patterned into what we call various substances of matter. Briefly put, matter is but the motion of light, and motion is not substance. Our creative thinkers must look primarily to light to perform tomorrow's miracles."

Light, energy, intelligence, whichever of the three you choose to acknowledge as the moving force behind the universe, the primary thing is to be able to acknowledge that substance is only relative, not a solid and absolute thing at all, but representative of the working of mind and always subservient to mind. A desk is not a desk except in the most crudely sensual way. In actuality it is an enclosure or series of enclosures in which molecules are speeding about at many times the swiftness of rifle bullets. A million times more volume exists outside the molecules than in them, and if those in steel, for instance, were to cease their movement for a moment, you could poke your finger through the steel with the same ease as you poke it through air.

Basic behind the construction of matter is an innate symmetry, a kind of mathematical ideation that can only be attributed to a thinking mind. The atom itself, the smallest building block of substance, has a cohesiveness and esthetic composition that, beyond all things, implies individuality. The atom indicates purpose and it indicates an urge to survival, and when a sufficient number of atoms of the right electronic make-up were combined to make a protein molecule, then it was a very short time indeed before arms and legs and eyes and brain were grown and there moved about on the surface of matter an autonomous being seeking dominion over his environment—man.

CONSCIOUSNESS IS PROPORTIONAL TO COMPLEXITY

When we turn our reflections back to the origins of life and the purposes of evolution we are struck at once with the picture of increasing complexity. From amoeba to man has taken many millions of years, and the two seem scarcely related. Yet the step from inanimate matter to animate matter, as is represented by the amoeba, is perhaps more breathtaking than the step from amoeba to man, for the latter represents simply an increase in complexity while the former represents something entirely different from what preceded it. Out of the masses of slag and rock and steam emerged an element that moved, that grew and maintained itself—life. Yet even growth there was not so much the evolution of one thing out of another dissimilar thing, but rather an adding unto one thing of characteristics lacking in its predecessor, so that the difference in condition between an animate and inanimate thing is primarily one of complexity as against simpleness.

No physicist or chemist will deny that the protein molecule is more complex than the molecules of inorganic elements. Some great change once transpired in nature for life to grow from inanimate substance, but in order for this to ever happen, consciousness had to be inherent in all matter. It is consciousness that is responsible for form. Wherever form is, there also is an intelligent presence. It inhabits the rock and the mountain just as surely as it does the human being. The form of the thing is dependent upon the idea that holds its whizzing molecules within boundaries, and this contour is just as surely mental as the concept of mathematics, and just as surely is held by a thinking being whose presence is always found within.

This leads us dangerously close to the established province of religion, but we are not concerned here with a father image who has created children and is raising them to knowledge. What we are concerned with is the bottom root of intelligence, how and why it manifests in the universe, and whether man is divorced from that originating intelligence, subject to it as slave to master, or umbilically tied to it in such a manner that he is it and it is he.

HOW THOUGHT CONDITIONS THINGS

Those who see chaos as the originator of the worlds, coincidence responsible for the formation of man, and futility as the earmark of life, find at every hand just such a universe. Those who perceive a hardened creator ordering his vassals about cannot help but be impressed by the inequality of the human lot and perceive in the world much bitterness and pain. Those who see an inhabiting presence in all things instinctively know that all forms of the world are only ideas given substance, that the mind which upholds each is resident within themselves, and that therefore they are part and parcel of all peace, perfection, and effectiveness. The world, as always, turns out to be exactly what our consciousness is conditioned to see. It is this astounding and tremendously dynamic premise that life is built upon, the central law upon which evolution itself hinges.

We see only that which we think we will see, and in consequence the world is peopled with things and events all dredged up out of our consciousness. A thing or a person or an event is not changed because of our consciousness, but inherent in each are all qualities, and we sift out only those that already occupy our awareness. It is for this reason that men are villains in one circumstance, heroes in another, that each in his time plays countless roles. It is not so much that the man is different in each circumstance, but that he is being constantly perceived by different persons who view him only through a narrow slit of individual vision and accept him for the thing they expect him to be.

Consider an ordinary knife. To the baker it is an instrument with which to divide a loaf of bread into parts. To the irate householder it is a weapon with which to dispose of the object of his wrath. To the surgeon, come to a sickbed without instruments, it is a life-saving tool that will allow him to take from the abdomen of his patient a diseased appendix.

To the young boy passing through the kitchen it is part of a game—mumblety-peg. Yet what it actually is is a compound of inanimate elements and previously living molecules—steel and wood, shaped a certain way and fashioned so, but even this is but an indication of what it truly is, for our senses reveal only a tiny part of the total qualities of anything that seizes our attention.

So a thing is the kind of thing it is only because of the personal relationship of the beholder, and it actually never has any true qualities at all because our senses are too crude to perceive any truth about it other than that which proceeds out of our consciousness. And it is this that affects us most of all. For when we see the knife we do not think of the kind and quality of the steel and whether it has substance or is only idea, but we look at the knife only to determine its relationship to us, and that is the only thing we see.

MATTER IS MOVEMENT

Just to understand the scientific premise that matter is not matter at all but intense movement confined within spatial limits is to arrive at a pinnacle of mental and spiritual freedom that will never again allow you to be intimidated by the things and circumstances around you. In deepest truth they are no more real than the conditioning of your consciousness, and you can, by an act of increased mental awareness, change them from the things you think they are into something totally and completely different.

Here we knock on the door of the occult. The ring of the foregoing indicates we will be able to move mountains, change water into wine, still the winds, and indeed we might once we learn the testing but veil-breaking truth that all mountains are in the mind, as are all limitation and lack, all storms. Make this encompassing decision, that matter is subservient to mind, and you will see at once that the world and everything in it is only an effect of consciousness, a partial manifestation of thought; and inasmuch as it remains always a reflection of idea in the mind of the beholder, it exhibits at once another of its infinite reflections the moment the thought in the beholder's mind changes. What that means is this: things show only a side that reflects the individual's thought about them. They don't truly change when the thought about them changes, but they contain all possibilities and reveal to the beholder only an aspect that his consciousness is prepared to perceive.

This metaphysical breakdown of the universe is a great help in adjusting one's self to the premise of working first with mind and allowing events to develop from an inner impulsion of their own. Once we are fully convinced of the mental causes behind all things, we no longer feel impelled to run about, lay on hands, attempt one way or the other to coerce the world to fit the pattern in our minds. One intelligence lies at the center of all events and things, and it is at the core of your own nature. Once you have gained sufficient wisdom to be concerned only with your own consciousness and the inner discipline that widens its awareness, then you can be sure that the outer world will be a reflection of the inner, that you are working with the root causes of your environment.

All possibilities exist in each person because each is a manifestation of a mind that is totality, infinity, unity and each is only less than the total according to his isolation from it, and when he expands his mental nature he approaches original perfection, power, omniscience. Mind over matter is not so much a mental dominion over material things as it is an awareness of their many-sidedness and unlimited potentiality. Acceptance by the observer of any one facet of a thing as the totality of that thing automatically confers such limitation on that thing as far as its influence upon him is concerned. In this respect our lives are guided by shadows, by the meaningful aspects we give the things and events we meet in the world, and our consciousness is never as much a product of circumstances as circumstances (in this subjective way) are a result of our consciousness.

OUR SKIN-DEEP SELVES

A little reflection on the conditioning quality of consciousness is all that is necessary to quickly realize how continuously it works in our lives. Love is blind because the lover always perceives the mental image of his beloved. The divorce rate is a product of disenchantment. It is not *because* of disenchantment that love leaves; disenchantment comes *after* love leaves. Places of triumph revisited always seem strangely small and shoddy. They do not fit the magnificent arenas cast up by our emotionally-charged memories. And when pain commingles with places and events, we can no more bring ourselves to visit them or have contact with them or even dredge them up from our memories than we can sprout wings and fly, so capricious is the pain-avoiding pleasure-seeking ego in its efforts to hide our true selves.

This veil-shrouding, fan dancing, now-you-see-it now-you-don't quality of the ego is what makes each of us use a thousand selves in the conduct of his life, and never actually be any one of them or even all put together. Because we do not truly know who we are we seek in every situation a role to be played, usually feeling no sense of deceit or sham whatever, but blithely accepting the fact of a chameleon self which adapts its colors to its background. In the office we are a different self to the boss than to our subordinates. At home we are a different self to our spouse than to our children. We are a different self at our club than with a small group of confidants. And we often present a different self to the neighbor on one side of us than to the neighbor on the other. We seldom know how it is that we get into the various roles we play, but play them we must, and when we have a dinner party and carefully select the guest list with an eye to their getting along, it is not the homogeneity of the guests that our eye reviews but whether we have played the same role with all of them and therefore can be a single self at the party that night. If perchance an uninvited guest arrives, this sudden dropping in is greeted with deep consternation as the necessity of playing two different roles is foisted upon us. It awakens deep within our psyches the uneasy undertones of schizophrenia.

Great dramatic coaches, in an effort to lead their protégés to understanding of the characters they portray, always seek an under-the-skin approach, instinctively realizing that a person is only truly understood from the inside, that any other position deals with symptoms only. Man's investigation of the world itself has taken this inner and outer course, the inner exemplified by psychology, religion, parapsychology, the outer exemplified by the physical sciences. Science has made the greater progress by far, but the race is not always to the swift. Science has pursued substance in its laboratories, from mountain to atoms, but unravelled no enigmas other than a kind of elementary construction, and its sole accomplishment in its search for the secret of life has been to chase matter off the physical stage into some realm of invisibility where it no longer can be perceived, much less understood by the methods and instruments available.

INTUITIVE PERCEPTION

Man is a reactive animal and generally plays the role expected of him. Rare and wise is he who is able to shuck off this automatism. He is able to do so only by recognizing that within each man resides the identical animating spirit. By inner understanding he is able to allow events to develop through their own inner impulsion. This intuitive perception permits him to take his place in each event according to the best interests of his own nature.

We are all born into a bondage of the senses, and insofar as we place absolute credence in their evidence, we remain slaves to them. Only when we arrive at a mystic intuition of the universality of intelligence are we finally able to realize that matter in essence is only mind and that innate in each of us is the same resident being, which exists everywhere at all times and in all things, appearing to be different according to the form into which it has entered but essentially remaining one, indivisible, and infinite.

Once in a while a man arises who by some strange evolutionary leap seems to have surmounted the bondage that holds others. Such a man was Edgar Cayce, the wizard of Virginia Beach. Not only was he able to read minds, see things and events at a distance, but he also seemed able to call upon universal mind for all the knowledge within it. Cayce's perceptions circumvented time, space, matter, and his carefully documented exploits have never been disproved. He became in hypnotic trance the most erudite of men, having at his fingertips all the knowledge in the fields of medicine and religion, yet in his normal waking state he was totally lacking in education. And Edgar Cayce does not stand alone as a mental phenomenon. Nearly every child prodigy, every genius exhibits this strange power to transcend the limitations of matter by a gigantic leap of mind. Mozart, Einstein, Gandhi, Jesus Christ, geniuses all, used some secret power of the mind to perfom their miracles. Though the man in whom genius lives hour by hour is rare, each of us sometime in his life usually is privileged in a moment of mystical intuition, sometimes several, sometimes many.

INNER KNOWING

A young man named George suffered intensely from migrain headaches. One night during a particularly painful siege he took to the streets in the hope that walking would reduce his pain. Suddenly he was overcome by the absolute knowledge that breathing pure oxygen would relieve him. He went immediately to the emergency hospital, won over the attending physician's objections, breathed oxygen, was immediately relieved. Such treatment is generally accepted in the medical fraternity today, but at the time it was rarely used and George had never heard of it. Another man named Tom, in the grip of a depression resulting from his loss of a job, awoke one morning with the feeling that he would be very successful in the valve manufacturing business. Tom's acquaintanceship with valves was cursory. He knew they did something inside pumps and engines, but he didn't know just what. He had had no training in engineering and scarcely any in business, but that didn't deter him. He went to a valve company and arranged a tour of the premises. He was immediately enchanted, sure that valve manufacturing was for him. Two weeks later he met at a party a man who identified himself as an inventor. He drew designs of his new valve on the hostess's tablecloth. Two days later Tom and the inventor found themselves in the bank arranging financing. Today their valve manufacturing firm is one of the largest in the nation.

THE LATENT FACULTY

Intuition is the power by which all things are done. Nobody ever built a building by piling blocks. A building is built first in somebody's mind; someone sees it towering to the sun, clear and solid in his imagination, long before the first physical movement is made to construct it. Those who go through life totalling facts accumulate only the smallest percentage of the knowledge that exists in the universe. That kind of man wants facts to tell him what to do, but facts never do; there simply aren't enough of them.

"In every man," writes R. Steiner, "there are latent faculties by means of which he can acquire for himself knowledge of the higher worlds." It is inner certitude, intuitive hunch, that leads us into right action. Modern man takes inordinate pride in the powers of his reason, but he has put the cart before the horse. He actually seldom follows his reason; his reason usually follows him. A look at the world's history shows us how true this is. Reason told Columbus the world was flat, intuition that it was round. Reason would have had him sail the safe seas around his native Europe; intuition led him across uncharted waters to a new world. Reason told Pasteur that disease was caused by fevers of the blood; intuition led him to search out bacteria and a whole new area of preventive medicine. We attain skill in works and action when we learn to trust ourselves completely to an inner impulsion and to cease acting in response to the events and circumstances around us.

DOCTRINE OF MIND OVER MATTER

There are three principal points in the doctrine of mind over matter which must be clearly understood. 1) An invisible but real cosmic medium exists which supports the apparent world. 2) There is an established connection between this real but unseen world and the illusory world of the senses. 3) This connection may be discerned and this relationship controlled by the disciplined consciousness of man.

Taking these points in order, we are struck immediately by the fact that it is very difficult to prove the existence of the cosmic medium. Our methods of scientific investigation have thus far done little to subject consciousness to the laboratory microscope, though the most recent investigations of parapsychology have been somewhat fruitful. Dr. J. B. Rhine's experiments at Duke University have proved successfully that there exists some method of communication between minds beyond the purely sensual, but this whole area of man's existence lies largely uninvestigated, like a strange and dark continent. People have dreams in which they see themselves doing a certain thing at a certain place, and a few days later actually find themselves in that same place doing that same thing. People report the sudden knowledge of a friend's good or bad fortune, the inner conviction that a house is burning down, of a loved one's pain or danger. Never a day passes but what countless manifestations of this kind are recorded around the world. The dark continent of man's uninvestigated psyche beckons us. When we finally have given it our complete attention, the world will witness an evolutionary leap the like of which has never been dreamed.

COSMIC MEDIUM

The cosmic medium that connects one man with another and one mind with another is the universal intelligence that permeates all things, all people, all places. By it each of us has an umbilical tie with his neighbor, for in a very real and actual sense each of us is one with his neighbor since the same basic mind is in everyone. As soon as a man is finally convinced that the principle of infinite multiplicity is not valid in any conception of the universe, then he finally is led to the concept of inner unity, the absolute oneness of all things. When this new principle has really come home to him, he realizes that there is only one life at work in the universe and it is in him as well as in his neighbor. He sees that it works secretly in the heart of all things, and by this insight he is able not only to influence its manifestation within him but also its manifestation in other persons, in other things.

The world that is perceived through our senses is only a partially revealed representation of the world that exists within mind. Strange, then, that the things that we encounter in space and time seem so very real to us. We knock upon a desk and know it is hard and that it is there. But the existence of the desk as an extension of an idea is a concept we seldom entertain. We spend most of our days thinking and planning and scheming, trying to originate ideas, but our actions are always predicated upon the fact that the things that we encounter in the world are the things that are truly influential. When we are able to perceive all things as manifestations of thought concepts, then we look beyond each to the idea that gave it form. Once we have turned our gaze in that direction we have begun to deal with the basic creative power of the universe and we have begun to see the possibilities in the second point in the doctrine of mind over matter, the established connection between the world of consciousness and the world of substance.

ENAMOURING EGO

"The intellect by itself moves nothing," said Aristotle, and modern psychology has affirmed this law. We encounter those circumstances that reflect the quality of our deeper consciousness. In short, we see only that which we are, and it is this enamouring quality of our ego that deludes us about the world. Most people keep running into the same situations over and over again. Some are accident prone; others are eternally fretting about their health; still others make a failure of one enterprise after another. Some lives take on the tenor of an epic tragedy as fate seems to heap one misfortune on top of another. But it is not misfortune that such people are encountering; merely the outer manifestation of the inner working of their own minds.

Life keeps bringing us into contact with those things which we fail to understand. As long as our consciousness does not grow, as long as our inner sight does not penetrate, that long will we continue to run into the circumstance that defeats us, until our heads are bloody and bowed, until we finally understand or are beaten completely. The established connection between the unseen world of the mind and the outer world of the senses is this: the outer world is always a projection of the inner. Its emotional content is the same as the emotional content of the consciousness beholding it; its influence on the individual is always according to what he perceives; and what he perceives comes from within him, not from outside.

MAGIC IMAGES

The first two points in the doctrine of mind over matter allow us to understand how we are slaves to circumstance, how we never truly originate action, but take action as a result of being stimulated into it. These two points, if finally accepted without relief, would be a hopeless concept of life indeed, but in the third point of the doctrine we find the leaven by which the whole makeup of life is changed from the deadened aura of hopelessness into the rosy-hued sparkle of anticipation. The third point in the doctrine tells us that we can alter our environment and our circumstances by disciplining our consciousness.

"Magical operations," says Eliphas Levi, "are the exercise

of a power which is natural but superior to the ordinary powers of nature. They are the result of a science and of habits which exalt the human will above its usual limits." Will, alone, is not the answer, however. Will, alone, is more often a pathway to pain than to power. When we think of will power most of us think of exercising our will against other people and other things, but the only place where our will power can be used effectively is in disciplining our inner consciousness. We can, in final analysis, choose to think only those thoughts which we want to think, and it is this power of mental choice that gives man his freedom. By it he is given the power to remake himself into any image he can envisage. He can heal his body, heal his soul, alter and exalt his own personality, enhance his will power, produce hypnotic states, ecstasy. He can change himself from the lowliest of idlers to the most accomplished and effective of men and all this not because he hustles about in the world but because he gathers his own inner being around him, takes thought, alters the quality of his own mind. All the power of an individual lies in his disciplining his own consciousness, and all his effectiveness consists of his being able to produce faith within himself. For it is only faith that is able to develop in us a mental image contrary to the one we have been entertaining.

EVIDENCE OF THINGS UNSEEN

"Faith," wrote Saint Paul, "is the substance of things hoped for, the evidence of things unseen." Through faith we are able to act as if we *know*. When we have actual knowledge, we proceed with confidence; when we doubt, we are unsure of ourselves, apprehensive. This is the contrast between the man of great faith and the man of little faith: the former goes through life as if he had a special genie at his side, a supernatural power upon which he can call in every circumstance, while the latter acts out the blurred and distorted vision within, cautiously, doubtfully, fearfully.

The substance of things hoped for is a real substance, formed from pictures in the mind as concrete and detailed as in the world itself. The evidence of things unseen is an inner evidence gleaned through the image-making power of the imagination. It is absolutely impossible for us to act against our knowledge. A man will not step in front of a speeding automobile because he knows he will be killed; he will not walk upon the water because he knows that he will sink; sometimes he will not even venture into a new business because he believes that he will fail. No amount of persuasion can change his reaction to what he knows. But what he knows can be changed, and the most direct and efficacious manner is through changing the images within his consciousness. If he learns to visualize his goal clearly, one day he will be able to embark upon a new venture and be successful. The emotional content of the image in his mind will seep down into deeper regions of consciousness and provoke him into right action.

If we think of ourselves as being strong we eventually become strong. If we think of ourselves as determined we eventually arrive at tenacity. If we think of ourselves as endowed with power we eventually achieve ascendency over circumstances. The mind has infinite power to influence us, for we act in accordance with its conceptions as it casts up before us inner images that stimulate us into action and attitude. Eating, appetite, sexual activity, motor response, intellectual activity are all triggered by the images we entertain in our minds. We are stimulated into all things by ideas. The world itself is an idea, and we react to it. We can change the world's influence upon us, however, by originating idea in consciousness, thereby stimulate ourselves and cease reacting.

IDEA AND ACTION

Doctor José Delgado, a Yale University surgeon, reports that the behavior of animals and presumably man can be drastically changed by painless electric charges to the brain. In experiments, monkeys ate seven times more food than normal or suddenly became amorous or abruptly ferocious, and tests on humans brought on fear, affection, giddy laughter, and remarkable feats of memory, all depending upon which area of the brain was stimulated. It seems obvious that in these experiments electrical stimulation is simply substituted for what normally would be nervous stimulation, and when we reflect that nervous stimulation is always brought about through reaction to the ideas in our consciousness, then we become acutely aware how important it is to control our thoughts and to treat the image-making power of the mind with care.

We always tend to become that which occupies our thoughts. In the long run a man is not so much a body as he is the sum total of the ideas within his consciousness. You need only meet him for a moment to know many of those ideas. If he is genial, you know that he regards the world as a warm and comfortable place. If he is cold, then you know that he finds hostility around him. If he is indifferent, then you know that he is afraid of being hurt. Excess always provides the clue. A man who laughs too much may be hiding his tears, like Pagliacci. We eat too much as a substitute for love, or drink too much to still our fears, or play too hard as an escape from the responsibilities of life, or overwork to accumulate security in a changing world. But always our response is to the image in our minds, the ideas that occupy us, the ghosts we envisage, the demons that pursue us, the fancied pots of gold that lie beyond the rainbow.

We must learn to take up our positions with a steadfast belief in the rightness of our stand. Doubt casts a pall of indecision over everything. We must shut out doubt from our minds and crystallize the images there so that we can take positive action on all our problems.

> He who doubts from what he sees
> Will ne'er believe do what you please.
> If the sun and moon should doubt,
> They'd immediately go out.
> —William Blake

DESIGNERS OF LIFE

To start visualizing things clearly is not nearly so difficult as might be imagined. Each of us has a deep psychological tendency to use his imagination to envisage not only his present surroundings but also their potentiality. We are deterred from this proper use of the imagination because of an over-reliance on material things. We see, for example, the established form of an automobile; we accept this form and no longer allow ourselves to visualize anything different. Thus we give our creative imagination an opiate and shut off an important corner of our nature. Not the designer, however. He cannot afford to visualize the automobile in its presently accepted form. For him, there must always be a new form. His envisaging of it is his livelihood.

We are all innately designers of life, and insofar as we accept the creative power of our imagination we are able to influence life's shape and substance and its effect upon us. We change events and people not by altering them intrinsically but by changing our perception of them. Each thing, each event, each person has infinite potentiality. We see in each only that which our consciousness is capable of perceiving. When we learn to look longer and with eyes of wonder, we develop a kind of insight that enables us to penetrate into depths we hitherto had not suspected. Because we then see differently, we then react differently, and our lives are changed accordingly.

To many people mental power implies such legerdemain as moving objects by will power or materializing or dematerializing things, or leading others around by their mental noses, but in actual fact the mental adept works on no one but himself. His is the eye through which all things are seen and only insofar as he is able to influence his own perception is he able to influence the world. The greater his knowledge, the closer he is to the heart of truth, and the closer he is to the heart of truth, the more he identifies himself with other persons and other things. Through this inner identification, he achieves understanding of the law of each person's secret nature and his own life and the world he lives in.

CHANGE YOUR THINKING AND CHANGE THE WORLD

If there is a problem in your life that you would solve, do not set your will to work on it. You will conquer this problem in the end, not by fighting it, but by understanding it. The reason it exists in the first place is because of lack of understanding. You must allow yourself to be convinced of this simple premise, that all problems reside in ignorance, that they represent a block in the understanding of the person who has them. As long as that block exists, so long will the problem remain. There is absolutely no possibility of ever solving a problem without gaining insight into its nature. Life is a constant movement by which simplicity is resolved into complexity and complexity is resolved into simplicity, and the alchemy that causes the natural growth of things is simply widened consciousness. The most complex problem in the world yields to understanding, and once it has been solved it becomes simple.

To achieve the ascendency of mind over matter you must accept the basic premise of there being one animating presence residing in all persons and all things. Behind all form is a basic unity, an essential oneness that is never destroyed despite all differentiation. When we are able, through higher consciousness and increased insight, to penetrate the many masks behind which the all-encompassing one mind and one life is hidden, then we achieve effectiveness in all our works and actions through understanding the dynamic law of becoming that exists within each form. All this is by way of saying that there is nothing in the world that we cannot influence by first influencing ourselves, for everything in the end is colored by the quality of our consciousness. We can change our consciousness and thus change what we see, and the tool by which we can effect this change is imagination. We can learn to visualize in our minds only those things that we wish admitted into our lives, and when we have truly learned to do this, physical counterparts of those ideas will soon appear in our environment.

You can be anything you want to be if you will only trust your imagination. Picture your heart's desire; never let the picture distort or tarnish; keep it fresh and clear and bright. It will enter your life quietly and unobtrusively, without sound of trumpets or clashing cymbals, for it will be following a law that exists throughout the universe, that everything basically is idea and must first begin in the mind of the beholder.

6 MENTAL IMAGERY

"To have seen that Vision," says Plotinus, "is reason no longer, it is more than reason, before reason and after reason, as also is the Vision which is seen. And perhaps we should not here speak of sight, for that which is seen is not discerned by the seer, if indeed it is possible here to distinguish between seer and seen as separate things. Therefore this Vision is hard to tell of, for how can a man describe as other than himself that which when he discerned it seemed not other but one with himself?"

TO THINK IS TO BE

That which is visualized in the mind becomes part of the possessor of that mind because a man is what he thinks. It is strange how little we know about the mind. Not much more has been determined about it since the time of Descartes and his brilliant basic premise, *"Cogito, ergo sum"*—"I think, therefore I am." We only know we exist because we think. Should thought stop in us, we automatically would cease to be. Should thought begin at any particular point in space, that point immediately would begin to live. It is deeply significant that we exist by grace of thought, and it is even more significant that at any particular time we are the sum total of the thoughts we hold in mind.

It seems reasonable to assume that the thinking being that inhabits us is thought itself, that the more complex and universal our thoughts are, the more complex and universal we become. It is impossible to separate the image in the mind of a beholder from the beholder himself, because in a very real sense the two are one. That which achieves the attention of consciousness becomes that consciousness. When our attention is focused on something, we become that thing. It is this power of consciousness, that it becomes the thought it thinks, which gives the mind such ascendency over matter. Man's investigation of the outer world has practically conquered space and time, but he still knows very little about what his own mind is and what its influences are. Because thought is invisible it never has come under the scrutiny of the laboratory microscope. As a consequence, men are nearly as poorly informed about the qualities and processes of thought as they were at the dawn of written history. Even though it is recognized now that the thoughts a person thinks determine his whole life, the average man continues to think in response to sensual stimuli rather than in response to his inner wishes and desires.

MENTAL LAW

The thought first, then the thing, that is the law. But the vast majority of people live on the opposite premise—the thing first, then the thought. The power of mental imagery still works even in this reversal of form, but in this case it merely lends validity to everything they see and every situation they encounter. Such people are unable to grow beyond the limitation of their own emotions, for they give credence to all sensual stimuli. Each such stimulus becomes bound up in an emotional reaction. Whenever they encounter an event or thing which they have encountered before, they react in a predetermined manner. It thus becomes impossible for them to progress into any degree of effective living, for by the very nature of their mental position the things of the world control them, they never control the things. They are either fearful or hostile, resentful, envious, or sad, but each of these emotions is inspired by a stimulus from outside and never by inner convictions or desires. These are the people who are the most strenuous defenders of their mental aberrations. In argument they are easily provoked to hysteria. Since their convictions are encysted in emotion, they defend them with their lives, convinced of ultimate disaster should their delusions be dissolved. The most fortunate thing that can happen is that life reduce their egos to nothingness. To a great extent their eyes are then cleared, and they are able finally to see that they have always reacted rather than acted. When humility enters a man's soul, he at last is able to perceive that he does not live alone in the world but with millions of brothers and that hidden in the heart of each is the same animating spirit.

FORECASTER OF THE FUTURE

"To know is nothing at all, to imagine is everything," wrote Anatole France. That which seizes the attention of our consciousness is an infallible forecaster of the future. Indeed, were we to know the thoughts that occupy a man's mind, we might provide him an accurate description of his coming life, down to the most intimate detail. The success of fortune tellers, via whatever medium they use, cards, tea leaves, crystal balls, is always the result of a telepathic communication between seer and subject. The thoughts that possess us lead us around by the mental noses. There is in thought a motor impulse that compels us to do the things we think about, and this is a law far above moral or ethical considerations. It works just as quickly for what is considered evil as it does for what is considered good. If you keep thinking about robbing the corner service station, and you keep this image in your mind for several weeks, you one day will find yourself at the service station, gun in hand, prepared to empty the till. People who commit so-called "crimes of passion" often report they were in the grip of a compulsion they could neither control nor understand. Such compulsion proceeds out of their thoughts. Images projected into the moving screen of mind finally take root in the motor impulses of the body, and each person is propelled into the action he visualizes in the deeper recesses of his consciousness. The Dhammapada cautions us to guard our thoughts, and indeed we should. Everything that is admitted into our mind takes shape, form, and substance in our lives, and we can stop this from happening only by ceasing to live, for the law of life is the law of thoughts becoming things.

CLEAR THINKING

The quality of our mental imagery determines how quickly we get effects in the outer world. Since most people are relatively unaware of thinking at all, they give little consideration to how well they think, to the clarity and reality of the images they envisage. Most of us are fuzzy thinkers. When we call something to mind, it comes to us as a vague and shadowy presence. We do not really see it, feel it, hear it, touch it, penetrate it, take it unto us, but rather are dimly aware of it by means of some verbal grasp of its idea. We say, "My house," but the image does not call to mind the actual house, only a vague idea of it in terms of whether the taxes have to be paid, the outside walls painted, the lawn mowed, or a party given there Saturday night. We adopt meanings about everything in terms of personal significance, but we seldom conjure up images in our consciousness for the simple reason that we never have trained ourselves to think that way, never have truly understood the significance of such images.

Think about something familiar. Think of a room in which you spend a great deal of time. See yourself sitting in some particular chair in that room. Look around. What do you see? Are there pictures on the walls? Where and what kind? What are their colors? Where are the furniture, books, papers? Is there dust gathered in the corners? Where are the lamps? How do they operate? See yourself in that room with such intensity that you actually *feel* that you are there. See the color, the solidity of objects. Work on this for a few days. If you are lucky, you will have an experience that will startle you. During one of these meditation periods, while you are visiting this room in your mind, you will have the sudden feeling that you actually are there. When this experience comes to you, you *will* be there, in a very real though psychic sense, such is the tremendous power of correct and clear mental visualization.

A DOOR AJAR

There are other tests you can take to convince yourself how fuzzy your thinking has been and how much power lies in making it clear. If you are married, try suddenly to call to mind the face of your spouse. You may be shocked to realize how difficult this is. What you immediately call to mind is an *idea* of your spouse, and this idea has the wavering shape of a shadowy dream. Concentrate on making his or her face as clear in your mind as a photograph. Bend the entire effort of your attention toward this end. Gradually the picture will clear. Soon you will see that face before you, animated, alive, vibrant, so that you feel certain that if you reached out you could touch a cheek with your fingertips. Don't be surprised that evening if your husband or wife says to you, "I was thinking about you all day today."

This is not legend or superstition or wishful thinking. When we deal with the mind we are dealing with the most significant thing in life. There are undreamed of powers in consciousness, and they have not even been tapped. Our first fumbling attempts to understand the paranormal will be very amusing to researchers a hundred years from now. The current awakening to telepathy and clairvoyance and precognition have barely jarred the door into an enormous storehouse of fantastic powers and perceptions. We take our first step on the proper path when we realize the original power of mind over matter and how our thoughts influence the world we live in. Once we truly have apprehended the tremendous force that propels a mental image to become a physical fact, then we see that we must dedicate our efforts to becoming clear and concise thinkers rather than rushers-around-in-the-world.

PSYCHIC IMBALANCE

We must learn to visualize with complete clarity, so that an image called up in mind exists with the same solidity, color, and dimension as one in the physical world. Research conducted into the content of dreams has revealed that some people dream in black and white while others dream in color. Others dream in pantomime, still others with full sound effects. Some people's dreams are populated with folks without faces, and in some people's dreams it is always night, in others it is always day. Such research has proved pretty well that emotional blocks in the subconscious restrict the individual from completely visualizing things in his mind. A man might attempt to envision himself successfully completing a task which he desires to do, but no matter how hard he tries to focus his inner attention he never can quite see himself in that position. If it would finally involve a change of residence, for example, he might report that he is able to see the new home and everything in it but is unable to visualize himself there.

It is the subconscious that blocks him out from such visualization. Some fear or hostility or resentment has given him a deep mental block about moving and forbids the picture from entering his mind and thereby bars the actual event from happening in the physical world. It is no easy matter for him to overcome this subconscious censoring of his thoughts. It represents a wrong self-identification, a psychic imbalance. This psychic imbalance is universally caused by the centering of consciousness in the ego rather than in the deeper regions of being. A man who allows his surface self to control his life is in the grip of a Lilliputian ghost. He eventually will become bound up mentally by thousands of little prompters that proceed out of his subconscious. It is they that give form and substance to his ego, the thing he regards as himself, which is never himself at all but only the limitations that he has accepted and come to regard as real.

SUBCONSCIOUS PROMPTINGS

Modern psychoanalysis, in order to test the psychic imbalance of the individual, uses a test devised by Rorschach, in which the subconscious preoccupation of a patient is diagnosed from spontaneous images which he sees in complex ink blots. Since the ink blots are haphazard and multiform, it follows that the images that the patient sees in them represent the kind of thing that his consciousness is habitually focused upon. In other words, the test provides a key to the thoughts which occupy an individual's mind and gives the psychologist a method of interpreting neurosis. The premise that diagnosis is based upon is that each of us sees in all things the thoughts that, *a priori*, occupy our minds. Thus life itself turns out to be nothing more or less than a gigantic Rorschach test. Shape and form and substance have infinite meaning and infinite possibility. To the individual beholder each assumes color and quality directly taken from the thoughts that occupy his consciousness. When we choose the thoughts we think we choose our lives.

The fact of the matter is that very few people are free to exercise choice in their thinking because the bulk of their thought erupts from pain-insistent memories in the subconscious. They are not free because they have wrongly identified themselves. Their sense of self is primarily the memories of events and relationships. In consequence, they assume themselves to be a changing thing, an ego, a sense of self built upon dimly remembered and barely perceived relationships. The ego thinks always in response to the subconscious. Only the great self, the sense of self free of the limitations of the ego, is able to originate thought or to be receptive to it in an unbiased manner. We all put too much value on the ego. Personality represents for us both a fascination and a delusion. By its very meaning personality is restricted to the individual and thus represents a limited sense of self. Only from the wider and broader standpoint of the Secret Self is it possible for the individual mind to orient itself correctly with life. Thus it is able to grasp meanings and relationships from a larger and more encompassing standpoint and to know by immediate perception rather than by reason and deduction.

INSTINCTIVE PERFORMANCE

The ego thinks from a small standpoint in the center. It thinks outward. It seeks to know by groping into the unknown, attempting to rationalize what it finds there. Since infinite space surrounds it, it is impossible for it ever to grow into great understanding. Since what it thinks is colored by what it already knows, and since what it knows is based upon a strictly personal and infinitesimal interpretation, it therefore, by its very nature, cannot ever arrive at true knowledge. Before a man can be truly wise, before he can arrive at his birthright of power and understanding, he must in some degree shuck off the trappings of the ego and take on a wider kind of consciousness. Instead of being a central thinker, he must learn to be a peripheral or outer thinker. He must learn to allow thought to develop in him under the impulsion of something outside of and greater than himself. He must learn to be able to do things without focusing his attention upon them. He must learn to perform them through an instinctive understanding of their true nature and the job to be done.

The ego prevents a man from performing in this manner. To be self-conscious is to be fearful and restricted. The instinctive and natural performer thinks with his outer and wider mind. He who is enrapt in consideration of his ego and sense of self is bound up in fear and tension during the simplest of tasks. That which we do well we do not think about. We simply perform by grace of our outer and wider mind. When we lose our contact with this mind, we fall from grace with a bang; for all by ourselves, focused upon each little movement, we cannot perform the simplest of tasks.

The centipede was happy quite
Until a toad in fun
Said, "Pray, which leg goes after which?"
That worked her mind to such a pitch,
She lay distracted in a ditch,
Considering how to run.
　　　　　　　—Mrs. Edward Craster

There seems to be absolutely no limit to the feats the human being can perform when he is able to grasp them with his outer or peripheral mind. A man stands on the forefinger of one hand atop a hundred foot pole. Another walks a tight-rope across the chasm of Niagara Falls. Another springs from a board and turns three somersaults in the air before landing on his feet. Still another juggles a dozen balls at a time. Watching such performances, we are astounded. How is it possible, we ask ourselves, for a human being to do such things? It is possible because the man has mastered the knack of performing without thought. He has learned to shut off the thinking of his central self and to stand outside, as it were, grasping his whole action as a continuous thing, seeing it as a single, flowing, unbroken movement. As a consequence, arms and legs move, muscles coordinate, energy is expended, all at the behest of a complete picture held by his wider mind. He performs from the spine, unthinkingly, responds only to the image of what he wants to do, just as another man might walk down the street, thinking only of where he wants to go and never of the act of putting one foot in front of the other.

TRUSTING YOUR GREATER SELF

The reason why most people play such atrocious golf is that they have broken the golf swing down into a dozen dif-ferent small actions, each of which receives the focus of their attention when they stand up to hit the golf ball. It is a wonder they don't break their spines or snap a tendon. The miracle is that they hit the ball at all, since they are thinking about everything else but that. Those rare specimens who master the art of shooting par have mastered also the art of *not thinking how*. The great player stands up to the ball only after he has made up his mind *where* he wants to hit it. He doesn't think of *how* he will hit it. We can adopt his method in everything we do. We can stop thinking how to do things and start concentrating our attention only upon where we want to go. Once we have made a decision, we must learn to trust our greater, outer mind for the actual performance.

There is a deep, underlying psychological reason for this. The brain and the organs of the body are not to be trusted beyond the intelligence from which they grew. To subject all performance to the limitation of human reason is to subject all action to restriction and error. An infinite, eternal intelligence grew the brain and body and both now nestle in the lap of that intelligence, are products of it, and never its master. We must stop forcing our ego to act as an originator of action and thought, and instead learn to let thought develop in us, action develop in us, as a result of a complete reliance upon an outer and wider sense of being.

Chuang-Tzu wrote, "A drunken man, when he falls out of a cart, though he may suffer, does not die. His bones are the same as other people's, but he meets the accident in a different way. His spirit is in a condition of security. He is not conscious of riding in the cart, neither is he conscious of falling out of it. Ideas of life, death, fear, etc., cannot penetrate his breast, and so he does not suffer from contact with objective existences, and if such security is to be got from wine, how much more is to be got from spontaneity?" What we are driving at is an attempt to function through the totality of our psychic being, rather than some small part of it, like the brain, or the reason, or the memory. It should be obvious that the whole is always greater than its parts, and if we can learn to think and act through the totality of all our psychic functioning, then it is apparent that our effectiveness must be vastly increased. The important thing to remember is that the center of the mind's activity is not in the conscious, thinking process, but in something greatly above it, outside it, and yet in a manner within.

ACTIVE MIND

When a man learns to let his mind alone, it begins to function in a spontaneous manner that is natural to it. It rids itself of inhibition and restriction, and the person's effectiveness and energy are greatly increased. There are large rewards to be gained from learning how to function unconsciously. It is through painful awareness of self that all our imperfections spring. We are able to stifle the nagging voice of self-consciousness through immersing it in the great sea of being that is the Secret Self. There it merges and is lost as a drop of water merges and is lost in the ocean. We become natural men instead of artificial ones, and all our actions and all our thoughts take on a spontaneity that springs directly out of the Divine. Unthinkable ingenuity and creative power lie within universal mind, and to the degree that you learn to trust your life and being to it, that much of its power is yours.

The most remarkable thing about man is his mind. The mystery that surrounds another person is the fact that he thinks, that his thoughts are invisible and therefore strictly his own. Within the boundaries of his own being, he lives in a world that no one truly penetrates. It is populated by shapes and structures, events and persons known only to him, with a significance that is rooted in symbol. And this world in his mind has greater meaning for him than the materialistic world in which he moves. He retires from the material world when he goes to bed, but even in sleep the world in his mind is still with him. This mental world has even greater meaning in sleep. Now his thoughts, though still couched in materialistic terms, take on symbolistic significance, and the things he dreams come to him as disguised meanings, playing out upon the screen of consciousness the conflicts that exist in his subconscious.

A man is with his mind twenty-four hours of every day, and he never ceases to think. He is influenced a thousand times more by the thoughts that cross his consciousness than he ever is by the situations he encounters in the sensual world. He is truly a mental creature, and those animal qualities he possesses are residual only, left over from an evolution whose great thrust, in the first place, was its effort to produce mind. Just as consciousness has evolved out of matter, to eventually control matter, so will it one day be free of matter, for the very nature of being presupposes a greater existence than any that is likely to occur as long as it is bound to the flesh. The cycle of birth, growth, decay, and death is bound to a physical world with its necessary constant production of different forms in an effort to find the most effective one. Such a cycle, however, no longer is mandatory for the mind, which has settled on an absolute form and no longer is changing in kind, only in degree. Evolution has brought us to the point where a mental being might best serve advancement by being free of the cycle of birth and death. Such a step is undoubtedly part of the evolutionary plan; it may be set for a time somewhere in the future or may be upon us now. Meantime the fact has become apparent that the pathway to man's salvation lies in emphasis on mental existence and gradual turning away from physical bondage.

TO THINK IS TO DO

Up to now no one has been able to stop the physical aging of the body, and currently every man is subject in the end to a physical death. As long as our activities, our pleasures, and our sensations are rooted in our physical bodies, we have no alternative but to eventually suffer pain, dissolution, and decay, but when we turn away from our physical bodies and take up residence in our minds, then we are able to experience a constant growth that lends us not only a deep personal satisfaction but fulfills the fondest wishes of life and evolution. To once make up your mind that intellect is superior to and supersedes matter is to take the most important step of all in the living of a serene and effective life. The soul grows within even as the body decays without, and that man who is able in the end to merge his sense of being with that of the Secret Self has perpetuated himself into eternity, has achieved immortality.

Images that play about in our minds lead us inevitably into action. This is a law of life, and we can neither start nor stop it. Whatever we think about we must do. Since we cannot stop our thinking, we inevitably are led into action by our thoughts, even if this action be of the most negative kind. Since a human being is a dynamic entity, choosing not to do a thing is just as much an action on his part as doing it would be. Fear of failure, for example, predisposes a man not to attempt any venture that carries a risk. As a consequence, he is apt to allow all things to pass him by, deterred from taking action because of the nature of the images in his mind. Usually these images are placed there by fear, or one of fear's cousins, and these negative emotional qualities spring out of the subconscious and have been placed there by the ego. The individual may rid himself of them by achieving a proper relationship between the ego and universal mind. He may become whole by getting rid of his sense of surface self, by immersing the ego in his wider being and becoming one with all things and all people.

GETTING RID OF MENTAL BLOCKS

A man is not able to force himself to think different thoughts from those that he habitually thinks. He cannot exclude certain thoughts from his mind or force others to enter by an effort of will. Thought originates in the deeper recesses of his being, an area that largely is unavailable to his conscious mind and one that for the most part simply will not respond to coercion. A psychological transformation is not possible without a spiritual awakening, and before a man can change his kind and type of thinking, it first is necessary that he alter his conception of self. A little reflection on the ego reveals what a delusional trap it is, for it is primarily a sense of separateness and it feeds upon a sense of comparison. It is pleased to be better than others, extremely sad to be worse, and it performs all actions for selfish motives —avarice, applause, power. The greatest sickness in the world is to be satisfied in the ego, for then we are blinded to the real nature of life and our own potentiality. Only when we are dissatisfied in the ego through defeat or disillusionment are we close to the veil that separates us from our true selves. It is at this moment that we suddenly may see, that our eyes and souls may open and penetrate into the deeper and wider being that gives a universal quality to all people.

We immensely improve our ability to visualize when we rid ourselves of the mental blocks and prompters that are stored in our subconscious. These we are able to clear away through a proper psychic balance between the ego and the Secret Self, and we achieve this balance by surrendering ego and turning our lives over to the Divine. This is not nearly so difficult as it sounds. We are not responsible for our existence in the first place. We didn't choose the bodies we inhabit or the life into which we were born, our language, customs, education, even the people we know have been chosen for us by a greater power. When we learn to trust this power completely, to turn over to it our sense of self, our actions, our mind, our ability, our talent, we are enlarged by it because of that very act. It uses us for its purpose and many times more effectively than we could ever use ourselves. There is tremendous energy to be gained by surrender of the ego to the Secret Self. A man becomes a power doubled. He suddenly seems free of restriction, cleared of restraint; his health, energy, and resources know no limit.

LETTING GO

Terry was a brilliant youngster. He had a straight A average in high school and was awarded a scholarship at a leading western university. But he was an intensely nervous and high strung young man, seemed constantly fearful and apprehensive. He would jump at the slightest noise, was shy and awkward in the presence of strangers, became tongue-tied when given an opportunity to speak, was afraid of heights, was afraid of closed places, was sick a good deal of the time. Even though he was graduated from college with honors, he nevertheless had great difficulty in finding a job, so unfavorable was the impression that he made upon prospective employers. His record prevailed, however, and he eventually found employment in the laboratory of a large industrial firm, where he helped in the research department. Then for no apparent reason he suffered a nervous breakdown and was confined to a sanatorium. Some months later he left the sanatorium, but he was too distracted to readjust to life, and he was directed by a friend to a religious retreat.

The retreat house stood on the bluffs overlooking the Pacific Ocean, and on a clear day a hundred miles of the California coastline could be seen. The brown hump of Santa Catalina Island stood off shore like a camel rising from the sea, and a light breeze generally blew off the ocean, carrying with it the salty tang of seaweed and kelp. Terry sat for hours on a stone bench, gazing out over this panorama. The magnificence of nature dwarfed him, and he could feel his ego subside. During such a mood, his advisor came to him, and they sat on the stone bench and talked.

"I see you are better now," the advisor said. "It stands in your eyes. You are not so concerned with yourself."

"That's true," answered Terry. "It's because it's so peaceful here."

"It is peaceful anywhere, my son, if your soul is properly centered."

"How does one properly center his soul?"

"By getting rid of self-consciousness."

"That's very difficult to do when one has an inferiority complex."

"An inferiority complex is a delusion."

"It may seem a delusion to you," answered Terry, "but it is not a delusion to me. I am fearful and apprehensive in all I do because I feel inferior, because I am afraid I will not do well."

"Then get rid of the sense of yourself as doer. Accept yourself only as instrument. Make up your mind that a power greater than you are is working through you to accomplish its ends. It is not embarrassed or fearful or apprehensive. It is dynamic, irresistible, and eternal. If you can manage to put yourself in its hands completely, you never will be embarrassed or fearful again, and you will accomplish such things as you never thought possible."

Terry listened to his advisor well. In the days that followed, he gazed out upon the sea and sky, and the truth came to him. When he left the retreat and returned to his home, his illness was gone, and he experienced a vigor in mind and body that he had never known. He undertook his work with serenity, became able to talk freely in front of people, mixed with them gladly, eventually came to lead them. Today he heads his own research company. He is well-to-do and respected, has not had a sick day in years. He credits everything to his religious awakening.

"I always thought that I was the one who was carrying the ball," he says, "and the responsibility frightened me. Once I learned that the world and its events and my life were in safer hands than mine, I was able to get myself out of the way and see the working of a master intelligence everywhere. The things I seem to have accomplished have been accomplished by something outside me. It works through me just as it will work through you. All I do is let it."

THE PERFECT LEADER

To free the mind of the restrictions imposed by egoistic thinking is the first thing to be done. This is accomplished by turning your life over to the Secret Self. Place your hopes, your dreams, your ambitions, your talents, your very self, on a mental silver platter. Hand it over to the Secret Self. Say, "Here, you take it. You run it. I will listen, follow your advice, execute your will.' If you take this mental stand without reservation, your life will be changed forthwith, and you will have embarked upon the highest adventure possible.

Moreover, from that time on, the images in your mind will manifest in the world exactly as you visualize them.

People who have never experienced a centering of the self outside the ego believe that when they make the declaration that they no longer will take action as a result of egoistic choice, then henceforth they will sit like lumps on a log because there will be nothing to stir them once they have surrendered volition. How wrong they are! We never move ourselves into action anyway. All our lives we are moved into action by the Secret Self. Our difficulties are all caused by the fact that we have a delusional sense of self which clutters up the subconscious with negative emotions, causes restrictive pictures of limitation, lack, and fear to be projected onto the creative screen of mind and therefore restricts the amount of energy that can flow through us. The ego is an impediment in the natural dynamic of being, yet even when present in all its full distortion, the individual is still directed by the Secret Self, with his power filtered and ineffectual. The man who has been cleared sits like no lump on a log. More likely, he thunders across the human scene, such is the power that manifests through him. Yet he himself does nothing. The power uses him to manifest through, and he simply hitches a ride, acting in the midst of conflict serenely and surely, an instrument of a power that has everything under control.

THE POWER OF THOUGHT

Once a psychological balance has been obtained, it is startling how clear images become in our minds. It is as if the inner world takes on even more reality than the outer, more dimension, more possibilities, for through our new psychic perception we become aware that there is the same consciousness in all things. When we visualize something in our minds we thereby sense the manner in which we affect the physical world; we see that consciousness affected in us affects consciousness in the thing visualized. We become aware that it is impossible for anything to externalize in our world without first being pictured in our minds. The simplest of actions takes on a new significance. We cannot reach for a pen, get up and walk to the door, answer the telephone, without first having a mental picture of such acts. We become cognizant of this sequence as the natural cause and effect of all things, and we become exquisitely aware of the fact that we can by an act of mental visualization cease responding to stimuli from the sensual world.

If, when we hear the doorbell, we visualize not answering the door, we will not answer it. In even this trivial circumstance we will find tremendous significance, for it teaches us that we can, in any instance, refuse to draw the mental picture decreed by sensual stimuli and draw the exact opposite. By that simple realization we become enlightened and disciplined beings, free from bondage to the world of senses. The process by which thoughts become things is rooted in the one intelligence from which all things are made. Everything is conscious, has a form that is determined by the awareness entrapped within. When the idea of a thing is changed within the one supreme consciousness, then the thing itself changes, for it was nothing but idea in the first place.

The mind's image making power is affected by its knowledge of itself, and by its inner sense of effectiveness. This sense of capability never is sufficient when it springs out of the surface self, but it is always equal to the task when it results from an identification of the individual with the Supreme. Spiritual awakening allows a man to visualize clearly, but even before that awakening he can discipline himself to exercise faith and belief in the things he desires. Jesus, who was certainly one of the great mental teachers, stated that it is done unto us as we believe. He repeatedly illustrated by deed and parable that the answers to our dreams come when we first have accepted their reality in our minds. The man who achieves a dynamic success in life has mastered the art of acting as if it were impossible to fail. Such a bold approach frees within him an energy and insight that fits him for every occasion. Nothing is impossible to anyone if he is capable of envisioning it in his mind, clearly, without reservation. Universal Subconscious Mind is the doer of all things, and it responds to the conceptions that we project into it with our conscious minds.

VISUALIZING THE OBJECTIVE

There is no objective too important or too trivial for universal mind to manifest it just exactly as it is visualized, but the truth is that few people take the trouble or time to visualize the things they want. They let such matters be decided for them by the events they encounter in the world. If, for example, they meet a friend who has acquired a new car, they are likely to avow to themselves and to family that what they want most of all is a new car. Next day, however, this desire fades, for now an associate in business has been promoted into a new job and they see that it is this they want most of all, not the new car after all. Next day, it is something else; the day after, something again. The desire of a week ago is long forgotten unless some event occurs to inspire in them the same reaction. Such people project a constant parade of changing pictures into the subconscious, which moves this way and that and never gets anything done at all. Since they really do not know what it is that they want, it is small wonder that they achieve nothing. It takes mental discipline to want something and to stay with it, to understand that all things are gained by sacrifice, that nothing is free, easy, or simple.

When we look upon the man of prominence and wealth, it appears to us that he has been favored by nature, gifted more in mind and body and with material things. But if we have had a little spiritual awakening, we arrive at an insight that allows us to see behind all successful men the years of unremitting toil, sweat, and tears that have disciplined them into the effective human beings they have become. Control and effectiveness do not come lightly; they are the products of a good deal of surrender of self. An aspiring youth, focused in ego and personal concern, has as little connection with a successful man as does an acorn with an oak. A thousand egoistic selves have paraded across the successful man's consciousness in the years of growth. In a manner he is all of them, in another, none. In all things he relies upon a power outside himself, which he courts daily.

AFFIRMATION

Visualize we must, and what we visualize manifests in our lives. If we would change our lives, the tool with which to change them is imagination. We must learn to visualize at the behest of a conscious mental choice, and we must teach ourselves to envisage all things clearly and concretely. An effective way to accomplish this is to set aside a period of affirmation each day, and the most beneficial time is just before going to sleep. Then the image is able to settle down into the subconscious without the distractions that result from activity. When we affirm our mental image, we have to know what it is we wish to achieve, whether it is success or health, improvement in personality, greater happiness, whatever. And we have to clearly conceive ourselves as possessing it. Be sure that it is something that is right for you, something that you are willing to devote time and effort to obtain.

The important things are a clear conception and a willingness to make all necessary sacrifices to effect it. The picture we form in our minds should be so clear we can almost touch it, and it should be projected with feeling. Affirm this image verbally. Write out a short and clear affirmation and be able to repeat it to yourself as you visualize your objective. Consciously relax your mind and body when you go through this affirmation period. Get the feeling that you are not making something happen, only accepting it. Feel that this thing is real in your mind, where all true cause exists. Finish your affirmation with a feeling of faith and expectancy and serenity. Know that your image will manifest in the world just as surely as you keep it sharp and clear in your mind. During the day, think and feel and act as if your desire were already manifested. You will then behave as if you have it, and this complete change in your psychic position will attract the situation to you.

It is a wonderful thing to experience the power of mind over matter. Once you have been able to bring some desired circumstance into your life by an act of faith and visualization, you will never again feel alone and friendless and helpless, will know that you have within yourself the key to all creation. Abundance and happiness and success and achievement are unlimited. The power to provide all exists in your mind and your imagination.

7 THE POWER OF CHOICE

Ask a hundred people if their lives had turned out to be what they wanted them to be, and probably not one in the hundred would answer affirmatively. Most people live dissatisfied lives, unfulfilled in most aspects of their natures, but unable to decide what these aspects are or how to go about fulfilling them. They have turned out to be what they are because they have not chosen for themselves, but have allowed events and circumstances to decide for them. They have been molded by a million different sensual stimuli, and they will continue to be so molded as long as they fail to exercise their power of decision.

THE ONLY TRUE ACTION

Man's only true action is his exercise of choice. How he grows and matures and the kind of person he becomes reside in the countless decisions he makes as he journeys through the years. The power of his choice is that it makes him what he becomes. It is the hub of a wheel of countless spokes, each spoke representing a way to be taken, and a man stands always in the center of an infinite number of possibilities. If his choice is made freely and consciously, then a man is enlightened and is consciously molding his own life. If his choice is made as a result of emotional response to the circumstances in which he finds himself, then a man is an automaton and life is molding him. To become free of reaction and to initiate thought from within is the evolutionary goal of mankind.

Once a person takes a step in this direction, no matter how small or tentative, he is forever unchained. He has broken out of the reactionary prison of sensual response and has discovered the completely transforming fact that there resides within him a power to grow in any direction he chooses. A man can choose what he will think regardless of the circumstances around him. He can choose whatever his consciousness will be focused upon, and thereby he can determine the direction in which he will grow. Whatever he thinks about he becomes in the end, and it is this astounding law that enables individuals to rise above their environment. A saint may emerge from the slums, a rich man from poverty, an enlightened mind out of ignorance, the leader of a nation out of an obscure log cabin. The history of mankind is a record of the overcoming of obstacles. The person who refuses to accede to the limitations of his environment is led into such aspiration by the images that form in his mind. He wants something; wanting, visualizes; visualizing, is led into the action that will lead to materialization of his desire.

LINEAR THINKING

For the most part people are unaware of the fact that their lives are decided by the thoughts they think. They are inclined to feel that circumstances are either beyond their control or that power over them is gained only by an intrinsic knowledge of their physical workings. The ability of a man to affect his environment by the way that he feels has largely been lost sight of in the western world. Western education teaches us to be linear thinkers. We gain the overall idea of a thing by examining it piece by piece. Feeling or intuition is largely ignored. Education in the older societies of the east aimed at grasping an intuitional sense of the basic idea of a thing. The eastern athlete works at his event by feel, trying to grasp a sense of the entire motion. The western athlete is more likely to break down his event into a number of correlated small actions, a leg bent here, an arm crooked there, a hip turned here, a shoulder turned there. As a result, he tends to lose feel, and only constant repetition and practice allows proper action to seep into his subconscious so that eventually he can perform unthinkingly.

It is very difficult to teach someone to dance by drawing diagrams of the proper steps upon the floor, but a man who instinctively moves in rhythm to music hardly needs to be taught at all, so apt a pupil is he. The eastern musician uses only a rough notation on his sheet of music to remind him of the melody, preferring to play by feel. The more complicated method of western musicians is represented by a double scale of notes and half notes, delineating completely both melody and harmony. This is not an apology for western methods of education, for the west produces its share of inspirational thinkers and instinctive athletes. This is only to say that the linear method of thinking, while proven effective in scientific investigation, is certainly not the only or even the best approach to be used by the individual in dealing with his surroundings. Our contacts in our daily lives are so profuse that we never can hope to understand them by trying to understand their parts. We must rely for our perceptions on an awareness of each thing achieved by an intuitional understanding of it.

INTUITIVE THINKING

It is often said that banking is a cold-blooded, logical business, based entirely upon reason, but one of the leading bankers in the southwest recently electrified his audience when he told how his bank processed loan applications. Oh, the paper work was done, all right, a financial statement substantiated, receipts and expenditures examined, accounts receivable assessed, a record made of the applicant's background and capability in his business, but when all these factors had been considered the question that the president always asked the examining officer was this: "What kind of feeling do you get?" If the examining officer reported a favorable feeling, the loan was made; if he stated he had mixed feelings, the loan was tabled to be reconsidered later; if he said he had negative feelings, the loan was denied. So in one of our leading financial institutions ultimate decisions are being reached on the basis of intuition rather than the reasoning power of the mind. It is interesting to note that the loss ratio of this particular bank is the lowest in the southwest.

In our society in the past, intuition simply has not been considered academically and philosophically respectable. Thus we have hardly begun to realize its possibilities. No doubt within its scope is the potential synthesis of all our more cumbersome calculations like mathematics, theology, metaphysics, logic. When we have learned to exercise our power of choice and to leave the working out of details to a greater intelligence than is embodied in our conscious minds, we will have arrived at a position of complete psychic effectiveness.

The power of choice is inseparably allied with the power to perceive. Things influence us according to the possibilities that we see in them, and we obviously cannot make a choice concerning that which we do not see. All possibilities are inherent in every situation, but we see only those which our limited consciousness is able to perceive. The wider that consciousness, the more possibilities are apparent, and the more significant become the choices open to us. To the Supreme all possibilities are actualities. The Secret Self is engaged in creating infinite multiplicity out of its own essential oneness, and this is its delight, its inscrutable play. To the human being laid down amidst this incessant change, it is of paramount importance not to become static and to seek constant growth, so that the field of choice widens through the lifetime.

THE EXERCISE OF DIVINITY

The man who knows only one thing exercises no choice. He proceeds along a single path because he sees no other. All around him is an unknown forest, and to his limited vision it would be unthinkable for him to veer off the pathway before him. Knowledge illuminates. The more we understand about our environment the less strange that environment appears. The more our consciousness expands, the more likely we are to perceive the myriad pathways that lead off the road we currently are following. There are as many ways to arrive at salvation and effectiveness as there are different people. The human soul is a direct opening into the world of things from the secret presence of universal self, incomplete, yes, partially manifested, yes, embarked upon a self-seeking journey called life, and this is the drama of existence and evolution being played out upon this mortal sphere.

To choose is to exercise divinity within. It is choice alone that is indicative of higher spiritual and mental development. By it we recognize both intellect and character. The person who is able to transcend the limitations and blandishments of the sensual world stands like a colossus on the evolutionary stage of life. He has likened himself to God by uncovering essential freedom within, through deciding the direction in which he will grow. Choice always presupposes sacrifice, for one does not decide in favor of one thing without deciding against another. Nothing is ever achieved or gained without giving up something else. It is this law of sacrifice under which all things live, by which they grow and evolve and aspire. The acceptance and knowledge of sacrifice alleviates much pain, for when we truly understand that we can have one thing only by giving up another, we hold onto all possessions with loose hands, prepared to let them go at any time. They do not belong to us alone; they are ideas proceeding out of universal mind and therefore under the mutual ownership of everyone.

PAIN AND GROWTH

Life sometimes seems to bend us terrifically, to put us under a strain we scarcely are able to bear, to involve us in conflicts that are beyond our scope to solve; but we are what we are only because we aspire to be greater, and the obstacles and the pain we meet with in life are only the result of our efforts to break out of the encysting shell of the ego and to grow outward in effectiveness and understanding. "The Archer," writes Kahlil Gibran, "sees the mark upon the path of the Infinite, and He bends you with His might, that His arrows may go swift and far." The ends of things do not reveal themselves to the finite mind of man, are only partially available to his intuitive faculties and then only insofar as he understands that life's goals and methods are in the hands of a greater power than he. His real vocation is to fathom his relationship to this power, to develop complete faith and trust in it, to realize that nothing rests in his own hands except the determination of the direction in which he will grow.

Choice implies freedom, and whether man is free or an automaton has long been a favorite argument of religious sects and philosophers. Any power capable of creating the world and overseeing the orderly process of evolution must know exactly where it is going and how it intends to get there. Its course cannot possibly be altered by any one of the finite minds it has created. All the events that have happened in the world must have been preordained, for only through their orderly occurrence has it been possible for life to take the direction it has taken. Yet within the absolutely rigid scope of the occurrence of these events the individual is free, because he has innate within him the power to assume any of the roles that have to be played within any event; and it is he, himself, who chooses in the end the role he will play. Since the universal self creates all things from itself it is in actual truth all things, and therefore does not consider life in terms of people but only in terms of events. Events would approximate thoughts in the mind of a supreme being, whose split into myriad manifestations would be to insure that it participated in all areas of each event in a form best suited to that participation. Thus the Secret Self permeates all events, and the countless forms it assumes, the multiplicity of masks that it dons to play its various roles, appear separate and unique only to other incompletely manifested beings, never to itself.

FREEING PSYCHIC ENERGY

Our egoistic sense of separateness is an illusion deliberately fostered in our mental and psychic makeup so that we are able to perform within the scope of the kind of people we are. Yet there is no absolute decree that we must do so, for at the same time that the illusion was fostered in us, power to break it was implanted also. By recognizing our ability to condition our own consciousness we can expand that consciousness to encompass any role we choose to play, and that is why we inherently are free and why each man carries within him power to master his own fate.

Decision looses a terrific psychic energy. It frees within us potentialities and possibilities we are not even aware of. To make up your mind is a wondrous thing. It directs you toward your mental image, sets you on the path to its realization with an energy that springs out of subterranean recesses. Whatever you do you will do twice as well if you make up your mind what you wish to accomplish. Even such a simple thing as trying to cross a street becomes easier once you make up your mind that you will not attempt it until there is a break in the traffic. You will not stamp the pavement then, apprehensively watching the approaching cars with an eye toward making a sudden spurt. You will know that such energy is wasted. You will stand patiently, serene and sure, because you have made up your mind. Every task in life can be likened to this simple illustration.

The man who enters into activity without making up his mind what he wants to do and how he wishes to accomplish it wastes his energies considering unsuitable possibilities as he proceeds. Some people say that to make up your mind gives you tunnel vision; you never alter course because you cannot see your surroundings. But all possibilities are inherent in all situations at all times. They exist in each situation before we enter it. Only those possibilities appear to us that we are able to envisage in our minds, but the picture we have should be the result of our choice. People to whom possibilities appear other than the one they set out to accomplish are those who have not made definite decisions; they have allowed the images in their minds to change and this changing alters the situation in which they find themselves.

DECIDE AND THE TOOLS ARE GIVEN

Decision is such an important part of everyday living. The coach before his team in the locker room attempts to inculcate in each member of that team a decision to win. Failure to make this decision is almost certain to result in defeat, for without it the pictures that form in the mind are too easily changed in favor of defeat when negative circumstances develop. When you *decide* to accomplish something you mentally toughen yourself to undergo the rigors and privations necessary to attaining the goal. This, above all, calls for tough-mindedness. The athlete who makes up his mind that he will swim the English Channel has to make up his mind at the same time that he will continue swimming, no matter how tired he gets. If he makes a decision to swim the channel and that decision does not include a knowledge of the tiredness he is bound to encounter, then he has not truly made a decision at all, and the first time tiredness seeps through to his consciousness, pictures form of *not* swimming the channel, and he is finished.

The kind of mental picture that assures success is the kind that is set into the mind with a conviction that is unshakable, that survives all onslaughts, obstacles, detours. Such inner conviction inspires great courage and energy. It is the mental picture held by all who achieve and accomplish, who get things done. Many people think they want things, but simply do not have sufficient desire to maintain their mental image in the face of negative circumstances. One has to want something badly in order to persevere in the face of misfortune and defeat. If we accept the sidetracking of our plans as evidence that they never will be realized, then it is a certainty that we never will accomplish anything. No path is easy except one that leads downhill. If we aspire, we must climb, and climbing takes effort and sweat and a willingness to continue in the face of all difficulties. A man climbs a mountain not just because the mountain is there but because he wants to get to the top. It is this inner instinct to overcome obstacles, to rise above circumstance, to win out over all odds, that has carried life on its triumphal emergence from amoeba to spaceman.

MENTAL TOUGHNESS

We have to be tough with ourselves because it is easy to sink into lethargy and forget our aspirations. If we want to hitch a ride on life's express and really go somewhere, we have to be prepared to be shaken up en route; we have to know we will undergo pain, and we have to be prepared to endure it. All of us are inclined to be too soft with ourselves. We want to be sure that we don't work too hard, that we guard against tension, but the truth is that a man makes himself strong by lifting weights, by entering conflict. We achieve physical health by exercise, by the constant use of our bodies to reach some goal. We achieve mental health by the same path, by keeping our mental efforts bent on learning, by always seeking to grow. Sleep is a panacea and one of nature's wonders, but worlds are never conquered by men who lie abed, only by those who are out in the world and doing. Men of purpose never have to decide between action and lassitude. The image in a man's mind, if it is one of accomplishment, propels him into action.

Purpose, however, is more significant than just accomplishment. Lack of purpose can destroy a man, bring sickness, alcoholism. It is purpose that holds the organism together. When that purpose disappears, the organism begins to disintegrate. Men who retire from active lives are excellent illustrations.

Puttering around the garden, playing golf, and fishing are insufficient purpose to hold a man together in his later years. The human organism was not built for enjoyment, but for accomplishment. When we focus ourselves on pleasure-seeking ends it is not long before we disintegrate both intellectually and physically; even our senses become surfeited, and we are no longer able to enjoy our pleasures. The man who works all his life toward the end of retirement usually is frustrated and confused after two or three years of enforced leisure and seeks desperately for some way to get back into harness. Usually, however, his disintegration during this period has been rapid, and he no longer can make a place for himself in the world of achievement. Then he becomes embittered and lonely, and old age really sets in. How much better if he stays on the job in the first place; if not in the same job, then in another found on retiring, so that he can continue to live each day with a purpose, so that he can feel part of the great human effort to progress, so that his abilities and talents do not rust and disintegrate but are kept sharp by constant use.

USE OR LOSE

There is a law that is apparent throughout all life. Simply stated it is, "Use or lose." If we put our right arm in a cast for three months it has shriveled to almost nothing when the cast is taken off. Only months of regular exercise will restore it to normality. As we grow older and our lives become more sedentary, we cease to put regular strain on our muscles, and they become flabby and flaccid. Abdomens tend to protrude; fat gathers on hips and thighs; and if we are forced to run across the street we are out of breath and fear a heart attack. We lose our physical condition through failure to use the muscles of the body, and as a consequence we are easy prey for disease and malfunction. Regular and systematic use of our muscles prevents this, so with the more intangible parts of our natures.

We must use our courage or it deserts us; we must use our determination or it leaves us; we must exercise our power of decision or we soon find that we have none. Taking a mental stand on things is not only important to success and achievement, but is also basic to mental health. The man who never knows where he stands and allows himself to be swayed on every issue is bound to put enormous strain on his emotional makeup, for he is led from peak to valley of victory and defeat without the slightest idea of what motivates him or what causes each circumstance to be attracted to him.

Faith in one's self and one's destiny is the seed from which all decision springs. Doubt is the essence of old age and death. Cynicism, pessimism, and despair are harbingers of failure, disease, and disaster. All things spring from mental images and emotional projections, and the ability to decide, to make up one's mind, is automatic to the man who sees his unity with all creatures and his umbilical connection with the Secret Self. To be unable to make up one's mind, no matter how trivial the problem, is an act of cowardice and contaminates the soul. To be unable to come to a decision is in fact a kind of quitting, a sort of refusal to enter conflict, and mentally dams up the flow of energy that proceeds into the individual from out of the universal, retarding, limiting, bringing about dissolution and decay. To be unable to make up one's mind implies a moral weakness. Such lethargy is not to be coddled but to be overcome. You will not conquer fear by acceding to it; only by meeting it head on; and if you do, your victory is assured, for fear itself is a coward and never stands before a direct onslaught.

MAKING YOUR OWN LUCK

Whatever you are afraid to do, do it, and you will be startled that you no longer are afraid. Whatever you are unable to decide, decide it, and you will be amazed how correct your decision has been. It is never the rightness or wrongness of our decisions that we are afraid of, but the fact that once we are committed to them we must stand and fight for them. It is the shying away from conflict that renders us unable to make up our minds. It is easy to lose your temper, to loaf and be mentally lazy, to eat what you want and as much as you want, to go into debt, to feel sorry for yourself, to go down and down, to put the blame elsewhere. But it takes courage to keep your temper and to be patient, to exercise and keep your body fit, to push your business and save your money, to say no, to accept complete responsibility for your own actions, to have faith, not to worry. A sign on the wall of many football lockerrooms says, "A winner never quits, and a quitter never wins." It sometimes seems that nothing more is going on in life than that nature constantly tests us to see if we are afraid. There are cycles of good and bad luck, to be sure. Every card player knows them and plays his hands accordingly. Such proverbs as "It never rains but what it pours" and "Misfortunes never come singly" are indicative of mankind's age-old recognition of streaks of good and bad fortune.

Nature deals us her cruelest blows when she desires to make us grow. Once we see the logic of this, we never again will quit in the face of adversity. When luck is running against you, that is the time to play harder, to cinch up your belt, pluck up your courage, smile, and be unafraid; that is the time to muster that little extra bit of mental alertness. Stick in there and fight. No matter how bleak the prospect, no matter how dismal the outlook, stay in there. Keep doing your very best, and above all things be unafraid. Visualize steel up your spine; call upon your inner resources for an indomitableness that will not yield. Nature is watching you; the Secret Self is watching you. Burdens and misfortunes are being placed upon your shoulders for a reason, and if you do not become scared, if you just plain stick in there and refuse to spook, you are satisfying the innermost purposes of life and soon or later you will be handed the keys to the kingdom of heaven.

TRUE AND FALSE ACTION

It is not difficult to distinguish between true psychic motivation and false psychic motivation, to be able to recognize when one is following the will of the Secret Self or simply the dictates of one's own ego. Action that proceeds out of the will of the Divine is always dynamic and constructive.

It is never ringed around with negative emotions and negative outlooks. It carries with it an inner conviction and absolute serenity, so that the individual knows beyond all doubt that he is following the right course. Conversely, action that comes from the ego is nearly always harrassed by doubt. The ego-initiated action is always an endgaining action. An individual performing at the behest of the ego seldom takes joy from his work or is completely engrossed in it. He seeks only the goal desired by the ego, and this end invariably is glory, riches, power, prestige, or one of the other accoutrements that bedazzle the little self.

Still another test that we may apply to the psychic motivation of our actions is whether or not they are effective. Action that is motivated by the Secret Self invariably is effective. The individual performing under universal will is irresistible, doing something that *must* be done. On the other hand, action that is performed under the impulsion of the ego rarely is effective and then but for that moment that ego-will coincidentally parallels divine will. Such an occurrence is rare indeed, but when it happens the individual is carried to dizzying heights with an absolutely erroneous idea of how it all happened. He credits his achievement to the use of his ego-will, and so he continues to exert it. In consequence it is not long before he makes an abrupt descent to the place where he started or even below it, becomes a picture of complete confusion and absolute frustration and knows not which way to turn. Such men have been known to commit suicide. They are the ones who suddenly seem to lose talent and ability, turn to alcohol and narcotics. But sometimes, if humility becomes ingrained before complete distintegration sets in, they find understanding and are able to remake their lives from the proper psychic position.

THE GENERAL MANAGER IS UPSTAIRS

Jim was a high-spirited, strong-willed young man, and when he was discharged from the army after World War II, he was offered a television job in a west coast city. Jim was ambitious, and vowed to rise to head his station, then to make it the leader in its market. He worked hard, for he wanted prestige and money, and within five years he had attained both. He became general manager of the television station, and it became the leader in its market.

During this period, of course, the entire television industry mushroomed. It grew ten times in size, and those employed in it were carried upward in the process. Then competition set in. Talent was recruited from advertising agencies, radio stations, motion pictures studios, the Broadway stage. Jim watched this influx of new faces and resolved to be better than all, to make more money, to be the leader. He worked around the clock, but nevertheless things began to go badly.

No matter how well he laid his plans, something always upset them. No matter how carefully he thought out a process, some unknown factor always cropped up and spoiled it. He began to think he was unlucky. People whom he was positive were inferior often bested him by what seemed an amazing stroke of fortune. He grew bitter, suspicious and hostile to associates. Two years later, he was fired.

One day, when his spirits were at their lowest ebb and he had about given up, he came across a book that depicted the joys of surrendering one's will to universal will, and since he was about to give up anyway, he decided to try this. He was astounded at the peace and serenity that came to him from the simple act of psychological submission. He took a humble job in a new television station, started on the road back.

His friends noticed the change in him. He had ceased being an agitator. He no longer undertook action for the primary reason of getting something done, but now seemed to do things through an inner joy in their actual doing. There was about him a quality of tolerance and understanding, of humility, that made his presence on the team a delight to all. Within a few months he was given a responsible job; within two years he headed the station. The title, "General Manager," no longer is on Jim's door, though. Asked why not, he replies, "The General Manager is upstairs."

THE ETERNAL SOURCE

Lecomte Du Nouy wrote, "Let every man remember that the destiny of mankind is incomparable, and let him above all never forget that the divine spark is in him and him alone and that he is free to disregard it, to kill it, or to come closer to God by showing his eagerness to work with Him and for Him." This, of course, is the exact psychic position that we must strive for if we would lead an effective and enlightened life. The knowledge of our eternal source and our subsequent identification with it leads us into actions and attitudes that have a broader and more universal viewpoint than any possible to the egoistic self. Our power of decision enables us to grow in any direction that we choose, and once we have shucked off the limiting and restricting presence of the surface self, we then are able to expand into a kind of cosmic perception that enables us to perform all work intuitively and with an effectiveness and skill heretofore denied us.

You may be sure that you will not be a victim of lethargy when you surrender your life to the Secret Self. Instead, you will become much more dynamic. The meaningless pattern of your human existence will be altered completely, and you will come to see the invisible shape of your destiny. When the veil is lifted at last, you will find that the desire to hasten or retard or change events has gone; what will be will be, and that is enough. Just to be able to recognize that there is a greater plan enables one to abdicate from any attempt to run it. This does not take one out of the arena, it plunges one in more deeply. All that is sacrificed is the limited view of the surface self. Your outer mien may be full of action and thunder and dynamics, but inwardly you are serene, sure about all things, because, as Trimalchio says, "Our Mother, the earth, is in the middle, made round like an egg, and has all good things in herself, like a honeycomb."

CONDITIONING THE SUBCONSCIOUS

As long as we are focused in the sensory area of our awareness, we are never master of our own house, for our true motivations spring out of subterranean areas that we are not aware of and do not control. That is why people often are unable to achieve results through positive thinking. The subconscious always directs us; the conscious mind is only its agent. The more self-sufficient the conscious mind seems, the more it is used as a tool by the subconscious. You cannot issue orders to the subconscious; that is the wrong psychic approach. The subconscious must perceive, then accept. It does not respond to coercion. But even though the conscious mind cannot order the subconscious about, it can condition it to react differently. If a man is fearful, he cannot make himself brave by an act of will only by conditioning his subconscious to promote feelings of bravery in him.

For this reason periods of meditation are very important. Through them we can change our awareness of prosperity, health, and happiness as the conscious mind impinges a conditioning quality upon the subconscious.

We can choose consciously the path to follow, but only the long lines of it. Our daily choices are enforced in us by the subconscious, for we always act and think intuitively and instinctively. If we are displeased with our actions and our circumstances, we must condition the subconscious to inspire in us different thoughts and different actions. This power of auto-conditioning is available to all. We can accomplish it by daily periods of meditation or simply by keeping within our consciousness at all times an awareness of the thing that we want to become. Realize this: when the chips are flying, we have to go with the personality and sense of self that already has been installed in the subconscious, for in times of action all our thoughts and movements are instinctive.

FACING HIDDEN FACTS

It takes firm-heartedness to face the fact that you have chosen every circumstance and thing in your life, not consciously, of course, but subconsciously. A man who is sick usually is appalled at the idea that he has chosen to be sick, dumbfounded at the effrontery of anyone suggesting that he can get well by simply choosing to be well. If somebody explains the conditioning quality of positive thinking, he sometimes tries it for a time but usually without visible results, for he thinks positively negatively, is telling himself that he is well while he knows that he is sick. A man can become well by choosing to become well, but he seldom becomes so the moment after making his choice. It first is necessary for him to embark upon a program of conditioning his consciousness into awareness of health. He has become sick because his consciousness picked up an awareness of sickness, and this must be cast out, replaced, and the task will not be accomplished in a day. Curiously, other persons sometimes have more effect on our subconscious than we ourselves do. A good hypnotist often is able to effect amazing cures. These are usually temporary, however, because the hypnotist-instilled idea is soon dissipated and replaced by the prompter that caused illness in the first place. The individual's conscious mind put the sickness prompter in the subconscious and will continue to do so until the pattern of thinking is changed.

GRASPING SHADOWS

There is no short and easy road to reconditioning your subconscious. Hypnotism and psychoanalysis are no panaceas. The reconditioning can be done only by yourself, and it takes concentration and continued effort; but there is always the great consolation that in the end you will be master of your own life. It is curious how often the things that we set our minds to evade us. It sometimes seems that the mere act of focusing our attention upon some objective causes that objective to become impossible of accomplishment.

> Follow a shadow, it still flies you;
> Seem to fly it, it will pursue:
> So court a mistress, she denies you;
> Let her alone; she will court you.
>
> —Ben Jonson

There is a deep underlying psychological reason why our conscious purposes are often defeated, and that is because they often are at odds with our subconscious purposes. If we fail, it is because we subconsciously wish for failure, even though our conscious minds seem to desire success above all things. But the conscious mind of itself can do nothing; it is always in the grip of the subconscious. It can only condition the subconscious and thereby receive its cooperation in the accomplishment of conscious objectives. All decisions are made subconsciously, and if we do not fight them, they are made swiftly and easily. Attempting to make our choices consciously in the heat of action only sets up conflict between the conscious mind and the subconscious mind, and in the end the choice is made by the subconscious anyway. If the choices made by the two minds are opposed, then we may see failure growing out of our efforts at success, or illness growing out of our efforts at health, or hate growing out of our efforts at love.

The sphere of effectiveness that the conscious mind has over the subconscious is this: by it we can choose consciously to become the sort of people we would like to be. We can become courageous and energetic and loyal and trustworthy and full of love and kindness and tolerance by the simple use of conscious conditioning methods, by concentrating our attention on the things we would like to become, by allowing these impressions to seep down to subconscious levels via our imagination. If we do this continually and with regularity, sooner or later we begin to act and think in just the way that our consciousness is focused upon. We then are able to behave in every situation instinctively and naturally, in the manner we always have desired. We literally have remade ourselves in the image of our desires through focusing our attention upon that image and allowing it to seep down into the subconscious. We are able to act and think according to a sense of self that we have made up in our minds. Our power of choice stems from our power to become, and we are always a reflection of an image that we carry in our minds. We can become anything we desire by changing our psychological viewpoint.

CLASH OF OPPOSITES

To have a mind is a wondrous thing, but a responsible thing too. Rudyard Kipling wrote, "There are forty million reasons for failure, but not a single excuse." And when we have come to a realization of the liberating and creative nature of our minds, we soon are made aware that we are finding in the world about us the images projected within consciousness. Take the time and have the courage to face the fact of the power of your choice. You have decided everything that has come into your life by taking a mental stand about it, by allowing that stand to take form and shape in your subconscious, by your willingness to accept it. If you are rich, you have accepted an awareness of abundance; if you are poor, you have accepted an awareness of poverty; if you are well and vigorous, you have accepted an awareness of health; if you are sick, you have accepted an awareness of illness.

All of life is the clashing of opposites, the black and white of extremes, the gray area in between. High, low, broad, narrow, dark, light, strength, weakness, always we choose between them; and through our choices we make ourselves into the kind of people we become, and shape the events and circumstances of our lives. No one else is responsible at all, only ourselves. Choice is always with us. We make it, and thereby decide our lives and our fate.

8 OVERCOMING OPPOSITION

The world is populated by many different kinds of people. The little girl stripping petals from a daisy in quest of a future husband while she recites the well-known chant is like each of us as he stands at the threshold of life and seeks his destiny. "Rich man, poor man, beggar man, thief, doctor, lawyer, merchant, chief." Which shall I be? Some become merchants, others manufacturers, some teachers, others artists, some warriors, and the world appears different to each, for what he sees there prompts him in his choice, dictates each step of his way. The warrior sees opposition. To him the world is girded around with opposing forces, and in the clash and resolution of these forces he seeks to find his role. Competitiveness and conflict come from perceiving obstacles. Sensing hostility in the environment makes every man a warrior in a psychological sense. No matter the area he has chosen, whether schoolroom or battlefield, mercantile store or library, each encounters opposition in everything he does, for it is by the stress and strain of conflict and the resolution of forces and ideas that the evolution of life itself is taking place on earth.

OPPOSITION MAKES FOR GROWTH

Opposition is the natural environment of life. Remove opposition from a man's surroundings, and he shortly withers and dies. A muscle grows strong by exercising it. Calluses protect the hand that daily performs hard work. The mind that is used constantly becomes alert and facile. But when we are unopposed we flounder and are frustrated, and our organism goes to pieces through lack of intent and purpose. We grow by meeting obstacles and overcoming them. By this effort and aspiration we are refined into better persons, into more intelligent and aware beings than we ever could become if we vegetated in a completely benign environment. When we realize that opposition is important to growth, then we learn to seek it constantly, not in the sense of falsifying it, but rather in looking about to find out where it already exists, and then, by the development of insight and awareness, to overcome it.

Nobody ever broke down a wall by running headlong into it. When we are opposed it is always by inscrutable and implacable forces. All opposition is blind because our own eyes are blinded. Once we have seen the truth about opposition, that opposition no longer will be there. Our efforts should not be bent upon breaking down a wall but upon raising our consciousness so that we are able to perceive methods of egress and ingress. Some people meet opposition enthusiastically and without hostility; those who do not are either broken by it or eventually turn and run. Hate, hostility, and resentment blind our eyes to the sort of thing that opposes us. In such a psychological state we never can see the truth about an obstacle, and its inscutability eventually will defeat us. You cannot throw yourself against the world and expect anything but defeat and despair.

EMOTIONAL BLIND SPOTS

All obstacles are not in their truest sense obstacles at all but merely mental blocks in the mind of the person who perceives them. He overcomes them not by opposing them but by attempting to understand them. In the end all obstacles are reduced to one—a false sense of self. To overcome opposition we must seek first for self-control and enlightenment as to the thing that opposes us. If it is a friend who competes for a job, we will neither gain the job nor keep the friend if we allow feelings of hostility to develop within us. Such emotional blocks blind us to the true nature of the job and the best way to go about getting it; they close our eyes to the qualities in our friend which might enable him to hold and perform the job as well or better than ourselves.

Recognizing that opposition is really a block in our understanding is the biggest step in overcoming obstacles. Once we know what we have to do, it is fairly easy to take the necessary action. Doubt and confusion produce no work. The made-up mind, even if made-up erroneously, at least gets the job done, is dynamic and creative and at work in the world. Opposition surrounds the man who cannot make up his mind, but doors appear in blank walls for the man who comes to a decision.

> I shoot the hippopotamus
> With bullets made of platinum
> Because if I use leaden ones
> His hide is sure to flatten 'em.
> —Hilaire Belloc

WILLINGNESS TO ENTER CONFLICT

There is a right and wrong way to do all things, but we do not necessarily choose the right way the first time we set about doing something. The immersion of the individual in events enables him to come to an understanding of those events, but if he does not enter into them, if he stands aside and attempts to view them from a distance, it is extremely unlikely that he ever will come to understand them at all. He will arrive at only an academic grasp of what is happening. He will have to measure the thing he is thinking about by some past experience, and since that past experience can have only the remotest bearing on the thing he now attempts to analyze, it will be most difficult for him to see its real relationship and potentiality. We get to know the things we are attempting to master only by doing them. No amount of teaching or studying ever made a craftsman. Whatever you wish to do, do it, and you will find your skill increase. The steps to mastery lead up a long hill replete with obstacles, and each when met and overcome increases your understanding. The job to be done has a right way to do it, and the right way to do it is made apparent by performance, and performance involves a willingness to enter into conflict, to meet opposition without fear, hostility, or resentment.

The quality most necessary in the conquest of life is courage. It is very difficult to undertake any dynamic action unless there is resident in the person a boldness that refuses to be intimidated by obstacles. There are three principal reactions possible to the human organism when faced by danger. It can run; it can fight; or it can freeze. We see evidence of all three in the animal kingdom. The lion faced by danger fights; the antelope faced by danger runs; the possum faced by danger freezes. Such reactions are usually all present in the same person. The one that is triggered when he is faced by danger depends upon his emotional conditioning and his perception of truth. If we run from danger it is obvious we have given in to fear. But the person who is frozen has given in to fear just as much as the person who runs away. However, few people run away today. We have been taught that fear is bad and must be overcome. Society admires the man of courage, and our fear of others considering us cowards usually is greater than our fear of dangerous circumstances. In the face of danger, the average person is rooted to the spot, mesmerized by the fear that permeates him. He could not possibly react in a worse manner. At least the man who runs away lives to fight another day, but the man who cannot either fight or run can only be destroyed.

FACING FEAR

In our modern society each man is engaged in a constant bout with fear. He must work to provide a living, and the fear is always with him that he will not earn enough for himself and his family. He usually is employed by an industrial colossus in which he is a mere cipher on the payroll, and since he cannot help but perceive his dispensability, insecurity constantly haunts him. He sees that he neither called himself into existence nor can he stay his eventual death, and because he cannot see beyond these ends of existence he turns his psychological face from any consideration of his spiritual side. He usually lives out his life with his awareness fronted in the ego, and as a consequence he forever is comparing himself with others. He is either better or worse but never equal, and so he is either patting himself on the back or berating himself for being inferior. Though fear is his constant companion he often fancies he has overcome it because he does not run away; but the fear remains and announces its presence by ulcers, high blood pressure, heart trouble, arthritis, cancer.

If we do not want to run away from danger and if we do not want to be frozen by it, then our only alternative is to fight it, to face it and allow our own particular dynamic to work out the overcoming of it. This involves above all things conquering fear, for when emotion permeates body and brain, the individual is unable to think; he closes himself around with a shell through which the true essence of the dangerous situation cannot possibly penetrate. He isolates himself from his own subconscious, freezes or runs away.

Conquering fear means to subordinate fear, to force it out of the level of awareness so that the psyche is free to appraise the situation, so that the individual consciousness may penetrate the essence of the situation confronting it and perceive its meaning independent of the ego. When a man does this, he is able to take action against his dangerous situation in such a manner as to reduce its threat to nothing. Take the lion tamer. As a novice he steps into the cage and experiences the frozenness that comes with fear. He would not be in the cage in the first place if he had not already overcome the running-away reaction, but now he must overcome his frozenness. He looks into the great beast's eyes and is mesmerized. He can barely bring his limbs to move in response to the dictates of his mind. But as the weeks and months go by and he is constantly in the cage with the lion, he begins to understand it and the barriers between the animal's subconscious and his own are lowered. Then he comes to an instinctive understanding of the lion, and the lion becomes aware of this and follows his orders docilely. There comes a day when stepping into the cage and putting the lion through its tricks no longer involves any danger at all. He has become so skilled in perception of the true relationship between himself and the lion and has so disciplined fear that he performs the task of running the lion as easily as he drives his automobile. No matter the situations that seem to imperil you, you can overcome all; you can act in the midst of them with great bravery, with an otherworldly boldness if only you will squeeze fear out of your consciousness, recognizing that it proceeds out of the ego and must be surmounted before any obstacle can be overcome.

INCREASING UNDERSTANDING

Marcus Aurelius wrote, "Do not think that what is hard for thee to master is impossible for man; but if a thing is possible and proper to man, deem it attainable by thee." In order to reduce each obstacle to its proper size we have to grow. We only meet an obstacle in the first place because of some smallness in our nature, and when we have gotten rid of that smallness we will have gotten rid of the obstacle too. All obstacles are in actual truth illusions, and to the extent that we are deluded by them is indicated a side of our nature that needs more maturity and understanding. Generally we only recognize opposition when we fail to pass beyond a certain point with our methods of action. If a bridge lies before us and we seek to cross it, we recognize opposition when a barrier is put in our path and a man asks us for a toll. Then we see very clearly that we must pay a price for our desire. Each of us, as he moves along without opposition, considers that he has evolved a formula that will make his path serene. There is no such formula, and no path will be serene for long. We are all sailors on a stormy sea that appears to be uncharted, but to some higher knowing mind the depths and the deeps are specifically known. Each of us sails this gigantic ocean according to his understanding.

All men are created equal in potential, but at any particular stage of their development the primary thing observable about them is their absolute inequality. Each is shorter or taller or fatter or leaner or smarter or bolder or more vigorous and seems to have no counterpart. Though we all set forth on life's journey with the same potential, present development of that potential is an individual matter; and the opposition that confronts us as we move from hour to hour of our temporal span is directly indicative of our understanding. It is what we cannot do or be or see that comes into our life as a problem. If our problems revolve around love, it is because we cannot love. If our problems revolve around success, it is because we are insecure. If our problems revolve around health, it is because we are spiritually and emotionally repressed. Always we seek to surmount the problems in our subconscious, and we generally do this by any means possible, sometimes creating the most fantastic illusions in order to substantiate our position. If we are unsuccessful, for example, we create a world of mean and capricious people whose sole purpose is to defeat our particular aims. If we are unloved, we relate by the hour the number of times we have done things for people and they have repaid us by ignoring us. If we are unhealthy, we recount at great length the tremendous drama of our struggle against the countless bugs that attack our weak and ineffectual organs. If we are fat, we think everybody else eats more and stays thin. If we are poor, we think everybody else works less and makes more money. If we are weak, we envy the strong, but seldom have the courage to strengthen our minds and our bodies by exposing them to tension and pain.

DECISION DETERMINES GROWTH

In every obstacle lies the key to another level of awareness. Until we find the key, we cannot grow and our perception is ringed around with barriers. A man looks at a hurdle and decides whether or not he can leap over it. In that decision he determines his fate. He may look at the hurdle and decide that he cannot leap over it no matter how high it is. He may look at the hurdle and decide that he cannot leap over it at that particular height, but could if it were lower. He may look at the hurdle and think that he could leap over it if it were twice as high. And according to his mental conception his trial will be. We are all on trial in life. Problems are posed to each of us, and we either face them or we don't but if we face them our growth is assured. Some people appear to conquer their problems easier than others, but this appearance sometimes is misleading. The enlightened man does not spread his troubles about. He keeps them to himself, preferring to create impressions of control and serenity. He has the inward realization that all people are equally troubled, that each has the same number of problems, perhaps on different levels, but equally important, nonetheless.

The most psychologically sound philosophy is a religious philosophy because it recognizes that life is aspiration, seeking to grow beyond its present understanding toward a goal that is as limitless as space. No man stands alone on the top of his mountain, no matter how small that mountain be. He is sustained and energized by a power beyond him, which in the end he must surrender to, which he must seek to express and effectuate upon the earth. What is going on in the universe stretches far beyond the imagination of the individual. We are in the grip of a power that knows exactly where it is going, that uses us as instruments to execute its will in the world. But the ennobling and heartening fact is this, that the individual may become anything he desires, may fit into any conception he is capable of conceiving, for no man is limited to what he appears to be, but has innate within him a quality that enables him to become anything he is capable of envisaging. He may reach out and touch the stars, for his creator can, and he is his creator, part and parcel, no different from at all, lacking only in understanding.

DESTINY AND UNDERSTANDING

If a man opposes his will to events he is opposing only his mental blocks. That which seems to be opposition, when truly perceived, is not opposition after all. Life is proceeding toward some great end. Nothing is small or unimportant in the achievement of that end. The pinpoint of a diamond may support a thousand revolving tons, and the individual is just such a support for his creator. The will of the Supreme prevails, and man serves it, but man is a manifestation of the Supreme, and therefore can alter his destiny. He can change what he is by taking thought. He can change what he will be by determining the direction of his growth. The will of universal mind is a will toward enlightenment. The Secret Self has incarnated in each being and seeks through that particular manifestation to add to its self-knowledge. A man does not exist to satisfy his senses or his ego, but has been created and put upon the earth to find himself, to grow into awareness and self-knowledge. All the obstacles and events of life are for this purpose alone. It is not money we serve or pleasure or vanity but an urge within us to grow, to become more than we are, to find our true selves and to achieve dominion over the circumstances around us.

Fate assigns to each man a personal destiny based upon his understanding. He may alter that destiny by altering his understanding, but he cannot change it by fighting it with the vain weapons of ego-will. Oedipus, in Sophocles' tragedy, strives with all the effort of his ego-will to escape his doom, and in so doing takes the very steps that eventually bring it about. A man serves false gods when he serves the senses and ego-desires. Following these false masters eventually leads him into a blind alley, where he either destroys himself or in some other manner courts tragedy. The Secret Self has placed the delusion of individual ego in us, but not so we will tilt at windmills, like Don Quixote.

The delusion of ego-self has been given us in order that

we might grow from the knowledge of a part to the knowledge of the whole and in so doing aid the Secret Self in its ultimate ascension out of matter. Providence combines predestination and human freedom for the reason that all things are the Divine and the will of the Divine is free. Lost in egosense, however, the individual is bound by the terms of a personal destiny based on sensual reaction. He can alter his life only by altering himself, and as long as he clings to the ego as knowledge of self, he serves the will of the Supreme as he serves a master. He does not know this, of course. He fights and rails against the blows of fate. He peers out from under suspicious brows at a world that seems to be his enemy. He seeks to conquer, to control, and failing to do so is convinced that a conspiracy is afoot to thwart his desires.

THE TEMPERING PROCESS

Even as Oedipus brings about his doom by struggling against it with his ego-will, so Aeneas in Virgil's *Aeneid* fulfills his destiny with honor and reward by submitting to the will of God. Aeneas was divinely appointed to bring the Trojan race to Italy and found the Roman Empire, and in this appointment was to be an instrument of the Gods. He was tempted to evade his mission, but finally accepted it, and with divine will as his guide brought a golden age of Roman law and peace to the world. These two classical characters, Oedipus and Aeneas, illustrate the age-old dilemma of man, whether to serve himself and his sensual nature in the world or to seek beyond himself for a guiding principle that is infinite and eternal. The path of Oedipus is the path of pain and frustration. The path of Aeneas is the path of enlightenment and serenity. Yet the ego is so strong in us that nearly every man chooses the path of pain and frustration. He has identified himself falsely with a vanity that demands recognition. He wants applause, fame, money, and he makes gods of these instead of the Secret Self in whose purposeful hands all things lie. Still, no man escapes the tempering influence of conflict and pain. No matter how far along the path of enlightenment he has traveled, he still pursues occasional blind alleys at the behest of the ego, still carries about in the subterranean recesses of his psyche many delusions and blind spots that prompt him to move in wrong directions, to adopt attitudes that are opposed to truth. Inevitably, he meets pain and frustration, but if he has come far enough on the path of enlightenment to recognize these symptoms for what they are, then he does not endlessly beat his fists against walls that will not yield, and recognizes as soon as he meets the pain that a block has been encountered in his understanding.

> It is not learning, grace, or gear,
> Nor easy meat and drink,
> But bitter pinch of pain and fear
> That makes Creation think.
> —Rudyard Kipling

THE PSYCHOLOGICAL OR SPIRITUAL WORLD

There is a power of extra-sensory perception inherent in each of us which we can call upon for enlightenment when opposition appears to have brought us to a dead end. The enormous psychic self which our surface minds are tied to permeates all things and all situations, so that we can penetrate the true nature of our opposition by a kind of mystic and occult process. Dr. Rhine's parapsychology laboratory at Duke University has proved the existence of the mind's extra-sensory powers. Many thousands of documented cases of Edgar Cayce's psychic ability also have proved that a door occasionally opens in the opaque barrier between the individual and universal mind and allows an inner perception of things beyond space and time and limitation.

Such a man is Peter Hurkos. Hurkos is a modest Hollander who successfully predicted in 1959 that the Los Angeles Dodgers would win the National League pennant, when all authoritative preseason predictions had them destined for the second division after they had wound up next to last the year before. Hurkos claims to be eighty-seven per cent accurate in his predictions and has the proof to substantiate his claims. "I have a gift of God," he says. He has been hired by police departments all over the world to track down escaped criminals, and his record has been astounding. He has been employed by business firms as a sort of security officer, checking the books simply by handling them, able to pinpoint any discrepancy through his feelings. The psychic ability of this amazing man has opened a door into the unknown, makes more apparent than ever the coming ascendency of mind over matter, reveals that the most fascinating conquests in the years ahead will be in mental realms and the study of consciousness.

Dr. Haldane wrote in *Science and Philosophy*, "Nature just mocks at us when we attempt to divorce her from conscious perception. There is no such thing as a physical world apart from consciousness. It is true that Berkeley and Hume showed *by reasoning that has never been shaken* that if the physical world were real in the sense assumed by Newton, we could never come to know of its existence. What we interpret as physically determined is only what is imperfectly seen. It is thus only an imperfectly revealed world that we have taken for a material world. There is no escape from the conclusion that behind the appearances of a physical or biological world we are in the presence of a psychological or spiritual world."

When we give first credence to the physical world, we give substantiality to an illusion. When we sweat and fume at obstacles, it is because we are unable to recognize that they are mental concepts and that they can only be altered in our own minds. All the great mystics have realized this mistaken focus of man's consciousness. Swedenborg stated that there are two beings within us, an inner being of true perception and action and an external being of reaction. If, for lack of a lucid apprehension of his inner being, a man allows bodily reaction to dominate his life, all his powers become absorbed in the use of external senses; and the inner being, the being of true perception and true action, gradually perishes. By subordinating the external being of reaction to an inner quality of light and serenity and divine purpose a man's false duality is solidified into unity with his creator and he arrives at the pinnacle of his effectiveness as an individual. The secret of the philosopher's stone is that unity is the mark of the Absolute. When we fully realize this, we come to an understanding of the mystic bond that exists between ourselves and each obstacle we meet. That thing separate from ourselves which appears to oppose us is not separate from ourselves at all, but is permeated by the same spirit, is energized by the same principle that energizes us, and if we only are able to look within the depths of our own nature, we eventually are bound to see the truth of each obstacle, and when we do, it will disappear.

TO KNOW IS TO SEE

Henry Miller wrote, "The majority of men are prisoners of instinct. A small number attain to the level of abstraction, with the emergence of which society may be said to begin. It is from this level that the laws, the arts, and all social creations emerge. Specialism is the gift of intuition, which permits man to see the inner as well as the outer in all its ramifications. Intuition, consequently, is the most satisfactory and adequate, the highest form of knowing. *To know is to see.*" It is amazing how much we can accomplish when we allow our subconscious minds to perform the work. It is equally amazing how difficult it is to do the simplest task when we go about it with our conscious minds. There is an elusive quality about life that makes it gossamer to the conscious mind. The microscope reveals another world but yields no secrets of that world. We hold an object in our hands and peer at it with all our attention focused upon it, but what is revealed to us about it is but the merest suggestion of its totality, barely indicative of the infinite qualities hidden from us by the very nature of our conscious examination. We have no trouble walking along a two-foot path when we do not think about it, but put that two-foot path across a hundred-foot gorge and we begin to think about each step.

Chances then are very good that in crossing we will tumble off the bridge and fall into the ravine below.

We have to learn to trust our subconscious to do things naturally at the behest of a principle that is greater than our surface mind. Reason is not to be trusted because it does not know enough about what it is dealing with. The complete knowledge about all things rests in universal mind, and this knowledge is within us. If we learn to call upon this intelligence to deal with each of our problems, we soon find that there is no such thing as an insurmountable obstacle. We have within us a resource that enables us to penetrate the block in our understanding that caused the obstacle in the first place. Have you examined your own life lately for the place where your understanding is blocked? It is easy to recognize. Do you find the same situation repeating itself with monotonous regularity? Do you sometimes feel that you are traveling around the perimeter of a circle, over and over? Like a man lost in a snowstorm, each of us eventually comes across his own tracks in life, for the law of living is that we must cover the same ground until our understanding concerning it is complete.

PSYCHIC AWARENESS

People object to pain and suffering being instituted in a world that was made by a loving God, but the master intelligence that has created all, permeates all, and seeks through countless differentiations of its own being for manifold expression of its infinite and eternal nature. Pain is the path by which it grows, and has no other significance. Pain is related to pleasure only as pleasure represents the absence of pain. Things that feel good make us static. Pleasure is the earmark of self-satisfaction. He whose aim in life is the seeking of pleasure has by that very attitude stunted his spiritual growth. The Supreme sees the goal along the path of the infinite and uses each of us to attain it. Our brains and bodies and hearts and minds and egos are instruments of a greater intelligence and will; and in that greater intelligence and will we have our true identity, not in the surface mind and ego at all.

Basic in the spiritual realization that comes to a man when he has achieved the proper psychic balance between ego and Secret Self is the knowledge that he and God are one. This claiming to be God is mystical and should not be confused with factual language. A man does not suddenly come to the realization that he is God with any kind of implication that he personally is in charge of the universe. The God that he speaks of is defined by the limited semantics of language. The God that he knows himself to be is a mystical life force that he allows to use him. Any attempt by himself to act upon the world from the position of God immediately defeats itself, for he cannot coerce things to a personal end without separating himself from the Supreme and acting in the ego, thereby losing the psychic position from which his knowledge first sprang.

The world is not here to be used by people who attain psychic illumination; it is here as a field of action for the working out of the expression of the Secret Self. The man who is able to achieve illumination simply comes into position as knower. By subordinating his ego and surface self to the workings of a greater mind and being, he achieves effectiveness and serenity, but he does not change the world. The world is what it is because of what it must become, and it was what it once was because of what it had to be now. The egotistic and vain action of men carries with it a sense of personal responsibility and impending disaster. There are wars and rumors of wars, there are economic crises and political crises. There are plagues and diseases and crimes. Men run about, hurry with this and that, convinced that disaster can be staved off only by their individual and heroic efforts. If there is any sense or meaning to life at all, no philosophy could be farther from the truth. The intelligence that reveals itself in the design of a snowflake, in the photosynthesis of green and growing things, in the complex biochemistry of living protoplasm, is in charge of the world and of life, and destiny and purpose can be left in its sure hands. It is not our position to rant and rail against fate and circumstance, and to save the world from disaster. It is ours to understand, to attempt to penetrate the meanings of existence so that we can grow into higher levels of consciousness and thereby become better instruments for the manifestation of the Secret Self. If we take this very great and exciting step we fulfill the primary commandment of life.

Creativeness becomes the guiding principle of the enlightened life. The man who places himself in the hands of the Supreme soon realizes that the work to be done through him will be unique because he is a unique instrument. He will not attack his tasks; he will listen and allow the work to be done. If he lets the ego control or originate, he defeats his purpose, for he cannot serve two masters. The creative urge prods so deeply at some people that they must abandon all to serve it, and in the serving of it they find spiritual enlightenment. They go each day to the fount of selfhood, rededicate themselves as instruments, let universal mind work through them.

CREATIVE WORK IS A PRAYER

Harry worked as a bank clerk, and in his late twenties was aware of a gnawing dissatisfaction with life. He thought it was because he wasn't getting ahead, and he certainly felt that he had little talent for his job. Day after day he arose at the same hour, fixed his breakfast in his small apartment, took the bus to work, sat at a small desk behind a low iron railing, ate his lunch at the same restaurant, returned home at night to an evening of reading before going to bed. The monotony of this existence, its lack of creativity, palled on him. He became anti-social, was irritable and resentful to those about him. Returning home from work one day, he sprinted after a departing bus, slipped, fell under the wheels. Both legs were crushed, had to be amputated. When Harry returned to full consciousness after weeks of hovering near death and learned how the world had tumbled about his shoulders, he exhibited a strange reaction. Instead of being overcome by despair, he actually seemed happy. When asked about it, he replied, "I don't really know why, but for some reason I feel that now I can really be myself. I've lost part of my physical body, but gained something else, I think."

After Harry was discharged from the hospital he took a cottage at the beach where he lived on a small income derived from insurance. He began to write. He sat all day in a chair, propped up before a typewriter, and turned out reams of copy. After a while, some of it was published. Within three years, he was comfortably augmenting his income. Even more marked than his success as a writer was his transformation as an individual. He was radiant. His clear eyes focused far away as he spoke of what his creativeness meant to him.

"It's religious," he said. "Like praying, I think. It's like being visited each day by a supreme mind that works through you because it needs you to do a particular work. I sit here all day in my little house, apparently all alone, but I must tell you that I feel more needed now than I ever have felt before in my life."

He gestured toward the manuscript scattered around the room. "All this has been done through me. It doesn't matter whether people think it's great or mediocre or even poor. It has been done by a power greater than I am, and this power works through me." The joy on Harry's face was testimony to the tremendous spiritual transformation that had taken place within him. "I lost everything," he continued, "my job, my health, my legs, but in losing them I found something of far greater importance. I learned that material things, even limbs of the body, are unimportant. The main thing in life is that a man should awaken to his true self and serve that self all his hours. This I have been privileged to do." He laughed then and showed his humor was still with him. "But I don't recommend that you cut off your legs to do it."

INDOMITABLENESS

In every conflict there are a few people who exhibit staying power, and this staying power nearly always represents the difference between the champion and the also-ran. Boldness of spirit and tenacity of purpose attend the man who acts in accord with his own nature. Confusion destroys purpose. The man who takes a stand clears away doubt and is able to act on his problem in harmony with all sides of his nature. He gets things done. His optimistic good nature survives in the face of all odds. Despair and gloom find no handholds on his soul; he casts them out of his nature by the simple psychological decision to perform at the behest of the will of the Secret Self.

Everyone cheers the underdog. A man who refuses to quit, who keeps on trying in the face of defeat, who does his best against superior forces, unloosens within us a sympathetic chord that is tied deep to subconscious racial memories. We all are aware that life is not easy, that the lessons it teaches are learned through pain and tension, and we recognize that the tempered stuff of which the enlightened man is made has been subjected to fire, that he only has survived at all through courage and perseverance. Greater than courage is tenacity, the willingness to stick in there and keep trying. By this patient and determined positioning of ourselves in life, barred doors eventually open and stone walls dissolve. A drop of water persistently applied wears away granite. Tender flowers lift their petals to the sun through solid concrete. Nothing resists persistent effort, and tenacity is the *sine qua non* of achievement.

We must not let circumstances influence our thinking. The appearance of obstacles must not cause us to lose heart. We must have faith in our basic position, know that we are capable of doing anything and being anything we can visualize. The same animating presence is within us as is within every obstacle, and we need only understand our true relationship with each in order to perform effectively. An inner knowing is necessary to effective action. We cannot even reach down and pick up a piece of paper unless we first visualize the action in our mind, with complete surety that we can perform it. This inner knowing is compounded of equal parts of faith and intuition. The image is born of intuition and faith holds it in the mind. Our development as individuals only comes when we encounter opposition. Recognizing this, we will find ourselves thankful for our times of pressure and pain, for then we are being urged to higher consciousness.

NO ENDEAVOR IS IN VAIN

Opposition comes to every man who aspires. By the mark of the encountered obstacle he realizes a time for growing is at hand. He does not turn away from the obstacle; he does not assault it or treat it as if it is not there. The ostrich hides its head from impending danger; the possum topples over and plays dead; but the enlightened man neither turns away from the fact nor ceases in his effort. Patiently, with a persistence that never tires, he examines his own mind and consciousness to determine where it is that his understanding is blocked away from true perception of the encountered obstacle. He will grow because he must, and when his period of growth is over, he will find himself beyond the obstacle; looking back along the path he has traveled he will not even find it there, for what we know seems simple when understanding has been achieved.

There are a thousand reasons for not doing things, and each one is valid if accepted. When we undertake a new venture or attempt a new course of action, we find obstacles to success at every hand if we choose to look for them. Getting the job done is not life's primary aim. Each task is only a test of human aspiration and self-knowledge. Raising human consciousness to constantly higher levels is the primary purpose of nature. Material ends are secondary, side-effects rather than goals. It is not so important to succeed in the eyes of the world as it is to attempt something bigger and greater than we have ever done. From this test, expanded consciousness comes, no matter the physical fate of the venture. No one ventures without reward.

No endeavor is in vain;
Its reward is in the doing,

And the rapture of pursuing
Is the prize the vanquished gain.
—Henry Wadsworth Longfellow

THE CONQUEST OF SELF

Opposition is the testing ground where life evolves constantly higher levels of awareness. In this arena the master spirit holds court, bound on a meeting with the completely evolved man. Evolution bends us and kneads us, tries us and sometimes breaks us. We serve a greater intelligence than we are consciously aware of; we are growing toward an eventual oneness with that intelligence; and if the path be marked by pain and trial, these are only urgings toward greater understanding and awareness.

The conquest of each obstacle is a conquest of self. The man who disciplines himself and searches for increased awareness finds no such thing as a permanent obstacle; his psychic position surmounts all. Nothing can stand in his path as long as he realizes each obstacle exists within. Progress always depends upon discipline. When we make ourselves do the thing that has to be done, we hold our sensual self under short rein, guiding and forming our destiny. Distasteful tasks serve a great purpose in the maturation of the soul. When we accept uncomplainingly the burdens placed upon us, we are given increased strength to handle them. A puerile philosophy bent on making money and living a life of ease eventually must wither the soul because it is a product of the ego. There is no easy path to goodness and greatness, which are always arrived at through hardship. Awareness and fortitude and tenacity and loyalty cannot be gleaned by easy mental exercise. Neither are they medals to be worn as marks of combat, but are automatically conferred upon the man who throws his heart into life's tests without reservation or timidity or doubt. He gains all because he gives all.

GUIDING PRINCIPLE

The fleshpots of self-indulgence are to be avoided at all costs. He who seeks primarily to avoid pain and hardship and to satisfy his senses eventually must dull those senses and corrupt the flesh. The discipline of Abraham Lincoln as against the indulgence of the Roman Emperor, Nero, gives us a clear mental picture of the way our nature is honed according to the paths we follow. The ideal within the man determines the man, and when we set forth on life's journey, each of us carries within him an image of the person he aspires to be. His whole life is determined by this image. If the image is Lincoln-like he disciplines his ego-nature and seeks within himself for a guiding principle; gradually the demands of his ego-self lessen, he is able to control his sensual nature, and the Secret Self illuminates his life with love, understanding, and courage. He moves calmly in the midst of the most crucial events, sustained and soothed through faith in his actuation by the Divine for a purpose that is good and great.

Let no obstacle dismay you. It has been put in your path for the purpose of your growth. Do not attack it headlong, but do not turn away from it. It is but a reflection of your lack of understanding. Do not cease in your calm and steady effort, and do not despair. Keep firm your resolve, keep clear the image in your mind, keep faith in the power that sustains you. Eventually, you will find yourself carried to a higher level of understanding, and the obstacle will disappear. Above all things, remember that opposition is a time of growth, that our effectiveness as individuals is in direct relation to the number of obstacles we have faced and surmounted in life.

9 DEVELOPING SKILLS

Each man contains all possibilities within him because he is a manifestation of an eternal and infinite being. P. D. Ouspensky states, "Everything exists always. There is only one eternal present, the Eternal Now, which the weak and limited human mind can never grasp and conceive. Our mind follows the development of possibilities always in one direction only, but in fact, every moment contains a very large number of possibilities, and all of them are actualized, only we do not see it and do not know it. We always see only one of the actualizations and in this lies the poverty and limitation of the human mind. But if we try to imagine the actualization of all the possibilities of the present moment, and then of the next moment, and so on, we shall feel the world growing infinitely, incessantly multiplying itself and becoming immeasurably rich and utterly unlike the flat and limited world we have hitherto pictured to ourselves."

CLEAR CHANNEL TO UNIVERSAL MIND

A man may develop any skill he desires. The essence of his nature is to grow in the direction indicated by the images that form in this consciousness. Some people are born with a clear channel from one facet of their consciousness into universal mind, and they are gifted. They are our Balzacs, our Mozarts, our Einsteins, our Galileos, our Michaelangelos, and though they are superhuman in one corner of their natures, in all else they are normal and subject to the same weak and

190

ineffectual vision as everyone. Such unearned perception of universal mind is sometimes more a curse than a blessing, because the person possessing it expects illumination in other areas also and is frustrated at being unable to find it. Rage and self-hate may grow out of such an unbalanced nature. Van Gogh cutting off his ear is an excellent illustration, and the artistic temperament, when gifted with genius, is often manic-depressive, alternating between periods of elation and self-abasement.

Skills that we earn are the skills that delight us. Nothing in life is so exquisitely satisfying as the mastery of a skill. Whatever we do well adds to our stature as persons, increases our scope and effectiveness. From birth to death we acquire countless skills, use them daily, perform them unthinkingly, because they have become part of our nature. We learn to walk, we learn to run, we learn to talk, we learn to read, we learn to figure, we learn to cook, we learn to sew, we learn to drive, we learn to run a business; and the kinds of persons we become and our effectiveness as human beings have a direct bearing on the number of skills we have mastered.

People say, "Oh, I could never develop any skills. I don't have any talent." Well, lack of natural ability is no reason for curling up your toes and playing dead. The most important thing in life is growth, and it makes no difference where you start on the scale of capability, what is important is that you do not stay there, but progress. There is a quality in the psychic makeup of man that when impressed with desire and a picturization of that desire immediately sets about opening his eyes to the possibilities for achieving it in the material world. Knowing this, we eventually come to have deep faith that the thing which we think about will become part of our lives.

MODERN PIED-PIPER

The man with the voice of a bullfrog probably will never give a concert at Carnegie Hall, but if he spends the major portion of his life learning to be a singer he will be able to perform quite creditably someday. None of us lives long enough to develop completely in all directions. For this reason the Secret Self created multitudes of individuals, and through this multiplicity seeks expansion in all areas. The individual himself functions best when he is able to determine those abilities most natural to him and then sets about developing them to their highest possible level. To do this he needs insight, and he most certainly needs to be free of mental blockages.

A man sometimes seeks to develop his business ability because he desires to have money, when in truth he might find more fulfillment in other fields. The end-gaining philosophy that has become predominant in our civilization is a pied piper leading us down streets of frustration. One who works only to gain a result is seldom happy and almost never works well. He finds no pleasure in his tasks and no satisfaction in their growth possibilities. He can hardly wait to get on from one moment to the next because the only time that has any meaning for him is the time when his goal is reached. Should he never reach it his life is hemmed in with bitterness through having sacrificed all for something that never materialized. It is better to lie on your back and look at the stars than to chase shadows, if the chasing is not fun. A little child can run after illusions and take delight in every moment, but the man who pursues a wraith and is bound to it begrudges every ounce of energy expended in attempting to bring his illusory target to earth.

Three laborers were asked what they were doing. The first said, "I am working." The second said, "I am digging a ditch." The third said, "I'm helping build a canal." Obviously the third man took the most satisfaction from his labor because he saw that his work would create and he was glad to be part of it. One who labors only to make a living puts in time that he wishes were gone, begrudges the hours he must spend at his tasks. He looks at the clock at ten and wishes it were noon, and he looks at the clock at three and wishes it were five. He actually wishes away a large part of his life.

LONGING FOR MASTERY

It is not nearly as important that we possess a skill as it is that we desire to possess one. The longing for mastery is the key to the motivation of the Secret Self, the very basis of evolution, of each form's tendency toward unity with its creator. Life is fluctuation and change, a constant cycle of growth and decay, and we have to aspire to be better than we are even to stay where we are, and the moment self-satisfaction comes to us our dissolution begins. Constant excitement and challenge come to the man who seeks mastery. Every situation confronts him with opportunity, for he sees in each an opportunity to develop a part of his nature. Whenever he meets an obstacle he knows his knowledge is inadequate, and he sets about at once to rectify this deficiency. He learns everything he can because he sees the bond common to all knowledge. Eventually he learns easily and well, for he removes all limitation from his mind and like a sponge draws the knowledge needed for effective works and actions.

We have to love the things we do in order to do them well. We have to like to perform the work regardless of the result. We have to not even care about the result and take our entire satisfaction from the action. When people have undergone great shocks, such as prolonged exposure to death and danger or the loss of a limb or the death of a loved one, they often turn to work for work's sake as a preoccupation for their minds, and thus they discover one of life's deepest joys. A child fingerpainting in a kindergarten class puts colors on paper with no idea of a result, and this engrossing of his whole nature makes him part of the work he does and the work part of him. Mental hospitals have discovered the therapeutic value of putting patients to work at easels or with needle and thread or even in the garden, for surrender of self-concern to the task at hand rids the person of his tormenting ego and he is able to get completely outside himself through becoming part of the work he is doing. We develop our skills through an inner love for the action involved. We will become musicians if we love music. We will become writers if we love writing. We will become builders if we love construction. We will become business men if we love commerce. But we become nothing simply through a desire to be famous and rich. Such false desires are products of the ego. Even the slightest look at them gives us evidence of their insubstantiality.

If we undertake to be a business man, for instance, and we run into difficulties and our reaction is one of depression and failure, we can be sure that we were led into our business endeavors in the first place through an egoistic desire to be better or more powerful than others. The business man who loves business glories in his moments of trial, for it is then that he develops more understanding, more mastery. Since he loves business, he loves it when its nature is most acute, and therefore his times of trial are a joy. Such people inevitably are successful because they cannot be discouraged, because they love the thing that they are doing whether it is going badly or well. They are unaffected by apparent turns of defeat and fortune, assure their own growth through having taken their eyes from the goal and becoming engrossed in the doing of their work.

WE LEARN BY DOING

Learning to do a thing well is primarily a matter of performing it endlessly until all the ramifications of its action seep down into subconscious levels and allow one to perform unthinkingly. It is difficult to fly an airplane when one does not know how. To the earthbound man, flight in a plane operated by his own hand seems almost unthinkable. When he takes his initial ride, he at first is frightened, then exhilarated, sensing his transcendence of nature's law of gravity. Soaring high above the landscape, he feels like a bird, arrives at a sensation of flying far removed from any previous experience on passenger liners. Then he may bridge the gulf between his earthbound limitation and his aspiration toward the sky, and he may decide to become a pilot.

The first time up he is clumsy and awkward, tense and in-effectual, seeing all too clearly that if his instructor were not present the plane would fall and crash into the ground. This sense of being poised between life and death with no one to look to but himself may prove to be one of the most signifi-cant experiences of his life. If so, his eventual mastery of the airplane is assured. Seeking understanding in an area hitherto hidden from him, his growth in that direction is inevitable. Soon he will find himself alone in the airplane, flying it freely and confidently, transcending the limitations of his own thinking. His exhilaration then will know no bounds.

Always we learn by doing. No amount of information in-jected into a man by books and lectures will make him the master of a skill. A skill is its own teacher, and each of us who aspires to mastery must become an apprentice. Ideas, facts, and abilities all come to the man who seeks to make himself more proficient, whether his field is creative, adminis-trative, executive, or simply the performing of labor. If he dedicates himself to a task for the love of doing it, eventually he will find himself highly capable. When we attempt to learn a new skill, our initial efforts are always inept, and the ego-conscious man often is stricken with discouragement and sometimes gives up further effort altogether. The enlightened man will not be dismayed by his initial ineptitude. He will know he is coming to grips with a new knowledge that will take time to seep down into subconscious levels.

EDUCATING THE SUBCONSCIOUS

The person who buckles on a pair of ice skates and ven-tures out onto a frozen pond for the first time is a sight to behold. His arms flail, and his ankles bend. He fights desper-ately for balance, swoops forward and backward in a hair-raising battle to stay upright. He can neither start himself when he is stopped nor stop himself when he is moving, and the only certain thing about his performance is that he is bound to wind up on the seat of his pants. Compare this novice skater with an Olympic champion. It seems incredible there could be any comparison, but there is. Not too many years ago, the Olympic champion was just such a novice, and his proficiency today is only testimony to the power of the subconscious to direct the actions of body and mind with the utmost symmetry and perfection.

When we try to do something difficult or something beyond our ordinary grasp, we must first come to grips with it consciously, by focusing our attention upon it. This period of conscious striving produces a tension within the psyche that stimulates subconscious activity, directing relief of the tension, producing resolution, giving dimension and control to the organism. The more conscious the striving, the more tension produced in the subconscious, and the more the subconscious works to effect answers to the problems that confront the individual. The man who is handicapped by poor speech and uncertain delivery might desire to become a platform speaker and set his conscious striving toward that end. His initial period of effort will produce little noticeable result because his ineffectuality cannot be solved by his conscious mind. He cannot be given a confident, dynamic delivery simply by thinking about it. Reason will not provide the effects he seeks, and no amount of study a happy solution to his problems. But as he delivers speech after speech, as he continually works himself through the same blunders and errors, his suffering and consequent need produce such tension in the subconscious that one day, of a sudden, he will find himself delivering a direct and dynamic speech with the power and clarity that heretofore have eluded him.

TURNING EFFORT INTO INSTINCT

We develop our abilities when we make continued efforts to improve ourselves and never cease in the continuity of these efforts no matter how little progress we seem to be making. We can never judge our progress anyhow, for the simple reason that all real work is done on subconscious levels and we may be transported from very low to very high in one sudden sublime moment of insight. A young housewife recently told the story of how she came to be an accomplished pianist. "I had been laboring at the piano for four years," she said. "I had gotten to the point where I was able to play a number of compositions, but they were all wooden, came out with no feeling, seemed to lack rhythm. The few times that I played for my friends, I was actually embarrassed at their having to listen. I practiced every day, though, sometimes as much as three hours. It seemed incredible that I made so little progress. I had always learned other things easily, but playing the piano seemed too much. Eventually, I became convinced I had no musical talent.

"One evening at a party a friend suggested that I play. A refusal rose rapidly to my lips, but suddenly I was overcome with the most wonderful feeling that I would be able to play well. I cannot say just how the feeling came. It certainly did not form itself in so many words. I just knew deep within myself that I would be able to play well, and I had a sudden insight into the relationship between the music and myself. The piano, the keys, the notes, and the sheet music all blended together and merged with me. I knew that when I sat down and began to play, I would play well because I would be performing outside myself and wouldn't have to think about it. When I sat down at the piano, I played exactly as I envisioned. The guests applauded and gathered around, and I played the rest of the evening. I have been playing well ever since, and the whole thing taught me a great lesson. We must never quit when we seem to be making no progress. We may go from the most inept novice to the most accomplished performer in that single moment when the hours of our efforts break through and merge with our instincts."

A man sets out to do a thing because he is impelled by the images in his mind. He is driven to the performance of the work that needs to be done, and he cannot rest as long as one iota of the task is unfinished. Yet he does not work simply to gain an end. He is engrossed in his task, just as it is engrossed in him, and his actions are performed with an inner joy, for he knows he is doing what he should be doing. He takes complete enjoyment from each day because each day

delivers him all he desires—the work he loves, his performance in it, and the growth of his knowledge and capabilities.

> Look to this day
> For it is the very life of life.
> In its brief course lie all
> The verities and realities of your existence:
> The glory of action,
> The bliss of growth,
> The splendor of beauty,
> For yesterday is but a dream
> And tomorrow is only a vision;
> But today well lived makes
> Every yesterday a dream of happiness,
> And every tomorrow a vision of hope.
> Look well, therefore, to this day.
> —From the Sanskrit

THE ONLY REAL SECURITY

One skill that people seem most desirous of developing is
that of making money. But making money is not a skill, it is
the result of a skill. Money sought for itself will surely prove
to be most elusive. It is not evil; it is good, good because it
is representative of work; but those who attempt to take it by
avoiding work are corrupting its true purpose and shrinking
their own natures. Henry Ford made this statement: "If
money is your only hope for independence, you will never
have it. The only real security that a man can have in this
world is a reserve of knowledge, experience, and ability." As
a young man, Ford had little money, but he was sustained
by the vision of his automobile, and his days and nights were
full of work and thought. When that day arrived that every
tenth family in America owned an automobile, Ford became
a rich man. His fortune came to him not because it had been
sought, but because he had rendered a service to millions of
people. In our day and age and society, wealth is a natural
result of serving a large number of people. All work is repaid

in kind, and when we serve one person he serves us also, and this owing of service usually results in the exchange of money. If we serve one person we are paid so much; if we serve two we are paid more; if we serve ten, even more; if we serve a million, we are bound to become wealthy. We cannot help but create wealth when we find a work that needs to be done, and we cannot help but receive a portion of this wealth ourselves. That money breeds money is axiomatic, but only when such money is put to work creating wealth. When our savings are invested in activities that promote discovery and creation, they cannot help but make money, for they are being used in accordance with this primary law of life, that every service must be rewarded.

Proper performance is always unthinking performance. Any other kind of action is ego-centered and based upon partial knowledge. A friend reports he can cut an apple exactly in half when he is not thinking about it, but when he concentrates, the halves no longer match. Innate in each man is an original mind, and knowledge there is not limited to that acquired through the senses. Egoistic conditioning causes mind to acquire a fixed idea of itself as a means of controlling itself, and consequently a man thinks of himself as "I." The focus of his consciousness then shifts from original mind to ego-image, and it becomes impossible for him to use original mind in any of his mental actions. Everything performed in response to the ego is intentional, affected, limited, and insincere. We have to learn to let intention go, to let sense of self go, so that we can perform under the impulsion of a greater mind and will. We must learn to be spontaneous; we must learn to give up plan and effort, to do the natural thing when the time for performance arises.

SPONTANEOUS ACTION

Basic in Zen Buddhism is the doctrine of unintentioned action. A Zen Buddhist disciple, an archer, is reported to have practiced for three years to let his arrows shoot themselves. When at last he was able to release the bow string unconsciously, in response to an intuitive action that had more to do with the target and arrow than his purpose, the effectiveness of his archery increased amazingly; but the moment he began to think of results he no longer was able to let the arrow shoot itself, and his scores fell off at once. Spontaneity is the mark of the Absolute. Universal mind does not need to think out things. It holds within itself at every moment the proper answer to each particular problem. It acts quickly and without thought. That which we do well we do without effort because we have given over the doing of it to a will and power that lie outside our conscious intentioned ego.

Developing a skill is largely a matter of abdicating from performance. We must learn to let go personal responsibility and conscious control. Henry Miller wrote, "When you dwell on the prophetic, you come to realize that there is an invisible pattern to the events which mold our destiny, and that history, philosophy, science, art, religion, yield but a distorted, meaningless, even ridiculous image of this divine web. But the most interesting aspect of this experience, this lifting of the veil, is that all desire to modify, hasten, or retard events is nullified. What is, is, what will be, will be, and that suffices. Merely to recognize, if only for a moment, that there is a greater plan, enables one to abdicate. In abdicating one is not removed from the stream of life even mentally; one plunges in more deeply, more wholeheartedly, that is the curious thing. All that is sacrificed is one's limited, egocentric view of life, a view which caused one to swim against the current instead of with it."

A juggler keeps eight balls in the air, and people exclaim, "Isn't that incredible!" And it certainly is if we assume that the conscious mind is controlling the action. The conscious mind can hardly *follow* the action, let alone perform it. Juggling eight balls is done by the subconscious, which directs all activity that takes on the coloration of skill or talent. This mind is not a multitude of minds but only one; therefore all skill and all talent reflect the activity of a single person. All books are written by the same author, all pictures painted by the same artist, all music composed by the same composer; in every creative activity or accomplished performance the same mind is responsible. A thing done well reflects the direction of the Divine, and thus spiritual awakening is necessary to effective living.

THE SECRET DOOR

As long as we live and act in the ego, we cannot hope to develop our talents and capabilities except in the most limited manner. When you set out to learn something, you must first get yourself out of the way. This "I" that you constantly refer to, this sense of self that sits directly behind your eyes, is egoistic in the sense that it is separate, and will prevent your learning anything well as long as it controls your consciousness. There is a great deal of difference between egoistic trying and letting action develop through spontaneous impulsion from the Secret Self. Effort made through the ego develops because the ego has some result in mind. It wants to feel better than others, wants to control them, or it is afraid or hostile or insecure, and this end-gaining action, so limited in viewpoint and knowledge, has only the barest chance of succeeding, and then only by coincidence with the purposes of the Secret Self.

People try and try to master some skill and make only the barest progress. They finally despair and give up altogether, and this giving up, this release of the end-gaining aims of the ego, is exactly the time that skill may develop in them because the Secret Self takes over. Examples of this psychological phenomenon are so profuse as to be irrefutable. Pasteur, laboring over test tubes and microscopes, received his greatest illumination in the period of his greatest hopelessness. Galileo was inspired with the idea of a revolving solar system at the nadir of his despair over the ineffectuality of his telescopes. Every researcher knows that a secret door is often found on a dead end street. Every creative artist knows that his greatest work comes after periods of intense frustration. That it is always darkest before the dawn is a well known saying. We have to have our egos reduced to nothingness before the Secret Self takes over. We have to get ourselves out of the way so that skills can develop in us, so that work can be done through us by a greater mind and being.

How often have you wadded up a piece of paper and unthinkingly tossed it across the room and been amazed when it landed directly in the center of the wastebasket? You may have wadded up other pieces of paper and tossed them at the wastebasket without a single further hit, and probably you shrugged your shoulders and wrote off the first hit to luck. Well, it wasn't luck at all. It was simply that you performed the action without the interference of conscious mind. In effect, you allowed the paper to propel itself at the wastebasket, with yourself as only a medium of impulsion. This kind of psychic unification of the basket and the paper and the propelling energy allowed all elements in the action to become "one piece," and anything occurring within that unity had to have perfect symmetry and be absolutely effective.

BECOMING ONE WITH OUR TASKS

Now if there is one mind common to all things and exclusive to none, it follows that we basically are all part of a single organism, and our effectiveness within that organism depends upon our recognition of this fact. As long as we view ourselves as separate selves, we are moved by the delusion of egoistic desire and thus led into opposition to the will of the Secret Self. Any action that is conceived in the ego and entered into for egoistic purposes, if not doomed to failure from the outset, can result in only mediocre success. Its entire purpose and impulsion arise from a limited knowledge, set against the ocean of knowledge that is universal mind. We learn to do things well by becoming one with them, by so engrossing ourselves in our tasks that we pick up a sense of unity with them. This sense of oneness is impossible to the egoistic nature for the simple reason that the ego itself is a sense of separateness. When we become completely absorbed in things, we have a true spiritual experience, for by this psychological transference of self, we plunge deeply into universal mind and become the work that we are doing. Everyone who has great skill or talent goes daily to this fount of forgetfulness, plunges in and is renewed, and the temple of his religious worship is his own talent. Henry David Thoreau wrote, "If one advances confidently in the direction of his dreams, and endeavors to live the life which he has imagined, he will meet with unexpected success in common hours."

THRUSTING AGAINST PAIN

All barriers to accomplishment are in the mind. Education itself teaches limitation, and history establishes a definitive level that suppresses human aspiration. For years four minutes was thought to be the fastest time that any man ever would run the mile, then along came a group of Australian milers with a new philosophy and they broke down the mental barriers, and now any number of men have run the mile faster than four minutes.

This new philosophy might as easily be applied to any area of human activity. It is built around the premise of thrusting against pain, on the idea that pain represents a limitation in the mind. Those who train under this system drive themselves to run farther than they think they can, asserting the principle of mind over matter to do away with fatigue. Such a philosophy releases a human being from all barriers. Nothing is impossible to him as long as his guiding principle is to surmount each obstacle he encounters.

Directional drive is the most important single factor in achievement. Outstanding boxers are culled from the social groups that have to fight hardest to survive. Heads of corporations and government executives are often born in the most humble circumstances, and their climb to the top is allied directly to their dedication. Heaven attends the man who throws his heart into his work. In his absorption he loses his egoistic sense of self and becomes a clear channel for the energy and creativeness of universal mind.

CONSTANT ASPIRATION

The usefulness of goals depends on their ability to remove limitation from our thinking. A man exceeds himself by aiming higher than he has ever aimed before. It is not the goal that is important, it is the aiming higher. When a goal is reached, it actually becomes a limitation unless replaced by a higher goal. The man who achieves something and spends any time patting himself on the back is nullifying his growth, for when self-complacency enters the nature, ego grows and the individual stagnates. If we don't try to exceed ourselves, we disintegrate. If we do not try to be better, it is impossible for us even to stay as good as we are. The dynamic forces of life are growth and decay, and nothing is static; things move in one direction or the other.

A few years ago, a young man emerged from an automobile accident paralyzed from the neck down, except for the rudimentary use of the forefinger of his right hand. As he lay abed and pondered his situation he resolved to develop some skill with that right forefinger. He had a typewriter rigged on his bed, with his right arm slung before it so he could peck at the keys with his forefinger. His initial efforts were excruciatingly slow, and required great concentration and resolve. He labored for hours to type a single sentence. As the weeks turned into months he was able to type a page, then two, finally a dozen or more. After a year he not only was typing proficiently but was actually sitting up in bed to do it. Today, he gets about with crutches and has embarked upon a program of total rehabilitation. He seems well on the road to recovery. Such tenacity and purpose might be expected to belong to a very grim person, but this young man has deep humility and a wry sense of humor. When asked how he has been able to accomplish such miraculous results, he stated, "I was given this body, and I banged it up. The least I can do is put it back in the condition I found it."

Men have searched out the trackless wastes of the poles, journeyed to the depths of the seas, flung themselves miles into the air, and now contemplate journeying amongst the stars. Who can say that anything is impossible to the mind and effort of man? There exists within him a power to imagine a better world than the one in which he lives, and he never ceases attempting to find it. Our imagination should be treated with precious care, for it is the tool of our liberation from the bonds that hold us. We can be anything we are capable of visualizing, do anything we are able to imagine, for the images that form in our minds inevitably lead us into the work that effects their realization.

INNER ACCEPTANCE

Skills are developed by faith that one possesses the skill already. This *a priori* inner attainment of the skill allows the individual to act as if it were impossible for him to fail. He still will go through a period of ineptness, but such ineptness will not stay with him. He will surmount all, all fear, all ineffectuality, for he is sustained in all circumstances by an inner vision that he already has accepted as reality. If a man aspires to an ability, he becomes accomplished only after inner acceptance. No one can ever be any better or greater than his mental visualization. If we accept ourselves as exactly what we already are, it becomes impossible for us to improve. To become better we must think we *are* better, not in the egoistic sense of thinking that something is our due, but in the wider spiritual sense of realizing that all things derive from the image within. Such psychic positioning of the ego releases it from bondage to itself and allows it to accept on faith the fact of its wider being and effectiveness.

Skillfulness is primarily a matter of becoming an instrument for the action of a greater mind and will. Any egocentric effort to dominate the world or to originate action from the standpoint of the surface mind immediately raises the problem of the ego controlling itself. Any system of self-control, inasmuch as it approaches perfect self-control, also approaches perfect self-frustration, for control implies keeping something from doing what it normally is disposed to do.

The idea of acting in accord with our nature meets with objections on every hand. Taking the restraints off human nature supposedly would be like letting loose a swarm of locusts. Religious and social groups have adopted the idea that man is more a work of the devil than of God, that his bestial nature must be held in restraint by laws and inhibitions. Thus duality is forced upon man, the necessity of presenting one face to the world while living in solitude with another, and it is responsible for more mental and physical ailments than all the microbes ever discovered.

BE YOURSELF

We present one face to the world and behold another in the privacy of our rooms, and this knowledge that we are not what the world expects us to be manifests in a kind of social conscience that makes cowards of us all. Most of us are afraid to be ourselves. Like chameleons we change colors to suit our backgrounds. Our opinions are formed by what people expect us to think; our behavior patterns are based upon how people expect us to behave; and since we are always thinking in response to outside circumstances we scarcely know how we feel at all and never have any sense of self other than the one reflected in the eyes of others.

"To thine own self be true," wrote Shakespeare, "and it shall follow as the night the day, thou can'st not then be false to any man." It is important to act in accord with your own nature. When you live sincerely and feelingly, you become a pure channel for the expression of the Divine. Each of us is accorded a unique individuality. As long as that individuality is unhampered by inhibition and fear, it is capable of expressing something different and vital, but when it is restricted and limited by apprehension, it cannot express itself at all. The dammed up torrent of universal energy then turns upon itself, and the dual sides of the ego nature, like the gingham dog and the calico cat, "eat each other up."

Countless people are restrained from learning because they are afraid to try. In them is a false pride that is connected directly to the ego, and it will not let them perform awkwardly because it has no humility, and it will not let them begin anything and be novices because it cannot stand any idea of itself that is not better than others. If a man be rid of ego-self and have accepted that he is only an instrument of Divine will and action, he is able to embark upon the learning of a skill with the utmost humility and deep indifference to the opinions of others. He can be laughed at without shame; he can be jeered at without ridicule; he can laugh at himself; he can ridicule himself; but all the while his vision burns brightly, and he knows that one day he will have the attainment of the skill. He has no fear, for fear is possible only to the ego, and the ego has been subordinated in his nature. He embarks upon all enterprises with courage, persistence, and faith. Just because he toils endlessly at the door of creation, that door eventually yields, and marvelous works are wrought through him because his hand is moved by the Divine. Whatever your aspiration, remember this: the master of that skill is within you. He who already possesses it is greatest of all. Give over the doing of your work to him and get yourself out of the way, and you will find that you are soon performing with consummate knowledge and skill.

10 CREATING YOUR OWN TALENT

Creativeness contains a secret. The creative man exhibits a deep psychic tie with the inscrutable mystery of life. He performs in his work with the same naturalness as the flower grows from the soil, for he has attained to a unity in mental and spiritual relationships that make him seem part of the thing he is doing. The consummate artist becomes one with his task, so allied with it in movement and being that it becomes almost impossible to discern where the man ends and the work begins. Carl Jung states that it was not Goethe who created Faust as much as it was Faust that created Goethe. One seems absolutely dependent upon the other since each represents the same thing. Faust is an extension of Goethe, just as Goethe is an extension of Faust.

THE ARTIST INCARNATE

Talent is an absolute blending of the individual with his work. Paintings of the great painter become the painter, just as the painter becomes the great paintings. When we see a person who exhibits a great talent, we know at once a kind of ecstasy at this manifestation of a supreme mind and skill. All exhibition of talent is a kind of religious experience to those who behold it, for it establishes a communion between the Secret Self and the individual. There is a living and super-force whose sphere of action is largely invisible and outside the boundaries of our workaday world. There is

208

something more purposeful than atoms. There is a higher evolved intelligence than any that is contained within the human brain. There is a door into a world beyond, which sometimes opens and allows the individual to be seized by strange potencies tremendously above the level of his personal abilities. When that happens we see the artist incarnate, the man with a super-talent, who is able in one sphere of his activity to demonstrate directly to us the incalculable power and wisdom and beauty of the Divine.

The mystery of the talented man is that he is rooted directly in universal mind, that it manifests through him without any restriction or distortion by the ego. It is not the man who is responsible for his work, but a power beyond and above him that is manifesting through him, using him as an instrument. In deepest essence each man is an artist and only comes to his complete fulfillment as an individual when he gets his egoistic nature out of the way and allows the creative talent of the Divine to work through him, to accomplish those tasks that can best be done through his individually honed nature. When we live out our lives focused in the ego and bound to egoistic desires and satisfactions, it becomes impossible for us to achieve a spiritual awakening or to fulfill ourselves as creative persons. The world of material things is too much with us. Desires to be better, to have more, to live in material comfort, blind us to the long reaches of existence. This little life we live is important not for the creature comforts it brings but for the search it involves us in. Until we make our primary purpose the discovery of who we are and where we came from and what our relationship to life is, we must live out our brief sputtering of the candle in complete unawareness and blind automatism, following the pressures that develop in the outer world as they impinge upon our senses.

THE CREATIVE VISION

When the inner soul of man is touched by perception of the creative side of his nature, he sees at once the disaster inherent in a conduct of life based upon material goals. He sees that this thing he has always thought himself to be, his ego, is illusory, that the desires growing out of ego lead him into a maze of intricate by-roads that inevitably will lose his chance at enlightenment. Such a man may give up all possessions, all fame, all creature comforts, so as to be misled no longer, and take up his existence with a resolve to be motivated in all things through an inner light that proceeds out of universal mind. Such enforced asceticism allows the individual to engross himself completely in the service of the Secret Self. John the Baptist prowling the wilderness in search of his immortal soul is no more an example of it than is the French painter, Gauguin, giving up career and family to exile himself on a South Sea island to paint pictures. Each has been touched by the creative vision, each must serve it at all cost.

When a man's eyes have been opened to the creative nature of the Divine, he no longer can help himself, must serve it as an instrument, and nothing stands in his way. The creative process is impersonal; it seizes the nature and uses it to the utmost, and the person performs feats of creation far above anything possible to his normal conscious mind. When this force truly predominates in our makeup, it monopolizes our energy. In the awakened artist, life is ruled by the subconscious. Conscious intention means little, and the man is swept along on subterranean currents in which he is firmly enmeshed and in which he joyfully participates.

COMMON CONSCIOUSNESS

Participation mystique is the secret of artistic creation and consists of a swallowing up of the individual by the Secret Self, so that the man becomes an outlet for the manifestation of the beauty and variety and infinite complexity of universal mind. No one truly does a thing well when he does it with conscious intention. His effectiveness in action is always the result of unthinking naturalness. He does not come to skill in works through objective analysis of his action as separate from the action of others but through a complete identification of himself with the work to be done. Samuel Taylor Coleridge wrote, "From my very childhood, I have been accustomed to abstract, and as it were, unrealize whatever of more than common interest my eyes dwelled on, and then by a sort of transfusion and transmission of my consciousness to identify myself with an object." Participation in the life of another through a mystic medium of common consciousness is the essence of artistic creation. The man who affects to do something through conscious intention and at the urging of the separate and unique desires of the ego is performing by the light of one candle in an arena where thousands of kilowatts are available. He cannot possibly create a true and effective work through the limited knowledge and tiny scope of his conscious mind. All intentioned works of art are flat and useless and depict only clichés and are not truly works of art at all but only a kind of syncretism of the elements of knowledge available to the ego. Such effort in writing is journalism; in art, poster painting; in music, dollar mongering; and the individual who performs thus, even though masquerading under the mantle of artist, is actually destroying himself through knowledgeable corrupting of his talent.

Every man has a talent in some area of his nature, as big a talent as has ever existed, and if this talent has not manifested it is because his egoistic nature has dammed it up. No matter how long the dam has existed, no matter how tightly controlled the egoistic nature, the dam can be broken and the power can be let loose and a man can realize the highest level of his talent and live the life of the artist incarnate. To turn the eye within and to release the egoistic nature from selfish desire is the first thing to be done. Once the whole nature is turned over to a power greater than it is, to be used for whatever purpose, without aim or intention, then the power comes through, then the man begins to be transformed, performing naturally in all circumstances, guided correctly in all actions.

PSYCHIC POSITION

There is tremendous joy in correct psychic positioning of the ego. There is a feeling of usefulness that comes to the individual, a rooted certainty in his soul that he is performing in the best manner possible. This is the feeling of "grace" that comes to the religious man. This is the time of creativity that comes to the artist. This is the period of great productivity that comes to the business man. This is the time of superior skill that comes to the athlete. Each serves, performs under the impulsion of an intelligence and talent so vastly superior to the surface mind that the relationship is accepted as a happy child follows a loving father. Of this time of attunement and consequent creation, Friedrich Nietzsche wrote, "One can hardly reject completely the idea that one is the mere incarnation or mouthpiece or medium of some almighty power. The notion of revelation describes the condition quite simply; by which I mean that something profoundly convulsive and disturbing suddenly becomes visible and audible with indescribable definiteness and exactness. One hears—one does not seek; one takes—one does not ask who gives: A thought flashes out like lightning, inevitably without hesitation—I have never had any choice about it. Everything occurs quite without volition, as if in an eruption of freedom, independence, power and divinity."

It takes courage to push off into the unknown realms of the subconscious. It takes daring and boldness to abandon the little ship of egoistic self and swim to that uncharted island of the Secret Self that lies beyond the horizon. Many people cling to their egoistic natures as if they might be saved by them instead of inevitably abandoned. Pain and frustration and ineffectuality are the only rewards that come to the man who follows his ego, and yet he often clings to his false idol through thick and thin, much as a drowning man grasps at a straw. Often he has so educated himself to the existence of the phantom he worships that even when he sees he is deluded, he cannot bear to part with his ghost.

But part he must, push off into the uncharted regions of the subconscious he must, for finally his ego-self abandons him altogether, breaks down and disintegrates with the disintegration of the body. In the end he realizes that he must throw himself upon the mercy and grace of something infinite and eternal, which caused him to be born in the first place and now causes him to die.

NO DARING IS FATAL

Accident, perversion, illness, and ineptitude are the lot of the apprehensive. The prize is always to the bold, and the courageous own the universe. But despite these obvious facts, the majority of people cower in caves and refuse to abandon the flimsiest security and strike out in quest of the great and the good. If you have the courage to take a chance, you will not be abandoned by fate. The universe works on the side of the man who aspires. It gives wings to birds and fins to fish and touches the toes of the tightrope walker with magic. "No daring is fatal," wrote René Crevel. The Secret Self has a cherished place for its torch bearers. Along the tenuous lines of evolution the bold and the brave lead a mighty advance. An irresistible force proceeds out of the man who has courage and tenacity in his heart; he cannot be stopped because he is being used by an infinite and omnipotent power. But those who pull the shells of their egos about them and refuse either to dare or aspire are by this psychological act squeezing the juices of life from their bodies and their souls; they must inevitably disintegrate because they have refused to grow.

To let go of ego and to center one's self in the consciousness of universal mind is the greatest adventure possible because it means casting off from safe shores and voyaging beyond visible horizons. Yet once this initial step is made, once a man ceases responding to the material world, once he turns his mind and body and heart over to the Secret Self, he is astounded at once by his inner joy and serenity. Only the surface self can know fear, and once it has been subordinated, so is fear subordinated. The ego has something to lose only because it sees itself as separate. Once this idea of separateness has given over to a basic perception of unity, the individual no longer knows fear because he has nothing to lose. A sense of being a part of all things and a part of all life is a psychic condition that produces the most indescribable satisfaction. It is the ecstasy reported by mystics, the sense of creativity reported by artists, the religious revelation reported by the saints. It is denied no one, is possible to all. Once it comes to a man, it provides a springboard for the development of a talent by which he is able to express the infinite nature of the Divine.

METAPHYSICAL ADVENTURE

Religious revelation is exactly the same thing as creative activity. They are both metaphysical adventures. They involve the acquisition of a total instead of a partial view of the universe. They are out of time and space and individuality and are centered in eternal terms and whole significances. Talent develops in a person when his spiritual awakening has begun because talent is inherent in each of us, and the purpose of life is that we be creative. When the spiritual awakening is true, so will the talent be true, and not compulsive or obsessional, allowing the individual to perform his work out of sheer joy, dropping his fruits like a ripe tree. It then becomes possible for him to obey his instincts and intuitions and not to be inhibited in his actions by what others expect of him. He gets near the heart of truth because he sees the sham and hypocrisy that are bound to partiality. He subordinates this partiality completely in all his actions and thought, and the talent that is visited upon him is the talent of something beyond him.

Art speaks to us in symbols of the universality of our true being. By it we perceive a portion of that ecstasy and unity from which we have sprung. By it we are able to achieve an inkling of the great destiny that awaits man. Some day men will become thoroughly awakened spiritually and consequently completely religious, not just believers as a few men are now, but knowers, causers, prime movers, thoroughly enlightened, gods in fact, even as now in potential. The attitude that results from a man's discovery of his inherent talent is not one of intentioned action or thought, but one that looks for discovery. The creative writer does not take up pen with an idea of "making" a certain thing, but only to see what will come through him and manifest itself on paper. The man who truly uses his talent is able to do so only because he lets it use him. The correct mental attitude is that whatever is there will come through and need neither be started nor stopped. You do not have to know what is coming, what it will look like, but simply have an open mind, and let it through. Never even bother to look at it closely, for if you do, you may think you know what it is, and by that mental fixation you will make it static and it no longer will grow and be flexible and creative. All that is great and good and lasting springs out of the subconscious processes of the Secret Self, and when we are moved by our greater minds we exhibit the talents that are ours.

> God guard me from those thoughts men think
> In the mind alone,
> He that sings a lasting song
> Thinks in a marrow bone.
>
> —Amy Lowell

CREATIVE LABOR

A thousand faces has the Secret Self, approached by a thousand doors, and when one is opened and that face beheld, there bursts through the individual a torrent of creativeness, a kind of super-talent. Partial is the human being, barely aware, a surface manifestation of unlimited realms of subconscious intelligence, but there is a path by which each may penetrate universal mind, and when he does he creates his own talent, depicting for the world some particular aspect of the Divine. No man is denied talent except by himself. When he allows his consciousness to be hemmed in by the ego he is unable to pull upon subconscious levels for the inspiration and drive necessary to creative work.

Unique individuality is the vehicle which the Secret Self uses for the manifestation of talent, and is largely being stultified by our modern industrial society. Our education teaches conformity. The industrial machine needs workers, and workers must be predictable, and predictability, as far as society is concerned, is best obtained by inculcating the same social conscience in each man. Consequently, the individual lives a routine that is not of his own choosing but has been selected for him by society. His opinions also have been given him by the group, and he accepts them as part of the condition of his life. All thinking is done for him. He believes the political institution best that he belongs to, the labor union best that he belongs to, the state, city, and community best that he belongs to. He is unable to make an objective decision about anything he encounters but reacts to everything as it affects his preformed opinions. This egoistic basis for judging things is completely false and completely static because it does not allow the individual to grow. Truth in some final analysis may be absolute, but for the individual man it is an individual matter. What is good for one is not necessarily good for all, but neither is the good of all necessarily best for the individual.

As long as man continues to live in groups, social conscience will continue to have a distinct and necessary function, but such social conscience must make provision for individual growth and responsibility, for it now tends to defeat itself by making automatons of its adherents. Large industrial firms are finding that the idea box in the plant pays dividends. When a worker is encouraged to think creatively about the business in which he labors, his mental attitude toward that business is changed. He not only becomes more efficient in his tasks, but sooner or later contributes toward the growth of the business. No man is built to put nuts on bolts all day. That is the task of a machine. But a man may endure such a job if allowed to pursue means by which it may be done more efficiently. Naturally he will not be disposed to such activity if he feels that it may result in his being without a job at all, but only if he feels that he will be rewarded with a better job or a better income.

The basic problems in industrial advancement are delineated by the opposing forces of labor and management. Organized labor has grown as a protection to the worker from exploitation, but its psychological position has become static. It is largely opposed to advances in technology that may do away with job categories, and "feather bedding" in all industries has achieved such proportion as to be a distinct burden on efficient operation. The solution to effective industrial growth is not likely to be found in organized labor, but rather in an enlightened management which makes its labor force part of its creative effort, rewards each man on an individual basis and allows participation of every member of the organization in the fruits of that organization. When such industrial enlightenment finally is achieved, there will be a unification of labor and management because their aims will be the same, and each man will have a creative responsibility toward his work.

PRODUCTIVITY

Creative talent demands production. The displacement of ego in favor of the guidance of the Secret Self results in a man being driven to accomplish tasks that heretofore he would have considered impossible. No mountain is too high, no wilderness too broad, and the creative soul attuned to the Divine labors and produces unremittingly. Thomas Carlyle wrote, "Even in the meanest sorts of labor the whole soul of a man is composed into a kind of real harmony the instant he sets himself to work. Produce! Were it but the pitifulest, infinitesimal fraction of a product, produce it in God's name."

For the most part we are too inhibited and repressed to be able to express the personality that is uniquely our own. The ego-controlled nature acts always in accord with an idea of how people expect it to act. Since it does not know itself, it does not know how it truly feels, but adopts feelings from desire-goals rather from the individuality innate to it. The man who endures all to make money is a classic example of repression and inhibition. He swindles his inferiors and fawns on his superiors, and by this consequent warping of moral values so completely represses the Secret Self that it is impossible for him to be creative or spontaneous in any area of his activity. Making money is not an end in life. Pursuing the god, Mammon, has only fatal results. But achievement is one of life's primary aims, and achievement often results in monetary success. To be what we naturally are and to live and act as we naturally were created should be the primary aim of each of us. We have been put here on earth by a power greater than we are; we have been manifested in our particular form so as to reflect in humanity an image of the Divine. We cannot reflect this image or do the work natural to us if we become repressed by centering our consciousness in our egoistic natures.

Spontaneity is the secret of doing things well. A man acts in accord with his whole nature when he does things *feelingly* instead of thinkingly. Reason is valuable too, but it serves a limited world and a limited knowledge. When a man acts only according to his reason, he acts with the barest facts in his possession. But when he acts instinctively and intuitively, he acts as an instrument of the Secret Self, and behind his action lie all knowledge, all intelligence, all power. When you are spontaneous in your actions and in your thoughts, you are being yourself, and when you are being yourself, you are a hundred times more effective, more joyful, more creative than you are when you are ordering your life in accordance with the aims of the surface mind. The consciously controlled and intentioned man is suppressing his talent, for he is suppressing the action of the Divine within him. No talent ever is exhibited by the conscious mind or ego, and the man whose life is ordered by them never can be creative.

GET INTO THE GAME

Let yourself go. Shake off inhibition and fear, and be yourself. Learn to think and act naturally, spontaneously; harmony and symmetry will enter your life, and you will discover your inherent talent. Most people never find their proper niches simply because they inhibit the talent they possess. It takes courage to go out on a limb and do the things that are natural. It is much easier to sit on the side lines, watch somebody else perform, and criticize. Monday morning quarterbacks are notorious in football, and in the world of art it has long been axiomatic that the critic is a frustrated artist.

Fulton Oursler reports, "Once winter's night, many years ago, when I was no more than twenty, I was belaboring a typewriter in the newsroom of the *Baltimore American*. A copy boy summoned me to the office of the managing editor, a bald-headed old walrus with white mustaches like hanging gardens and a perverse sense of humor. Leaning back in his swivel chair he asked me:

" 'Do you play the piano?'

" 'No, sir.'

" 'Fiddle?'

" 'No, sir.'

" 'Sing?'

" 'No, sir.'

" 'Then go up to the Lyric and cover the concert. Our music critic just dropped dead. You've got the job.' "

If hindsight were foresight, we'd all be kings. It takes little imagination and absolutely no enterprise to recognize the errors of people who have the courage to try when the outcome is in doubt. Creative talent carries with it an element of deepest personal risk. Before the individual becomes a fit vehicle, he must figuratively hang himself from a cliff by his fingertips, suspend himself between life and death. In this psychological position of awareness of the basic elements of life, he no longer is confused about the purposes of the Secret Self, is able to pierce quickly the sham and subterfuge of egoistic action and thought, and to act always as an instrument of the Divine. A deep indifference to the opinions of others existing side by side with recognition of a common spiritual bond brings to the individual his true and unique personality, allows his whole life to be an expression of that particular facet of the Supreme that is best able to manifest through him. Thus he discovers his talent. It may be in the arts, the sciences, business, war, or politics; but wherever he finds his niche, he will fit into it as a hand in a skintight glove, as if he and it were made for each other, and he will perform his work in such a manner as to be completely indistinguishable from it.

TEMPERING BY FIRE

Every creative individual must undergo a tempering process during which he is subjected to fire, after which his toughness is increased. Life is not such a gentle thing as to be approached with dainty fingers. Look about and you will see that nature chooses her blessed ones by subjecting them to the most severe tests. Out of the crucible of conflict emerge the lion-hearted, and they are the ones who carry the banner of evolution onward. The man who subjects himself to the sternest of trials is in the end the best instrument for effectuation of the purposes of the Secret Self. It is he through whom mighty works are done, upon whom great events hinge. The exercised muscle grows stronger, the exercised mind grows smarter; the exercised heart grows bolder; but nothing destroys as quickly as disuse. Repression and inhibition do more toward girdling man around with limitation than any obstacle he faces.

If a thing were as easy to do as to say all of us would be saints. Exorcising fear, anxiety, and hostility from the consciousness is not a simple matter and is nearly impossible as long as the ego rules the nature. In order for the individual life to be natural, it is necessary that it be lived as an extension of the Divine. Reason must be subordinated as primary principle. Emotion must be subordinated as guiding force.

Action and thought must develop spontaneously and effortlessly, as a result of the consciousness being placed in the position of observation rather than origination.

The development of talent depends upon spiritual awakening. The unawakened individual is born with talent, but if unawakened during his lifetime literally is eaten up by the force that possesses him because he is unable to express it and the opposing sides of his nature are constantly at war with each other.

DO WHAT YOU ARE

Dale belonged to the United States Marine Corps during World War II and fought through five campaigns with extreme bravery. Prior to his enlistment he had gone to art school, and his early works in oil showed much promise. The danger and disaster he faced in the marines, however, altered his attitude, and once he was discharged he made up his mind that he wanted material possessions. He set about acquiring them, took a job in an advertising agency as a layout man, gradually advanced to art director, received a salary that enabled him to live in comfort. He was far from happy, however. Easel and paints were forgotten, and nightly journeys to cocktail bars took on such dimension that he seldom went to bed without being drunk. Before long, he was drinking during the day also, and it became obvious to his intimates that he was harboring a deep core of resentment.

When this resentment finally manifested in an arthritic attack, Dale was sent to bed by his doctor, and there had time to think. One day an old friend from his art school days, now pursuing a career as a painter, came to him and they talked. His friend looked at the sumptuous apartment.

"You must be making it pretty good," he said.

"Sure thing," answered Dale. "Twenty thousand a year and all the trimmings. Practically anything I want. How about you?"

His friend smiled. "I'm lucky if I do three thousand a year, and you could put my little studio in one corner of this apartment."

"Then why not give it up?" asked Dale. "Come into the ad agency. I'll start you at ten thousand."

Dale's friend shook his head. "No, thanks," he said. "I'm happy the way I am."

"You are?" asked Dale.

"Yes."

"Really happy, eh?"

"You bet. Aren't you?"

"I couldn't be more miserable."

"Then it strikes me that you're the one who ought to change. There isn't enough money in the world to lock me into an unhappy job. You're not painting, are you? I don't see an easel or a canvas in the whole apartment."

"I've given it up," answered Dale.

"So you've given it up and you're flat on your back and you've got lots of money and you're unhappy. I'll tell you something. There's a studio right next to mine, and the rent is thirty dollars a month. You give up your job and move in there and begin to paint again. Unless I miss my guess that's the cure for what ails you."

After his friend left, Dale thought it over. That evening he obtained brushes and oils and started to paint. By the end of a week he was deeply engrossed, and his arthritic pains had gone. He moved out of his apartment and into the studio and has been painting ever since. He smiles cheerfully now in his paint-stained smock.

"I made twenty-five hundred dollars last year," he says, "which is big money for a painter, but it barely kept the wolf away from the door. Still, I couldn't care less about that wolf. All I want to do is paint. When I paint, I am completely happy, because I'm doing something that is part of me."

CREATIVENESS AND COMPETITIVENESS

Somerset Maugham wrote, "The artist can, within certain limits, make what he likes of his life. In other callings, in medicine, for instance, or the law, you are free to choose whether you will adopt them or not, but having chosen you are free no longer. You are bound by the rules of your profession; a standard of conduct is imposed upon you. The pattern is predetermined. It is only the artist who can make his own."

When you turn your life over to the Secret Self the channel in you best adapted for expression of the Divine is cleared and developed, and a unique talent is exposed. A direction of growth is opened, within which you are perfectly free. It has little to do with your position in society or your membership in social groups. Your mind and talent develop independently of material associations because you have turned them over to the Secret Self to use as they are best fitted. Each of us most satisfies himself as a person and fulfills himself as a member of society when he lives the life of an artist, not necessarily that of a painter or writer but an artist in the sense that his attitude toward all things is creative rather than competitive.

The world of competition is the world of egoistic desire, for competition seeks ascendency over others. People whose ruling passion is to prove themselves better usually look upon the world with hostile eyes and regard every man as an enemy. Such limited perception of the nature and purpose of life clearly destroys more often than it blesses, for victory always is temporary, and defeat awaits all whose lives revolve around superiority. The ego is born, blooms, withers, and dies, just as the material body, and the individual whose aspirations center around it must follow a cycle that leads to eventual defeat and disintegration. Oh, the noon day of the ego is fine. A man in possession of his full powers may stand upon his individual mountain and beat his chest and defy the world, but noon quickly passes and the day of his life wanes, and noontime becomes a very dim memory as the shadows lengthen.

In order to participate freely and fully in all things, the wider vision that perceives the majestic onward march of evolution must be adopted by the individual as basic in his attitude toward life. Such a man may appear to be competitive through participating in competitive things, but he does not compete through egoistic desire to be better or superior, only as a result of having opened himself as a vehicle for the manifestation of the Secret Self. He is used in all things and is never the user, and because he sees his basic unity with all men he is able to enter competition without hostility, neither for gain nor loss. He is able to regard with equal mindedness those he vanquishes and those who vanquish him, for each represents to him the same immutable person whose manifestation he knows he is himself.

SURRENDER BRINGS CONTROL

The truly creative attitude is a passive one insofar as it listens and does not command. Yet what is wrought through the individual whose ear is attuned to the Divine is charged with the most vital energy imaginable, far surpassing anything possible to egoistic will power. It is ego-will that eventually breaks the individual through constantly throwing him against obstacles that are immovable because they are not understood. Will power seeks to batter down doors that are best approached with a key. The enlightened man is a talented man because he is a creative man, and this creativity is instilled in him by a sense of unity with all things. Obstacles and opposition and enemies have meaning for him only as they indicate a lack of understanding within himself, and he never seeks accomplishment by running headlong at things, but only by attempting to mentally and spiritually penetrate their true meaning.

My teacher is the conqueror knowing all
And seeing all, the Master Infinite

In pity, all the world's physician, he
And he it is by whom these truths are taught.
—Theragatha

Has the ship of your life come to disaster through running aground on uncharted shoals? If so, the greatest lesson you can learn is now possible, for your ship never would have grounded if the proper navigator were charting the course. Your surface self and egoistic nature have been at the helm, and the limited perception of surface mind could not possibly know of the uncharted shoals. Now your ship is aground, and the only way that it can be freed is to give over command to the Master who knows these waters well. Surrender is the principle by which ultimate control is gained. The bossy surface self continually tries to run the show and its enamoring cry of "I, I, I" may easily delude the whole consciousness into limited life and knowledge, but when a person runs into sufficient pain and difficulty, a crack appears in the hard veneer of the ego and a light is let through which illuminates all for one startled instant of awareness. Then a man knows that his life and self are in the hands of something greater than he is, that his identity with the surface mind has always been an illusion, which in this moment of enlightenment he is freed from.

Creative men affect us as being rich in possibilities. They are ripened trees that drop their fruit, and we scarcely can be near them without attaining to some unexpected good. The creative man's attitude has an aspect of abundance, as if he has some mystical tie with a horn of plenty, not of material things necessarily, but of ideas and of possibilities that give a universal note to everything he does. A good thing is effective and generative. It grows and propagates and makes room for itself. It springs into being through an irresistible creative urge of universal mind, and the vehicle of its manifestation always is the man with an artistic attitude toward life. Ralph Waldo Emerson wrote, "The true artist has the planet for his pedestal." He sees the possibilities inherent in all things, is a discoverer in the universe, and interpreter for his less enlightened fellows.

FREEING YOUR TALENT

Each man is by some secret liking connected to a particular aspect of life. When he has become freed of the repressions, limitations, and inhibitions imposed upon him by his education and training, he is able to expose this subconscious preference and by it attune himself with the creative talent that naturally is his. Such talent has limitless possibilities for manifestation. It need have no connection with the so-called arts, may be as simple a thing as a talent for kindness or love. It may be a talent for speaking, for persuasion, for teaching, for research, for study. It may be in science or business, but wherever it is it will prove on exposure to be vastly superior to the abilities of people who are guided solely by competitive aims and egoistic desires. It will proceed out of an inexhaustible fount, be superior to the person, seem to use him rather than he use it. His ordinary mortal self will live with his talent in a constant state of startled delight. He will know it is a visitation of something above and beyond him, will treat it at all times with loving care, follow it, obey it, never command it.

The most completely frustrating thing that can happen to the individual life is for inherent talent to fail to develop. Such failure only can come about through the ego controlling the nature, restricting the individual's growth in the direction intended.

The torrent of creative energy that exists in every human being becomes dammed up only with the gravest danger. Resentment, bitterness, hate, and hostility are the emotional maladjustments that result from a frustrated creative nature, and these inevitably find their counterparts in physical illness. Heart trouble, circulatory disease, arthritis, rheumatism, cancer, ulcer are all psychosomatic symptoms resulting from dammed-up creative energy. It not only is imperative that we free our talent in order to become fulfilled as individuals, but it also is important that we free it in order to live physically vigorous lives, in order to have healthy bodies. These ends can be accomplished only by lowering our egoistic barriers, by turning our lives over to the Divine to be used for whatever purpose our basic natures are best suited. When we are able to do this, we become natural persons, blend into our tasks and our work in such a manner that we seem an extension of our activities and they an extension of us. We achieve an effectiveness in action that is directly proportional to the degree that we have turned our lives over to the Secret Self, and the manifestation that comes through us of superior action and skill is not possessed by the surface self but uses it as an instrument to effect its purposes in the world.

YOUR SEPARATE STAR

True artists we all are inherently, for each of us reflects an image in the growing body of mankind of the one mind and intelligence that lies behind creation. We paint a picture as we go through life of that mystic and occult realm whence we originated and to which we one day will return. When we depart, the picture remains, with our signature in the corner, and is just as surely the representation of what we saw and felt and heard and attempted to communicate as is the picture of the painter, signed and hung upon the wall of the gallery. And in the final analysis who is to judge which vision is the most beautiful or worthwhile, for if a man live the life of an artist, his hand is guided by a will other than his own, and what is wrought through him is wrought at the behest of the Divine, whose deft brush strokes are gradually adding to the picture of eternity and infinity.

Throw off the egoistic bonds that hold you and allow the Secret Self to shine through. You will become the artist incarnate. A talent will begin to develop in you toward which your whole nature can be lent. You will begin to do the work that only you can do, that will fulfill you as a human being and as an aspiring soul. Wherever your heart leads, you may joyfully follow, with an inner certainty that you are acting in accord with the deepest motivations of life.

> Each for the joy of working
> And each, in his separate star,
> Shall draw the thing as he sees it
> For the God of things as they are.
> —Rudyard Kipling

11 HOW TO USE YOUR SIXTH SENSE

Today the existence of a sixth sense is well recognized. Super-sensory ability has been recorded through the centuries but only recently under laboratory conditions; now its existence is finally and irrevocably proved. Under sixth sense may be lumped all paranormal phenomena such as thought trans-ferrence, clairvoyance, and psychokinesis, which in para-psychology are called ESP, extra-sensory perception. Intuitive understanding of circumstances comes through the use of the sixth sense, and its range and scope are vastly greater than the other five.

THE DIMLY SEEN WORLD

The physical sensory organs reveal to us the barest indica-tion of what actually is encountered in the material world. They record vibrations. Each sense records a tiny segment of the total spectrum of vibrations. The recording of all five senses is only an infinitesimal part of that total spectrum. A million times more remains untold about each object we encounter than is ever revealed to us by our physical senses. We move about in a world that we obtain only the dimmest impression of. Objects that we regard as solid are not solid at all, are merely enclosures of higher vibrations, and every-thing exists in a constant state of movement and flux. Form is merely the imprisonment of movement within dimension, and in the final analysis all things are far more mental than physical.

Now that physical science has been able to reduce the smallest bit of matter to nothingness, has found basic substance to be energy or intelligence, even the most materialistic of researchers has been forced to the inevitable conclusion that all things are basically ideas, that they are held in form as concepts in some universal intelligence. It is through this universal intelligence that we discover the sixth sense, that we arrive at spiritual enlightenment. It is the immersion of ego in this intelligence that provides salvation for the individual man, allows him to live his life in a state of attunement and harmony. The psychological act of shucking off the little self and attaining to a larger self is what the great mystics speak of when they record their arrival at the "moment of truth."

There is a vast and great mind that is responsible for the construction of the universe, that is in a very real sense the universe itself, and this infinite and eternal intelligence creates only from its own substance, and everything which it creates is inherently itself, not something different, except through the limitation imposed upon it by its becoming partial and incomplete. Everything in creation is a manifestation of the one mind and intelligence that underlies all. Each man therefore has within him a super-mind which is free of limitation and restriction, and this mind, working beneath the level of conscious intelligence, is capable of absolute and truthful guidance in all things because it understands and perceives all things.

MOMENTS OF ILLUMINATION

Universal mind is a manifestation of the Secret Self, of that divine will that inexorably leads mankind upon the path of evolution. The surface mind and ego are products of the five senses, of that knowledge that a man acquires during the period of his lifetime, and since they are the results of limited knowledge and partial experience, they are the poorest vehicles for the conduct of action. Absolute effectiveness comes to the man who immerses ego in universal mind and allows the Secret Self to guide him. His psychological position is that of a listener; his inner mind and heart become attuned to a wider consciousness, a greater sense of being; impressions, knowledge, and intuitive urgings come to him from out of this source with an authority greater than anything received through his sensory organs.

"Ever and anon the trumpet sounds from the hid battlements of eternity," wrote Francis Thompson. And to each of us as he goes through life, a moment comes, however fleeting, when a crack appears in the hard wall of consciousness, and we see through briefly, into regions of eternal light and infinite knowledge, and in that moment we truly are possessed of a sixth sense; something paranormal happens, some example of intuitive knowledge; we read the thoughts of others or see at a distance or understand coming events. Such an experience leaves us shaken. Our absorption in the material world is forgotten for the moment. We begin to see the astounding possibilities of mind and consciousness. We become convinced that when we deal with material things we deal with results, not causes; we know that all causes exist in mind. We begin to perceive infinite possibilities, vast scopes, subtle nuances that have been hidden from us by our limited consciousness. Such understanding may come to us from a small event or large. It may result from a such a simple thing as the sudden apprehension of the thoughts of another person. A light may burst upon us and we may have sudden knowledge of a coming event. Perhaps one of our dreams comes true, or a loved one materializes and instructs us as to a course of action. In any case, intuitive phenomena come to all people. The dice player urging the goddess of fate to smile on his next cast does not always beseech lady luck in vain. Sometimes he opens up a channel between him and omnipotent intelligence, and the dice repeat magic numbers at such length as to reduce mathematical odds to absurdity.

INTUITION AND REASON

Intuition is much more reliable than reason, for reason charts its course with limited access to facts, while intuition has at its fingertips all the knowledge that has ever existed, that ever will exist. Using the sixth sense, however, is not such a simple matter as trusting one's life to one's feelings. It is very easy to fall into the trap of being guided by the emotions, under the misapprehension that emotions are intuitive feelings. Nothing could be farther from the truth. Emotion is a wild horse, running away with the inhabitant in the body, and he who is ruled by emotion is in the grip of something worse than limited knowledge; he is the blind tool of egoistic fears, hates, envies. Such a life is an idiot's tale, without design. Reason can control the emotions, and reason is a far better guide. Reason is limited in both effectiveness and knowledge, however, and when it has achieved sufficient supremacy over the emotional nature, it may safely be subordinated to the guidance of intuition; thus the whole life is brought to a level of competence and attunement.

Charles Steinmetz of the General Electric Company wrote, "Some day people will learn that material things will not bring happiness and are of little use in making men and women creative and powerful. Then the scientists of the world will turn their laboratories to the study of God and prayer and the spiritual forces which as yet have hardly been scratched. When this day comes, the world will see more advancement in one generation than it has seen in the past four."

Reason enables us to deal effectively with our immediate surroundings, but only within the scope of the information available to the five senses. Reason tells us we may go coatless on a sunny day, but the storm that is gathering over the horizon is outside the scope of reason, and when it rains in the late afternoon, reason has been wrong. The wider consciousness in the depths of the individual must be trusted before his actions can be guided with a knowledge of all factors. Reason is a tool, and logic is an effective method of thinking, but each is only a means and no more reliable than the information fed into it. In the eyes of the world the intuitive man often acts unreasonably, for his actions are based upon a secret knowledge that is hidden from more logical minds. The reasonable man has difficulty discerning between the emotionally-guided man and the intuitively-guided man. To him, they are both unreasonable. He sees that the emotionally-guided man is almost never right, and he correctly attributes this fact to such a man's psychic blind spots. He sees the intuitively-guided man act unreasonably but with continued success, and he attributes this to luck rather than to any effective means of coping with the world. In consequence, the reasonable man is almost as blinded as the emotional man, for he has shut his eyes to the possibilities of intuitive knowing.

LOGIC AND SCIENCE

Scientific approach to the solution of problems works from effect to cause. Knowledge of a particular problem is contained in those facts observable in the effect under scrutiny. This effect is the field of effort, and logic is the method by which science works from the effect to the cause which produced it. Such procedure has made remarkable advances, but for the most part they have been within the realm of known facts. Now and again a creative thinker joins the laboratory armies and in one intuitive flash spans years of painstaking experiment. Albert Einstein stated that his Theory of Relativity was revealed to him in a moment of inspiration, and the simplicity of the eventual mathematical formula, E equals MC^2, could not have been hidden from an army of researchers unless its significance was outside the scope of their consciousness. All science and mathematics are in the end philosophical, for they attempt to penetrate the mysteries of the universe and the secret of life, and they represent the efforts of mankind on the boundaries of awareness to extend that awareness unceasingly.

To recognize that there is a mind within us that knows the answers to all our problems is the first step to acquiring the use of the infallible sixth sense. It is not necessary to find a solution in the material world. In point of actual fact the solution can never be found there. The secret lies within ourselves, and we need go no farther than our very room to find each answer. There is tremendous comfort in discovering within one's self an infinite and eternal mind that holds the answer to each problem, to realize that the solution to each perplexing situation may be found simply by searching one's soul. But if a man be sufficiently out of joint with life, he may find it extremely difficult to commune with his inner and deeper nature, may even become neurotic through having severed psychic ties with his originator. When he looks into the reaches of his soul, those trackless corridors stretch toward infinity and appall him with their emptiness; he is frightened, seeks quickly to return to the uneasy security of his material existence. It takes courage to look upon the many faces of the Secret Self. The Divine does not reside alone in beauty, comfort, love, and harmony, but is equally resident in ugliness, hardship, hate, and discord. The Secret Self attains its purpose in all areas of endeavor by the conflict of opposites, and before we are able to live as mature human beings we must accept all sides of life as being part of an absolutely sure and perfect plan for the working out of the purposes of the Divine.

GOD SENSE

The sixth sense is a God sense, an identification, however momentary, with the Secret Self, which enables the individual, in that instant, to perceive future, past, and present in one instantaneous tableau, to contain all space and time within the confines of his own consciousness. Such awareness, if constantly possessed, would make all one's actions infallible, and the purpose of evolution must lie in just such an end as this; the beginnings of such a development are already perceivable in the lives of many men. The ouija board, the divining rod, the crystal ball, and the star gazer have been with us since the dawn of recorded history. Such phenomena definitely are indicative of man's recognition of a power of intuition—a sixth sense. This paranormal facility of the mind has been largely ignored in the past century of material conquest, but now that the searchlight of scientific examination is being brought to bear, it appears inevitable that mental and spiritual advances will overshadow material advances in the years ahead.

A new approach, a new concept is necessary before investigation of the paranormal will yield results. The methods of science have not demonstrated that they are adaptable to the study of a world that is invisible. By means of the microscope and the telescope, science has extended its vision enormously, but in the realm of the microcosm it disintegrated the atom and found nothing left, and in the world of the macrocosm it detected distant galaxies moving away at the speed of light into space that shouldn't exist. Ultimately, all investigations of matter have a common meeting ground, which is the disappearance of individuality into unity, into a world where space and time and separateness do not exist, and this world is not capable of representation by objects or material things but is primarily mental and not subject to the probing of physical instruments.

Investigations in the field of parapsychology have now proved that it is possible for one mind to communicate with another without any known organic means, and this has been labeled telepathy. It has also been proved that the human mind can attain to knowledge of coming events, and this has been labeled precognition. It has been proved that the human mind can see at a distance, and this has been labeled clairvoyance. It has been proved that the human mind can influence the behavior of objects, and this has been labeled psychokinesis. All these powers of the mind, however dimly discerned or barely understood, when lumped together indicate the existence of an absolutely unexplored area of vast and almost unimaginable possibilities that one day must liberate man from his bondage to the flesh. Moreover, there is indicated a coming revolution in the basic concepts of life.

THE SEA OF CONSCIOUSNESS

Science has always investigated a world of multiplicity, attempting to establish physical relationships between one thing and another. Man, the animal, exists in a world of action and reaction, but man, the mental being, exists in a world that appears to be without division, without space and time, for inherent in his mental makeup is the ability to transcend these. No enlightened mind can have any quarrel with the investigations of Doctors J. B. Rhine and S. G. Soal in the field of parapsychology, and from their results the only possible conclusion is this. There are not many individual minds in the world at all, but only one mind, and this mind is infinite and eternal and is the sustaining source of each of us, is in its truest essence all of each of us, just as each of us in truest essence is all of it. Now if each man exists in a sea of consciousness, and the consciousness in him is in everything else and in all other men, it then becomes possible to understand what we are dealing with when we deal with extrasensory perception.

It has been stated that a man's intelligence is like an iceberg, one third of it appearing upon the surface, two thirds existing below, but parapsychology reveals the relationship between conscious and subconscious intelligence to be one part to a million. Moreover, universal subconscious mind exhibits no necessity for being educated during the lifetime of the individaul. It provides eternal and infinite guidance because it has existed since the beginning of time; all knowledge is contained within it, and that very small "taught" intelligence acquired by conscious mind is the tiniest light compared to the illumination known when the individual life has been turned over to the guidance of the Secret Self. A thousand times more awareness is obtainable by the person through enlightened use of universal mind than through efforts in the world of material things. Once the Secret Self has been fully exposed to mankind, education, which today takes sixteen years of a person's life, will be accomplished in weeks, even days. When the powerful and penetrating aspects of universal mind become common enough knowledge to be taught at our schools, such buildings and bridges as now are constructed in six months will rise overnight.

There is no such thing as a particle of matter that is not possessed of conscious intelligence, however low, however restricted by the form in which it finds itself. All things exist by grace of the Secret Self, which is innate in each, has become each as part of an overall plan, and the urge to self-knowledge that exists within the heart of each creature is that impulsion to find in partiality that same sense of self-awareness and expressive joy that it knew in its complete and whole state. To develop the use of the sixth sense is to learn to use universal mind, to cease living in the separate egoistic nature and to turn over the whole life to a wider and more encompassing awareness than is possible to the surface self.

STEPS TO SPIRITUAL AWAKENING

The consistent use of the sixth sense depends upon spiritual awakening, depends upon a man recognizing the spiritual bond that unites him with all others, with all things. Dethroning the ego, removing the focus of his consciousnes from the surface self, he thereby attains to a state of widened awareness that emanates directly from his identification with the one mind and one life that is the true inhabitant in all bodies. When a man reaches this state of illumination, a new world opens up for his exploration. Physical effects take on secondary significance. He sees that things originate on an invisible plane, that all causes are mental, proceed out of ideas, out of visualizations. He begins to see that material things are not really solid facts at all, but only partially revealed manifestations of conceptions held in mind. Now he is able to perceive the secret of acting mentally, of altering things by altering the idea that exists within them. He begins to see that this altering is possible through complete identification of himself with the thing, that once this widened consciousness is achieved, he can change the thing merely by changing his idea of it, because the same mind is in him as is in the thing. Nothing is impossible to the man whose consciousness breaks out of the bonds of the ego. Once he shakes off surface self, there is revealed to him a world that is bounded only by eternity and infinity. He can become anything he desires, can accomplish anything he will, for in a very real sense all events and things have their existence in him. To achieve this state of spiritual awakening is the goal, to arrive at this state of joy and bliss and complete effectuality is beyond doubt the most worthwhile and rewarding culmination of life.

Steps by which spiritual enlightenment is achieved are the steps by which the sixth sense is brought under dominion, and they are four. These steps infallibly produce spiritual enlightenment, and to him who puts them into practice is brought not only the sixth sense but an expanded consciousness that allows him to live his life joyfully and effectively. The four steps are: 1) Consecration, 2) Surrender, 3) Sacrifice, 4) Love. Consecration means the focusing of the total mental and spiritual efforts of the individual on discovery of the Secret Self. Surrender means a wholehearted giving over of all action and goals to the Divine. Sacrifice means continual and deliberate subjugation of ego to the will and purposes of the Secret Self. Love means yearning for unity, longing to return to a state of wholeness and oneness. These four sacramental steps, if performed unceasingly, are bound to develop that wider consciousness in which the sixth sense becomes an integral part of the life. The first step taken, all others will follow. With the mind and being dedicated to a search for wider consciousness, the life inevitably will be transformed, a sense of intimacy will come into the consciousness, and the person will find resource by which he is able to give over his goals and aspirations to the Divine.

MAN IS MADE OF MAGIC

Once this psychological divestment of the ego has taken place, illumination is near. Now it becomes second nature to practice the sacrifice by which the ego is kept in subjugation. Little egoistic desires are daily given up in favor of that one encompassing search for unity that is now the total consecration of the individual. The ego does not cease to exist, far from it; in some areas it appears as vigorous as before, but now it recognizes that it is only a tool, not originator, not captain or master; and it performs its tasks, goes about its work under the impulsion of and following the guidance of a will and a power totally beyond and inexpressibly more powerful than itself. There comes to the individual an experience of the unity from which he has sprung, an experiential return to a source of absolute bliss and joy and power. He enters the Secret Self; the Secret Self enters him. This mutual penetration, this merging, is the union known as love, and when this takes place in the consciousness of the individual, his emergence as an enlightened and effective man begins. Now he realizes that man is not bone and blood and flesh or even brain, but is constructed of invisible essences that can only be called magic.

Jean Gebser wrote, "Telepathy, trance, precognition, telekinesis, levitations, dual personality, and many other paranormal phenomena are rooted in the magic structure of man. So called paranormal phenomena are not at all paranormal but fundamentally natural. Without certain telepathic powers, without traces of the magic structure, without a minimum of inner pre-vision (or the power of precognition), without sleep and light 'intuitioning,' not one of us could live another day. And all of these powers arise in the main from the magic structure of our consciousness." The effective use of the sixth sense is attained by the man who comes to the realization of the essential magic of human consciousness. He does not give his allegiance to the world of material things, but to a world of ideas and concepts and thoughts, which he perceives preexists and preordains the material world.

Perceptions of the sixth sense are never as concrete as those of the five physical senses. The reason for this is obvious. Our physical senses are used through all our waking hours; our sixth sense seldom, if at all. The sixth sense works in us as feeling, not feeling sustained by emotion, but inner certainty as to a course of action, as to the development of coming events. Reason is not renounced altogether, nor logic, nor knowledge, but all these are subordinated to intuition, and they are used only to bring into consciousness all aspects of a problem that needs to be solved. Intuition develops the solution, which emerges in the consciousness of the individual as a deep certainty that may have either visual or auditory manifestations, perhaps both. A man might list all elements of a problem confronting him. He might wrestle with the problem in terms of reason and logic, but he will draw no conclusion immediately. He will turn over the problem to his subconscious for a period of resolution, confident that the correct solution will be delivered to him.

FRONTIERS OF THE MIND

The enlightened man does not shut out one part of his nature in order to use another, but uses all he is all the time in all places in each thing he does. Reason and logic and intuition become a unified tool for his coping with life; the sixth sense merges with the five material senses so as to convey to his consciousness a constant impression of both the inner world and the outer. Because he exists on all possible levels of consciousness, he is able to perceive things and events in their true nature and thereby to guide his own actions accordingly. He does not oppose events because he sees their inevitable direction, and he takes up his tasks within the moving stream of history as if he were directing it, when in point of fact he actually is playing the part best suited for him in that moving stream. The sixth sense brings to us impressions and convictions that are impossible to attribute to memory or experience. We are moved to conviction from out of the inexhaustible resource of universal mind, and we eventually become as positive in the reception of this feeling as we do to our senses of sight or touch or hearing.

The Irish poet, George Russell, reports, "Once in an idle interval in my work I sat with my face pressed in my hands, and in that dimness pictures began flickering in my brain. I saw a little dark shop, the counter before me, and behind it an old man fumbling with some papers, a man so old that his motions had lost swiftness and precision. Deeper in the store was a girl, red-haired, with gray watchful eyes fixed on the old man. I saw that to enter the shop one must take two steps downward from the cobbled pavement without. I questioned a young man, my office companion, who was then writing a letter, and I found that what I had seen was his father's shop. All my imaginations were not imaginations of mine in any true sense, for while I was in a vacant mood my companion had been thinking of his home, and his brain was populous with quickened memories, and they invaded my own mind, and when I made question I found their origin. But how many thousand times are we invaded by such images and there is no speculation over them?"

The frontiers of mind and thought have barely been penetrated. Awaiting the human search for knowledge lies the most exciting, unexplored area of all—human consciousness, mind, being, mentality. Our lives grow into images of those things which our minds are preoccupied with, and if we are concerned with bolts and nuts we achieve a bolts-and-nuts mentality, and our very absorption by this infinitesimal slice of existence bars us from perception of the tremendous possibilities in other spiritual and mental realms. A man who takes up his tasks as he might approach an altar transforms his work, no matter how menial, into a sacrament. When a man puts intuition to work for him and closets himself with his consciousness in a searching effort to develop his sixth sense, he is bound not only to grow in effectiveness and power but also as a questing human soul in search of the uttermost. Nothing in life is resolved simply by facts. Facts shriek at us because they appeal to our conscious minds, but facts that human knowledge has uncovered up to now are but the tiniest representation of the total sum of knowledge in universal mind. The rational, logical man who prides himself upon acting only on known facts is not nearly so rational as he would have himself believe. In point of actual fact he is more often led to erroneous conclusions than true ones, not because he does not apply his reason and his logic and his knowledge, but because they are insufficient, deal only with a portion of existence, not its entirety.

YOU SHALL KNOW THE HIDDEN PURPOSE

Each of us has a job, each has a "row to hoe," and within our circumscribed tasks problems constantly arise which we are called upon to solve, upon the solution of which our lives often depend. To apply the use of the sixth sense to the solution of these problems is possible to every man, regardless of how obsessed he is with the material world. Even if he will not strive for spiritual enlightenment, will not turn over his life to the Divine for guidance, will not subordinate the ego by sacrifice, will not find within himself a longing for unity with the Secret Self, he still is not beyond the salvation offered by intuition. When his time of conscious striving with a problem is over, when he has considered all elements, pitted them against each other, weighed them, counted them, tabulated them, he then may visualize within his own mind a secret computing machine into which he can feed all elements of the problem and which will deliver him a true and accurate answer. Each of us, no matter how spiritually enlightened, can profit by this visualization. When your problem is upon you and you know as much about it as you ever possibly can, forget it completely. Envisage your secret computing machine, feed all elements of the problem into it. See them go in one by one until finally the whole problem is out of your hands. Know in your own heart that the problem will be solved, that you need do no more about it than act upon the solution when it is presented. Have no fear; the solution will come. It may be the following morning, perhaps the next afternoon, it may be a whole week, but it will illuminate your consciousness and you will know with the utmost certainty that the true answer has arrived. Once this highly significant experience has come to you, reason and logic and knowledge will have been dethroned as the principal activators of thought and action in your life, and enshrined in their stead will be that faculty of intuition that transcends and transfigures all situations and circumstances because it is infinite and eternal and speaks to the individual from out of his sixth sense.

12 THE MENTAL ATTITUDE THAT NEVER FAILS

Over most men hangs the sword of Damocles. They have fallen into the psychological trap of creating their problems by trying to solve them, worrying because they worry, being afraid of fear. There is a capricious quality in our psyche that denies us each object we try to grasp. Our wrong thinking, wrong acting, egoistic nature leads us to pursue things through vain desire. Acting and thinking in the small part of our nature, it is inevitable that we be frustrated in our purposes.

INSURING SUCCESS

The mental attitude that insures success is one in which the individual turns his work and the results of his work over to the Divine without attachment or desire. This psychological absolution from the aims of partial seeing allows him to follow the behest of a master will with perfect equanimity. He will not be dismayed by circuitous routes, he will not be bitter about apparent defeats, he will not rail against obstacles, because he knows that the ends of his actions are in the hands of an omnipotent being which insures his absolute development and complete success eventually. An enlightened man sees that the purposes of the Secret Self are the only true purposes. He adopts these as his own, dons the mantle of Divine as his true, inmost being. All his actions take on long-range significance. He understands that there is a secret purpose in the smallest task, that the eventual result of this purpose lies beyond the perception of his conscious mind. There develops within him a towering trust, a positive certainty as to eventual victory that makes him irresistible and impregnable in the midst of all action. He cannot be defeated, for defeat is possible only to a being bounded by space and time, and he has taken up his residence in a self that is eternal and infinite. He sees that all things are brought to him for his inner perfection, that victory and defeat are merely opposite ends of a scale of sensitivity by which his aspiring soul gradually is able to abdicate from masquerading as a separate, isolated ego and to recognize its absolute unity with the Divine.

To be undiscouraged and undismayed by whatever turn of fortune is encountered is always a mark of maturity and enlightenment. Such fortitude is possible only to a man who has forsworn desires to be better, to get more, to have power, or any other of the egoistic shortcomings that mark the individual at war with his fellows. The vital and animalistic nature hungers always for the fruits of its labor, and when these are denied, it becomes disconsolate, loses faith, may even give up altogether. Whoever is bound to his animalistic nature is bound also to constant hungering for the fruits of his labor, and in consequence takes up his tasks under a delusion that blinds him to the possibilities for success. Selfish striving for gain defeats enerprise at the outset because it is based upon the false belief that one manifestation of the Divine is innately better than another and therefore more deserving of reward. Such psychological misapprehension is based on partiality, sees a world of multitudinous and separate things to be conquered and achieved dominion over. The separate surface self never achieves dominion over anything, even over its own nature. It did not spring itself into being, it cannot stay itself from eventual oblivion, its growth and development are entirely reactionary, and all things lie outside the scope of its effectuality.

EFFECTIVE GUIDE TO LIVING

In almost everyone, however, the surface self achieves the illusion that it is able effectively to influence life. In consequence, through the years that his physical body flourishes, a man is mentally and spiritually bound to a delusion about who he is and where he came from and what his relationship to the world is. His lack of effectiveness in life, his failure to grow mentally and spiritually, his gradual dissolution into cynicism, into disenchantment with the material world, he seldom attributes to a psychologically wrong viewpoint but generally feels he hasn't "beat the game" because he hasn't arrived at the pinnacle of material sucess he envisaged as a youth. Even more revealing are ego-strivers who achieve their goals. The mountain they climb so laboriously overlooks a barren landscape. When they stand upon the highest spot and look out over the bleak vista, their souls are seized in the vise-like grip of fear, and they turn their eyes to the earth and never look skyward again.

Our cities and nations are populated with people who cannot stand to look into their souls because they never have discovered who they truly are. Infinity and eternity appall them by dwarfing the ego. What is needed most of all is an effective guide to living, a humanistic relationship between the individual and his creating source, so that each man is able to see with absolute clarity and perfect equanimity that his life not only is part of a divine plan for the development of consciousness in the universe but that he himself is both mentally and spiritually unified with that master spirit whose field of unfoldment the world is. Such spiritual illumination allows a man to put his life and his works in the hands of the Divine, with complete assurance that both will be used for the best purpose. Once this psychological dispossession of personal effort and personal victory has been accomplished, the individual never again suffers defeat. Apparent defeat becomes only a turning place in the road; all detours merge into one triumphal march to victory, become part of that plan by which eventual success is assured.

When the revelation comes to a man that the Divine is working through him, all his labor takes on a highly-charged spiritual significance alongside which material rewards pale. Such a man no longer works for money, no longer works for success, but only for the expression of that mind and consciousness within him which he now knows to be the Supreme manifesting upon the earth. He does the work of the Secret Self and never of his surface self. He subjugates the surface self to a master spirit that uses it as a tool for the effectuation of the divine purpose in the world. The faith that grows out of this knowledge sustains him under the most fierce, adverse pressure. Something higher than heart or intellect upholds him through the longest detours and the blindest gropings. His egoistic self has found that supreme master and highest philosophy by which it not only understands itself and its place and purpose in the world but also is admitted to a secret place of light and peace and understanding. In the heart of the enlightened man is the hidden knowledge that he is never at the mercy of im-mediate appearances, that he has within him the power to change all through his identification with the Divine, through his knowledge that the mind in him is the mind in all others.

PERFECT KNOWING AND IMPERFECT SEEING

This giving over of one self and assuming another is far more than just a merely psychological switch of viewpoint. The awakened man dies in one small part of his nature in order to be reborn in a larger and wider consciousness. To the onlooker the change may be imperceptible. He may do the same work, live in the same manner, forsake neither friends nor fun, but all actions now will be unified by spiritual awareness, so that there emanates from him an inner joy, an absolute acceptance of life. He may rise to a position of prominence in the world or he may not; it is indifferent to him. He serves not the causes of men, only the will and purpose of the Divine. "We are here to see what we can add to, not to see what we can get from, Life," wrote William Osler. In the enlightened man the egoistic nature has been so far withdrawn from the frontal part of personality that his impression upon others is one of constant giving, never of taking. He becomes a horn of plenty through which the Divine pours its infinite resource. To whomever he contacts there comes a sense of love and understanding and security, descending through him into the other from the Secret Self.

Those whose consciousness is focused in the surface self live within narrow horizons of awareness, are puppets driven by sensation. The world makes itself known to them through the tiny windows of their senses, and they react to it, never exert a mental or spiritual influence upon it. Their failures are failures of imperfect seeing. They see neither who they are nor what the true nature of a situation is; consequently their actions are always based upon partial knowledge. A sufficient number of failures stemming from this imperfect working completely defeats the individual, and his frustration is announced through physical ailments of the body. Emotional blockages and repressions inhibit circulation in certain areas of the body, and disease and malfunction set in. Repressed hostility, aggression, insecurity, and fear are root causes of arthritis, heart disease, arterial sclerosis, cancer, ulcer. A society that demands conformity of its members is bound to frustrate a large number of them, and this manifests itself as a gradual rise in physical infirmity. Since it is patently impossible for the individual to alter the social system under which he lives, solution of the dilemma must provide spiritual freedom while allowing for physical conformity. Arriving at the realization that the Divine dwells in you just as you dwell in the Divine dissolves the cares and frustration of the egoistic nature. Once you have been able to identify yourself with the master spirit of eternity it becomes possible to view existence on a long-term basis, to detach yourself from physical goals.

FAILURE IS A STATE OF MIND

Existence is essentially a fight. Man is tested in the crucible of conflict from cradle to grave, and the time of his most severe testing is the time of his greatest growth. Nature is not interested in winners. All too often victory is a signal for cessation of effort. Nature is interested in growth, and growth is possible only to one constantly at work expanding his abilities and talents. In any line of endeavor the man who has it made is going down hill. Our waistlines stay trim and our minds alert when we are kept at our labors through necessity. Our surface selves often find in victory or gain the opportunity to indulge sensation, and we are caught in a trap from which we may never emerge as aspiring individuals again. Havelock Ellis wrote, "Conquest brings self-conceit and intolerance, the reckless inflation and dissipation of energies. Defeat brings prudence and concentration; it ennobles and fortifies." Defeat, of course, is never a fact unless it is accepted as final. The man who realizes that all growth possibilities are within him never accepts defeat. He knows that he can do much better than he thus far has shown, for he has a secret pipeline into the source of all energy and talent.

Failure is a state of mind and never a physical fact. We try to accomplish something and if results don't come our way within a certain period of time we often throw up our hands and say we can't do it. If this psychological abdication from trying is done without a cessation of physical effort, we may find that suddenly we are getting results, for unconsciously we have turned our works and actions over to the Secret Self and they have become effective. But if the individual ceases to make any further physical effort, then the work will never be done for the man has turned his back on it.

BOLDNESS

Each of us best fulfills himself and the purposes of nature when he performs the task of torch bearer in some area of his activities. Boldness engenders its own success through liberating energies repressed by inhibition. If a man finds within himself the courage to go out on a limb, it will never break under his weight, will sustain him no matter how fragile it appears, and he will see from his new vantage point an entirely different world. Between the timid and the brave is but a single step, and that is the first one. Wild animals attack the prey that runs away but stand stock still and are intimidated by any that faces them. If a man will find within himself the spiritual resource to make his first step toward danger instead of away from it, he will find that danger disappears. But if he gives in to the impulse of fear and makes his initial step away from danger, life will chase after him, surely devour him.

> Let any man show the world that he feels
> Afraid of its bark and 'twill fly at his heels:
> Let him fearlessly face it, 'twill leave him alone:
> But 'twill fawn at his feet if he flings it a bone.
> —Edward Bulwer-Lytton

Fear engenders fear. The first step away from danger turns into a trot, then a shambling run, then a panic-stricken dash, and the innocuous cur that pursues us is now a fancied monster. Similarly courage engenders courage. The first step toward danger allows us to see our antagonist clearly. We examine his face and behold that it is not nearly so threatening as we imagined. We begin to see ways and means of coping with him, and just because we have confronted him head on, he stops his aggressive action toward us and considers whether we ourselves might not pose some danger to him. This is true of events as well as living things. A psychological aura emanates from events as from people. If something seems to threaten us, then it surely will pursue us if we run away, but if we advance upon it boldly, it stops its movement toward us. It hangs back to reconsider, eventually yields. Nothing stands before continued effort and nothing can resist the man who persists in the face of all discouragement. The mental attitude that never fails is one in which the individual dispossesses himself of the goal-seeking ego and lodges his psyche firmly in a consciousness of the Divine, viewing his own life as an opportunity for emergence of the master spirit, regarding the work that he does as being the work of the Secret Self.

PERSEVERANCE

Everything great is accomplished by men whose perseverance transcends mere human endurance. Galileo at his telescope, Newton beneath his apple tree, Einstein in his laboratory, Columbus on his ship, all are examples of illumination following a period of prolonged perseverance. No man performing at the behest of egoistic desire could possibly have accomplished the feats of these enlightened pioneers; long before illumination arrived, he would cease his searching and go on to other fields. The Divine uses the discoverer and the creator, each for the purpose for which he is best suited. Such men cannot fail for they are doing the work for which they were intended at birth. In consequence, their lives are completely absorbed in their tasks, so that the work is inseparable from the man, is in some kind of mystic sense the man spun out in space and time and perpetuated as a creative fact. When that psychological turnabout is made by which the individual life is surrendered to the Secret Self, there enters into the person an unearthly determination that impels him to perform his work in the face of all odds, in the teeth of the bleakest appearances. He takes his cue from a light within, and he is able to alter the psychological aura of things by bringing into the midst of events his own positive determination and absolute dedication to the accomplishment of his tasks. His impact upon events is not brought about through vain desires or selfish goals, only because he is doing those tasks that are natural to him.

Fear of failure is a deterrent to action in all those entrapped in ego-consciousness. The surface self does not possess that sense of equality necessary to the undertaking of perilous tasks. It is concerned always with appearances, and it cannot bring itself to undertake an adventuresome action because if such action comes off disastrously or comically it is made to appear incapable or a fool. Millions of people are afraid to try because they are afraid to fail, and such inhibition keeps them from realizing all but the tiniest fraction of their capabilities. This short-sighted focusing of consciousness in the surface self keeps the individual's attention upon transitory goals. He undertakes to sing a song, for example, not because a song in him must be sung but because he wants the attention and admiration of others. With this false viewpoint, it is even difficult for him to bring himself to get up before his audience, for he carries within a picture of the shame and defeat he will feel if his attempt to win admiration results instead in ridicule. The song therefore does not get sung, and if sung, sung poorly. The individual has not become the thing he is doing but is only using it for the satisfaction of his surface nature.

DON'T BE AFRAID TO FAIL

The mental attitude that never fails is one that is not *afraid* to fail. One must be willing to accept the conditions that follow failure before he has any chance of attempting a new enterprise. If it be such a simple thing as diving off a board into a swimming pool, one must be willing to accept the pain attendant upon a belly flop before he is able to muster the determination to dive. Once fear is gone, he will not belly flop; his dive will be swift and clean. He performs it because it is in him, and it performs him as much as he performs it. To get the surface self out of the way and allow the psyche to be possessed by a master spirit allows the individual to undertake his tasks without the slightest fear of failure because he not only has a sense of equality toward others but knows that a power greater than he is guiding his steps in the best possible manner. We need to realize that everything is the result of change, that there is nothing permanent in the entire world except that Secret Self from which we have sprung.

WILSHIRE SELF-IMPROVEMENT LIBRARY

ASTROLOGY
___ASTROLOGY—HOW TO CHART YOUR HOROSCOPE Max Heindel 7.00
___ASTROLOGY AND SEXUAL ANALYSIS Morris C. Goodman 10.00
___ASTROLOGY AND YOU Carroll Righter 5.00
___ASTROLOGY MADE EASY Astarte 7.00
___ASTROLOGY, ROMANCE, YOU AND THE STARS Anthony Norvell 10.00
___MY WORLD OF ASTROLOGY Sydney Omarr 10.00
___THOUGHT DIAL Sydney Omarr 7.00
___WHAT THE STARS REVEAL ABOUT THE MEN IN YOUR LIFE Thelma White 3.00

BRIDGE
___BRIDGE BIDDING MADE EASY Edwin B. Kantar 15.00
___BRIDGE CONVENTIONS Edwin B. Kantar 10.00
___COMPETITIVE BIDDING IN MODERN BRIDGE Edgar Kaplan 7.00
___DEFENSIVE BRIDGE PLAY COMPLETE Edwin B Kantar 20.00
___GAMESMAN BRIDGE—PLAY BETTER WITH KANTAR Edwin B. Kantar 7.00
___HOW TO IMPROVE YOUR BRIDGE Alfred Sheinwold 7.00
___IMPROVING YOUR BIDDING SKILLS Edwin B. Kantar 10.00
___INTRODUCTION TO DECLARER'S PLAY Edwin B. Kantar 10.00
___INTRODUCTION TO DEFENDER'S PLAY Edwin B. Kantar 10.00
___KANTAR FOR THE DEFENSE Edwin B. Kantar 10.00
___KANTAR FOR THE DEFENSE VOLUME 2 Edwin B. Kantar 10.00
___TEST YOUR BRIDGE PLAY Edwin B. Kantar 10.00
___VOLUME 2—TEST YOUR BRIDGE PLAY Edwin B. Kantar 10.00
___WINNING DECLARER PLAY Dorothy Hayden Truscott 10.00

BUSINESS, STUDY & REFERENCE
___BRAINSTORMING Charles Clark 10.00
___CONVERSATION MADE EASY Elliot Russell 5.00
___EXAM SECRET Dennis B. Jackson 7.00
___FIX-IT BOOK Arthur Symons 2.00
___HOW TO DEVELOP A BETTER SPEAKING VOICE M. Hellier 5.00
___HOW TO SAVE 50% ON GAS & CAR EXPENSES Ken Stansbie 5.00
___HOW TO SELF-PUBLISH YOUR BOOK & MAKE IT A BEST SELLER Melvin Powers . . 20.00
___INCREASE YOUR LEARNING POWER Geoffrey A. Dudley 5.00
___PRACTICAL GUIDE TO BETTER CONCENTRATION Melvin Powers 5.00
___PUBLIC SPEAKING MADE EASY Thomas Montalbo 10.00
___7 DAYS TO FASTER READING William S. Schaill 7.00
___SONGWRITER'S RHYMING DICTIONARY Jane Shaw Whitfield 10.00
___SPELLING MADE EASY Lester D. Basch & Dr. Milton Finkelstein 3.00
___STUDENT'S GUIDE TO BETTER GRADES J.A. Rickard 3.00
___YOUR WILL & WHAT TO DO ABOUT IT Attorney Samuel G. King 7.00

CALLIGRAPHY
___ADVANCED CALLIGRAPHY Katherine Jeffares 7.00
___CALLIGRAPHY—THE ART OF BEAUTIFUL WRITING Katherine Jeffares 7.00
___CALLIGRAPHY FOR FUN & PROFIT Anne Leptich & Jacque Evans 7.00
___CALLIGRAPHY MADE EASY Tina Serafini 7.00

CHESS & CHECKERS
___BEGINNER'S GUIDE TO WINNING CHESS Fred Reinfeld 10.00
___CHESS IN TEN EASY LESSONS Larry Evans 10.00
___CHESS MADE EASY Milton L. Hanauer 5.00
___CHESS PROBLEMS FOR BEGINNERS Edited by Fred Reinfeld 7.00

____CHESS TACTICS FOR BEGINNERS Edited by Fred Reinfeld 10.00
____HOW TO WIN AT CHECKERS Fred Reinfeld 7.00
____1001 BRILLIANT WAYS TO CHECKMATE Fred Reinfeld 10.00
____1001 WINNING CHESS SACRIFICES & COMBINATIONS Fred Reinfeld 10.00

COOKERY & HERBS
____CULPEPER'S HERBAL REMEDIES Dr. Nicholas Culpeper 5.00
____FAST GOURMET COOKBOOK Poppy Cannon 2.50
____HEALING POWER OF HERBS May Bethel 5.00
____HEALING POWER OF NATURAL FOODS May Bethel 7.00
____HERBS FOR HEALTH—HOW TO GROW & USE THEM Louise Evans Doole 7.00
____HOME GARDEN COOKBOOK—DELICIOUS NATURAL FOOD RECIPES Ken Kraft 3.00
____MEATLESS MEAL GUIDE Tomi Ryan & James H. Ryan, M.D. 4.00
____VEGETABLE GARDENING FOR BEGINNERS Hugh Wilberg 2.00
____VEGETABLES FOR TODAY'S GARDENS R. Milton Carleton 2.00
____VEGETARIAN COOKERY Janet Walker 10.00
____VEGETARIAN COOKING MADE EASY & DELECTABLE Veronica Vezza 3.00

GAMBLING & POKER
____HOW TO WIN AT POKER Terence Reese & Anthony T. Watkins 10.00
____SCARNE ON DICE John Scarne 15.00
____WINNING AT CRAPS Dr. Lloyd T. Commins 10.00
____WINNING AT GIN Chester Wander & Cy Rice 10.00
____WINNING AT POKER—AN EXPERT'S GUIDE John Archer 10.00
____WINNING AT 21—AN EXPERT'S GUIDE John Archer 10.00
____WINNING POKER SYSTEMS Norman Zadeh 10.00

HEALTH
____BEE POLLEN Lynda Lyngheim & Jack Scagnetti 5.00
____COPING WITH ALZHEIMER'S Rose Oliver, Ph.D. & Francis Bock, Ph.D. 10.00
____HELP YOURSELF TO BETTER SIGHT Margaret Darst Corbett 10.00
____HOW YOU CAN STOP SMOKING PERMANENTLY Ernest Caldwell 5.00
____NATURE'S WAY TO NUTRITION & VIBRANT HEALTH Robert J. Scrutton 3.00
____NEW CARBOHYDRATE DIET COUNTER Patti Lopez-Pereira 2.00
____REFLEXOLOGY Dr. Maybelle Segal 7.00
____REFLEXOLOGY FOR GOOD HEALTH Anna Kaye & Don C. Matchan 10.00
____YOU CAN LEARN TO RELAX Dr. Samuel Gutwirth 5.00

HOBBIES
____BEACHCOMBING FOR BEGINNERS Norman Hickin 2.00
____BLACKSTONE'S MODERN CARD TRICKS Harry Blackstone 7.00
____BLACKSTONE'S SECRETS OF MAGIC Harry Blackstone 7.00
____COIN COLLECTING FOR BEGINNERS Burton Hobson & Fred Reinfeld 7.00
____ENTERTAINING WITH ESP Tony 'Doc' Shiels 2.00
____400 FASCINATING MAGIC TRICKS YOU CAN DO Howard Thurston 10.00
____HOW I TURN JUNK INTO FUN AND PROFIT Sari 3.00
____HOW TO WRITE A HIT SONG AND SELL IT Tommy Boyce 10.00
____MAGIC FOR ALL AGES Walter Gibson 10.00
____STAMP COLLECTING FOR BEGINNERS Burton Hobson 3.00

HORSE PLAYERS' WINNING GUIDES
____BETTING HORSES TO WIN Les Conklin 10.00
____ELIMINATE THE LOSERS Bob McKnight 5.00
____HOW TO PICK WINNING HORSES Bob McKnight 5.00
____HOW TO WIN AT THE RACES Sam (The Genius) Lewin 5.00
____HOW YOU CAN BEAT THE RACES Jack Kavanagh 5.00
____MAKING MONEY AT THE RACES David Barr 10.00
____PAYDAY AT THE RACES Les Conklin 7.00

___ SMART HANDICAPPING MADE EASY William Bauman 5.00
___ SUCCESS AT THE HARNESS RACES Barry Meadow 7.00

HUMOR
___ HOW TO FLATTEN YOUR TUSH Coach Marge Reardon 2.00
___ JOKE TELLER'S HANDBOOK Bob Orben 10.00
___ JOKES FOR ALL OCCASIONS Al Schock 7.00
___ 2,000 NEW LAUGHS FOR SPEAKERS Bob Orben 7.00
___ 2,400 JOKES TO BRIGHTEN YOUR SPEECHES Robert Orben 10.00
___ 2,500 JOKES TO START'EM LAUGHING Bob Orben 10.00

HYPNOTISM
___ CHILDBIRTH WITH HYPNOSIS William S. Kroger, M.D. 5.00
___ HOW YOU CAN BOWL BETTER USING SELF-HYPNOSIS Jack Heise 7.00
___ HOW YOU CAN PLAY BETTER GOLF USING SELF-HYPNOSIS Jack Heise 3.00
___ HYPNOSIS AND SELF-HYPNOSIS Bernard Hollander, M.D. 7.00
___ HYPNOTISM (Originally published 1893) Carl Sextus 5.00
___ HYPNOTISM MADE EASY Dr. Ralph Winn 10.00
___ HYPNOTISM MADE PRACTICAL Louis Orton 5.00
___ MODERN HYPNOSIS Lesley Kuhn & Salvatore Russo, Ph.D. 5.00
___ NEW CONCEPTS OF HYPNOSIS Bernard C. Gindes, M.D. 15.00
___ NEW SELF-HYPNOSIS Paul Adams 10.00
___ POST-HYPNOTIC INSTRUCTIONS—SUGGESTIONS FOR THERAPY Arnold Furst ... 10.00
___ PRACTICAL GUIDE TO SELF-HYPNOSIS Melvin Powers 10.00
___ PRACTICAL HYPNOTISM Philip Magonet, M.D. 3.00
___ SECRETS OF HYPNOTISM S.J. Van Pelt, M.D. 5.00
___ SELF-HYPNOSIS—A CONDITIONED-RESPONSE TECHNIQUE Laurence Sparks 7.00
___ SELF-HYPNOSIS—ITS THEORY, TECHNIQUE & APPLICATION Melvin Powers 7.00
___ THERAPY THROUGH HYPNOSIS Edited by Raphael H. Rhodes 5.00

JUDAICA
___ SERVICE OF THE HEART Evelyn Garfiel, Ph.D. 10.00
___ STORY OF ISRAEL IN COINS Jean & Maurice Gould 2.00
___ STORY OF ISRAEL IN STAMPS Maxim & Gabriel Shamir 1.00
___ TONGUE OF THE PROPHETS Robert St. John 10.00

JUST FOR WOMEN
___ COSMOPOLITAN'S GUIDE TO MARVELOUS MEN Foreword by Helen Gurley Brown .. 3.00
___ COSMOPOLITAN'S HANG-UP HANDBOOK Foreword by Helen Gurley Brown 4.00
___ COSMOPOLITAN'S LOVE BOOK—A GUIDE TO ECSTASY IN BED 7.00
___ COSMOPOLITAN'S NEW ETIQUETTE GUIDE Foreword by Helen Gurley Brown 4.00
___ I AM A COMPLEAT WOMAN Doris Hagopian & Karen O'Connor Sweeney 3.00
___ JUST FOR WOMEN—A GUIDE TO THE FEMALE BODY Richard E. Sand M.D. 5.00
___ NEW APPROACHES TO SEX IN MARRIAGE John E. Eichenlaub, M.D. 3.00
___ SEXUALLY ADEQUATE FEMALE Frank S. Caprio, M.D. 3.00
___ SEXUALLY FULFILLED WOMAN Dr. Rachel Copelan 5.00

MARRIAGE, SEX & PARENTHOOD
___ ABILITY TO LOVE Dr. Allan Fromme 7.00
___ GUIDE TO SUCCESSFUL MARRIAGE Drs. Albert Ellis & Robert Harper 10.00
___ HOW TO RAISE AN EMOTIONALLY HEALTHY, HAPPY CHILD Albert Ellis, Ph.D. 10.00
___ PARENT SURVIVAL TRAINING Marvin Silverman, Ed.D. & David Lustig, Ph.D. 15.00
___ SEX WITHOUT GUILT Albert Ellis, Ph.D. 7.00
___ SEXUALLY ADEQUATE MALE Frank S. Caprio, M.D. 3.00
___ SEXUALLY FULFILLED MAN Dr. Rachel Copelan 5.00
___ STAYING IN LOVE Dr. Norton F. Kristy 7.00

MELVIN POWERS MAIL ORDER LIBRARY

HOW TO GET RICH IN MAIL ORDER Melvin Powers 20.00
HOW TO SELF-PUBLISH YOUR BOOK Melvin Powers 20.00
HOW TO WRITE A GOOD ADVERTISEMENT Victor O. Schwab 20.00
MAIL ORDER MADE EASY J. Frank Brumbaugh 20.00
MAKING MONEY WITH CLASSIFIED ADS Melvin Powers 20.00

METAPHYSICS & NEW AGE
CONCENTRATION—A GUIDE TO MENTAL MASTERY Mouni Sadhu 10.00
EXTRA-TERRESTRIAL INTELLIGENCE—THE FIRST ENCOUNTER 6.00
FORTUNE TELLING WITH CARDS P. Foli 10.00
HOW TO INTERPRET DREAMS, OMENS & FORTUNE TELLING SIGNS Gettings 5.00
HOW TO UNDERSTAND YOUR DREAMS Geoffrey A. Dudley 7.00
MAGICIAN—HIS TRAINING AND WORK W.E. Butler 7.00
MEDITATION Mouni Sadhu 10.00
MODERN NUMEROLOGY Morris C. Goodman 10.00
NUMEROLOGY—ITS FACTS AND SECRETS Ariel Yvon Taylor 5.00
NUMEROLOGY MADE EASY W. Mykian 10.00
PALMISTRY MADE EASY Fred Gettings 7.00
PALMISTRY MADE PRACTICAL Elizabeth Daniels Squire 7.00
PROPHECY IN OUR TIME Martin Ebon 2.50
SUPERSTITION—ARE YOU SUPERSTITIOUS? Eric Maple 2.00
TAROT OF THE BOHEMIANS Papus 10.00
WAYS TO SELF-REALIZATION Mouni Sadhu 7.00
WITCHCRAFT, MAGIC & OCCULTISM—A FASCINATING HISTORY W.B. Crow 10.00
WITCHCRAFT—THE SIXTH SENSE Justine Glass 7.00

RECOVERY
KNIGHT IN RUSTY ARMOR Robert Fisher 5.00
KNIGHTS WITHOUT ARMOR (Hardcover edition) Aaron R. Kipnis, Ph.D. 10.00
PRINCESS WHO BELIEVED IN FAIRY TALES Marcia Grad 10.00

SELF-HELP & INSPIRATIONAL
CHANGE YOUR VOICE, CHANGE YOUR LIFE Morton Cooper, Ph.D. 10.00
CHARISMA—HOW TO GET "THAT SPECIAL MAGIC" Marcia Grad 10.00
DAILY POWER FOR JOYFUL LIVING Dr. Donald Curtis 7.00
DYNAMIC THINKING Melvin Powers 7.00
GREATEST POWER IN THE UNIVERSE U.S. Andersen 10.00
GROW RICH WHILE YOU SLEEP Ben Sweetland 10.00
GROW RICH WITH YOUR MILLION DOLLAR MIND Brian Adams 10.00
GROWTH THROUGH REASON Albert Ellis, Ph.D. 10.00
GUIDE TO PERSONAL HAPPINESS Albert Ellis, Ph.D. & Irving Becker, Ed.D. 10.00
GUIDE TO RATIONAL LIVING Albert Ellis, Ph.D. & R. Harper, Ph.D. 15.00
HANDWRITING ANALYSIS MADE EASY John Marley 10.00
HANDWRITING TELLS Nadya Olyanova 10.00
HOW TO ATTRACT GOOD LUCK A.H.Z. Carr 10.00
HOW TO DEVELOP A WINNING PERSONALITY Martin Panzer 10.00
HOW TO DEVELOP AN EXCEPTIONAL MEMORY Young & Gibson 10.00
HOW TO LIVE WITH A NEUROTIC Albert Ellis, Ph.D. 10.00
HOW TO MAKE $100,000 A YEAR IN SALES Albert Winnikoff 15.00
HOW TO OVERCOME YOUR FEARS M.P. Leahy, M.D. 3.00
HOW TO SUCCEED Brian Adams 10.00
I CAN Ben Sweetland 10.00
I WILL Ben Sweetland 10.00
KNIGHT IN RUSTY ARMOR Robert Fisher 5.00
MAGIC IN YOUR MIND U.S. Andersen 15.00
MAGIC OF THINKING SUCCESS Dr. David J. Schwartz 10.00
MAGIC POWER OF YOUR MIND Walter M. Germain 10.00
NEVER UNDERESTIMATE THE SELLING POWER OF A WOMAN Dottie Walters 7.00

____ PRINCESS WHO BELIEVED IN FAIRY TALES Marcia Grad 10.00
____ PSYCHO-CYBERNETICS Maxwell Maltz, M.D. 10.00
____ PSYCHOLOGY OF HANDWRITING Nadya Olyanova 10.00
____ SALES CYBERNETICS Brian Adams 10.00
____ SECRET OF SECRETS U.S. Andersen 10.00
____ SECRET POWER OF THE PYRAMIDS U.S. Andersen 7.00
____ SELF-THERAPY FOR THE STUTTERER Malcolm Frazer 3.00
____ STOP COMMITTING VOICE SUICIDE Morton Cooper, Ph.D. 10.00
____ SUCCESS CYBERNETICS U.S. Andersen 10.00
____ 10 DAYS TO A GREAT NEW LIFE William E. Edwards 3.00
____ THINK AND GROW RICH Napoleon Hill 10.00
____ THINK LIKE A WINNER Walter Doyle Staples, Ph.D. 15.00
____ THREE MAGIC WORDS U.S. Andersen 15.00
____ TREASURY OF COMFORT Edited by Rabbi Sidney Greenberg 15.00
____ TREASURY OF THE ART OF LIVING Edited by Rabbi Sidney Greenberg 10.00
____ WHAT YOUR HANDWRITING REVEALS Albert E. Hughes 4.00
____ WINNING WITH YOUR VOICE Morton Cooper, Ph.D. 10.00
____ YOUR SUBCONSCIOUS POWER Charles M. Simmons 7.00

SPORTS
____ BILLIARDS—POCKET • CAROM • THREE CUSHION Clive Cottingham, Jr. 10.00
____ COMPLETE GUIDE TO FISHING Vlad Evanoff 2.00
____ HOW TO IMPROVE YOUR RACQUETBALL Lubarsky, Kaufman & Scagnetti 5.00
____ HOW TO WIN AT POCKET BILLIARDS Edward D. Knuchell 10.00
____ JOY OF WALKING Jack Scagnetti 3.00
____ RACQUETBALL FOR WOMEN Toni Hudson, Jack Scagnetti & Vince Rondone 3.00
____ SECRET OF BOWLING STRIKES Dawson Taylor 5.00
____ SOCCER—THE GAME & HOW TO PLAY IT Gary Rosenthal 7.00
____ STARTING SOCCER Edward F Dolan, Jr. 5.00

TENNIS LOVERS' LIBRARY
____ HOW TO BEAT BETTER TENNIS PLAYERS Loring Fiske 4.00
____ PSYCH YOURSELF TO BETTER TENNIS Dr. Walter A. Luszki 2.00
____ WEEKEND TENNIS—HOW TO HAVE FUN & WIN AT THE SAME TIME Bill Talbert . . . 3.00

WILSHIRE PET LIBRARY
____ DOG TRAINING MADE EASY & FUN John W. Kellogg 5.00
____ HOW TO BRING UP YOUR PET DOG Kurt Unkelbach 2.00
____ HOW TO RAISE & TRAIN YOUR PUPPY Jeff Griffen 5.00

LIBROS EN ESPAÑOL
____ CARISMA—CÓMO LOGRAR ESA MAGIA ESPECIAL Marcia Grad 10.00
____ CÓMO ALRAER LA BUENA SUERTE A.H.Z. Carr 10.00
____ EL CABALLERO DE LA ARMADURA OXIDAD Robert Fisher 10.00
____ EL CABALLERO DE LA ARMADURA OXIDAD (con cubierta gruesa) Robert Fisher . . . 20.00
____ LA PRINCESA QUE CREÍA EN CUENTOS DE HADAS Marcia Grad 10.00

Available from your bookstore or directly from Wilshire Book Company.
Please add $2.00 shipping and handling for each book ordered.

Wilshire Book Company
12015 Sherman Road
No. Hollywood, California 91605

For our complete catalog, visit our Web site at http://www.mpowers.com.

Books by Melvin Powers

HOW TO GET RICH IN MAIL ORDER

1. How to Develop Your Mail Order Expertise 2. How to Find a Unique Product or Service to Sell 3. How to Make Money with Classified Ads 4. How to Make Money with Display Ads 5. The Unlimited Potential for Making Money with Direct Mail 6. How to Copycat Successful Mail Order Operations 7. How I Created a Bestseller Using the Copycat Technique 8. How to Start and Run a Profitable Mail Order Special Interest Book Business 9. I Enjoy Selling Books by Mail—Some of My Successful Ads 10. Five of My Most Successful Direct Mail Pieces That Sold and Are Selling Millions of Dollars' Worth of Books 11. Melvin Powers's Mail Order Success Strategy—Follow it and You'll Become a Millionaire 12. How to Sell Your Products to Mail Order Companies, Retail Outlets, Jobbers, and Fund Raisers for Maximum Distribution and Profit 13. How to Get Free Display Ads and Publicity that Will Put You on the Road to Riches 14. How to Make Your Advertising Copy Sizzle 15. Questions and Answers to Help You Get Started Making Money 16. A Personal Word from Melvin Powers 17. How to Get Started 18. Selling Products on Television   8½" x 11½" — 352 Pages . . . $20.00

MAKING MONEY WITH CLASSIFIED ADS

1. Getting Started with Classified Ads 2. Everyone Loves to Read Classified Ads 3. How to Find a Money-Making Product 4. How to Write Classified Ads that Make Money 5. What I've Learned from Running Thousands of Classified Ads 6. Classified Ads Can Help You Make Big Money in Multi-Level Programs 7. Two-Step Classified Ads Made Me a Multi-Millionaire—They Can Do the Same for You! 8. One-Inch Display Ads Can Work Wonders 9. Display Ads Can Make You a Fortune Overnight 10. Although I Live in California, I Buy My Grapefruit from Florida 11. Nuts and Bolts of Mail Order Success 12. What if You Can't Get Your Business Running Successfully? What's Wrong? How to Correct it 13. Strategy for Mail Order Success   8½" x 11½" — 240 Pages . . . $20.00

HOW TO SELF-PUBLISH YOUR BOOK AND HAVE THE FUN AND EXCITEMENT OF BEING A BEST-SELLING AUTHOR

1. Who is Melvin Powers? 2. What is the Motivation Behind Your Decision to Publish Your Book? 3. Why You Should Read This Chapter Even if You Already Have an Idea for a Book 4. How to Test the Salability of Your Book Before You Write One Word 5. How I Achieved Sales Totaling $2,000,000 on My Book *How to Get Rich in Mail Order* 6. How to Develop a Second Career by Using Your Expertise 7. How to Choose an Enticing Book Title 8. Marketing Strategy 9. Success Stories 10. How to Copyright Your Book 11. How to Write a Winning Advertisement 12. Advertising that Money Can't Buy 13. Questions and Answers to Help You Get Started 14. Self-Publishing and the Midas Touch   8½" x 11½" — 240 Pages . . . $20.00

A PRACTICAL GUIDE TO SELF-HYPNOSIS

1. What You Should Know about Self-Hypnosis 2. What about the Dangers of Hypnosis? 3. Is Hypnosis the Answer? 4. How Does Self-Hypnosis Work? 5. How to Arouse Yourself From the Self-Hypnotic State 6. How to Attain Self-Hypnosis 7. Deepening the Self-Hypnotic State 8. What You Should Know about Becoming an Excellent Subject 9. Techniques for Reaching the Somnambulistic State 10. A New Approach to Self-Hypnosis 11. Psychological Aids and Their Function 12. Practical Applications of Self-Hypnosis   144 Pages . . . $10.00

Available at your bookstore or directly from Wilshire Book Company.
Please add $2.00 shipping and handling for each book ordered.

Wilshire Book Company
12015 Sherman Road, No. Hollywood, California 91605

For our complete catalog, visit our web site at http://www.mpowers.com.

A Personal Invitation from the Publisher, Melvin Powers...

There is a wonderful, unique book titled *The Knight in Rusty Armor* that is guaranteed to captivate your imagination as you discover the secret of what is most important in life. It is a delightful tale of a desperate knight in search of his true self.

Since we first published *The Knight in Rusty Armor,* we have received an unprecedented number of calls and letters from readers praising its powerful insights and entertaining style. It is a memorable, fun-filled story, rich in wit and humor, that has changed thousands of lives for the better. *The Knight* is one of our most popular titles. It has been published in numerous languages and has become a well-known favorite in many countries. I feel so strongly about this book that personally extending an invitation for you to read it.

The Knight in Rusty Armor

Join the knight as he faces a life-changing dilemma upon discovering that he is trapped in his armor, just as *we* may be trapped in *our* armor—an invisible kind that we use to protect ourselves from others and from various aspects of life.

As the knight searches for a way to free himself, he receives guidance from the wise sage Merlin the Magician, who encourages him to embark on the most difficult crusade of his life. The knight takes up the challenge and travels the Path of Truth, where he meets his real self for the first time and confronts the Universal Truths that govern his life—and ours.

The knight's journey reflects our own, filled with hope and despair, belief and disillusionment, laughter and tears. His insights become our insights as we follow along on his intriguing adventure of self-discovery. Anyone who has ever struggled with the meaning of life and love will discover profound wisdom and truth as this unique fantasy unfolds. *The Knight in Rusty Armor* is an experience that will expand your mind, touch your heart, and nourish your soul.

Available at all bookstores. Or send $5.00 (CA res. $5.41) plus $2.00 S/H to Wilshire Book Company, 12015 Sherman Road, No. Hollywood, CA 91605.

For our complete catalog, visit our web site at http://www.mpowers.com.